The Which? Guide to
Choosing a School

About the author

Christina Raffles is a parent and retired lawyer with expertise in personal accident claims. She deferred her career to bring up her two children, and has wide experience of the schools system, both inside and outside the staffroom (as a highly accomplished sportswoman, she has also coached sport at co-educational independent schools). She lives in the West Country.

Acknowledgements

The author and publishers would like to thank the following people and organisations for their help and advice: Advisory Centre for Education (ACE); Len Almond; Margaret Atherton; Dr David Cornelius (Association of Tutors); Department for Education and Employment; Dyslexia Institute; Headmasters' and Headmistresses' Conference; Professor L.B. Hendry; Cricket Kemp (Association for Neuro-linguistic Programming); Katie Mohamed; National Association for Gifted Children; National ISIS; Clare Roels (National Early Years Network); Graham Searle; Virginia Wallis; Juliet Wells.

The Which? Guide to Choosing a School

Christina Raffles

CONSUMERS' ASSOCIATION

Which? Books are commissioned and researched by
Consumers' Association and published by
Which? Ltd, 2 Marylebone Road, London NW1 4DF
Email address: books@which.net

Distributed by The Penguin Group:
Penguin Books Ltd, 27 Wrights Lane, London W8 5TZ

First edition October 1999

British Library Cataloguing-in-Publication Data
A catalogue record for this book is available from the British Library

ISBN 0 85202 794 X

For a full list of Which? books, please write to Which? Books, Castlemead,
Gascoyne Way, Hertford X. SG14 1LH, or access our web site at www.which.net

Cover and text design by Kysen Creative Consultants

Typeset by ensystems, Saffron Walden, Essex
Printed and bound in England by Clays Ltd, Bungay, Suffolk

Contents

Part 4 The determining factors

Appendices

★An asterisk next to the name of an organisation in the text indicates that the address can be found in this section

Introduction

Choosing a school is perhaps the most important decision you will ever have to make for your child, but it is one that is very far from straightforward. Many parents, facing the responsibility of finding the best, most appropriate, school available can be forgiven for feeling confused by the welter of recent legislation on education, and perturbed by some of the horror stories circulating.

Within both the state and independent (private) sectors, the competitive aspect of choosing a school has become more marked, particularly as the quality of educational provision can vary widely within a locality. A good school should provide the type of all-round education that will equip a child to meet the challenges of adulthood. The objective of this book is to help parents identify just such a school – a school that meets the unique requirements of their child.

Good state schools are much sought after but, contrary to the government's claims, parents may not be assured of obtaining a place for their child at their first-choice state school (see Chapter 16). It would be wrong, however, to assume that all inner-city state schools suffer deprivation, or conversely that schools in the leafy suburbs are guaranteed to provide a sound environment. This guide shows parents how to assess accurately the facilities and atmosphere at a school.

The national press continues to highlight the endemic problems afflicting the state system, including teacher shortages, the breakdown of discipline in some schools, and failing schools. The government, meanwhile, in an attempt to raise standards, has opened the flood-gates to a series of proposals, which supplement existing measures. The fear expressed is that children are being expected to jump through hoops in order to meet government targets. The book outlines these major legislative developments and explains their impact.

The independent sector, too, has been subject to reform. For the first time, full school inspection reports for fee-charging schools are to be made public to all parents, not just to those with children at that school; such reports have been available to parents in the state sector since the early 1990s (see Chapter 6). Thanks to this significant advance, parents will no longer be prohibited from knowing what they are buying.

However, the system still harbours pitfalls for the unwary. Proprietor heads have a free rein, with only market forces to check excesses, and unlike the state system there is no requirement for teachers to be qualified – in other words, the gardener could be seconded to teach French. This situation comes as a surprise to many parents. Shortages in the state sector have meanwhile compelled some schools to use instructors without qualified teacher status, while qualified teachers at state schools may be asked to cover subjects outside their specialist area (see Chapter 8).

Some parents assume that an independent education will be superior because they are paying for it; however, it is as well to be aware that some good state schools outclass some private schools. Needless to say, if you are paying fees, value for money becomes crucial. Chapter 17 lists ways to prepare for school fees, with specific emphasis placed on how to cut the cost. Choose the wrong school and you could seriously damage your wallet. This book aims to ensure damage limitation.

The statutory requirements at each Key Stage and subject choice are examined (see Chapter 12). Schools may also offer a range of extra-curricular opportunities that encourage personal growth and enable pupils to develop diverse interests: these are investigated in Chapter 15.

The league tables in the national press that list schools' academic results are now an annual event (see Chapter 13). In throwing the spotlight on to individual schools and enabling comparisons to be made, they have played a role in compelling schools to improve their performance. League tables can be of help to parents in assessing the merits of different establishments, but it would be wrong to rely solely on raw statistics, which do not take account of the many diverse socio-economic factors that may affect performance. While independent schools maintain an impressive standing in these tables, many select by ability and are, therefore, bound to outrank non-selective schools. This book demystifies the homage paid to these tables and exposes the distortions.

As long as parents adopt an objective approach, they should be able to sort out the real, factual evidence of school performance from schools' promotional gambits. Many of the descriptions in current guidebooks are subjective opinions based on information supplied by schools themselves. Since these titles feature the merits of numerous competing establishments, many are tempted to make exaggerated claims about their performance and facilities. Because the schools know the intricacies of how their system works and you as a parent probably don't, they hold all the cards. Parents, as outsiders, can find themselves at a great disadvantage. This book aims to reverse this by empowering parents with this insight.

It is crucial to involve your son or daughter in the process. This book shows you how to assess the various options open to you and draw up a shortlist of schools that meet your son or daughter's requirements (for more information, see 'How to use this book', page 21). It guides you through the application process, including how scholarships can be more easily won (see Chapter 17). Clear advice is given on how to obtain the most information out of an interview (see Chapter 19). While there is no magic formula for ensuring a satisfactory result, by following the advice in this guide you should greatly increase your chances of a successful outcome.

Part 1

Elements of choice

Chapter 1

Where to start

Education is a huge industry with nearly ten million pupils aged between 3 and 18 in over 33,680 schools throughout the United Kingdom. Parliament places a duty on parents to see that their child between the ages of 5 and 16 receives a full-time education suited to his or her age and ability. This duty may be satisfied either by full-time attendance at school, or in some other way – through home education, for example (see Chapter 5). The government for its part undertakes to guarantee a free place at a state school for each child during those years, as well as a place at a school or sixth-form college between the ages of 16 and 18, if required. Chapter 2 describes the different types of state school. While the legal duty to educate 5- to 16-year-olds lies with parents, the government has extended its undertaking down to the age of four (three in some areas), so parents may now expect a suitable nursery place for their child, if this is their wish (see pages 28–9).

School statistics

There are over 31,000 state or 'maintained' schools throughout the UK, of which primary schools, with over 23,000, make up the greatest number, followed by secondary schools, of which there are almost 4,500. Nursery schools, special schools and pupil referral units account for the remaining 3,500.

According the Department for Education and Employment (DfEE), in 1998 there were over 2,500 independent schools accounting for well over 600,000 pupils – about seven per cent of all children of school age. Many independent schools have more applicants than places and some are fully subscribed for years to come: numbers are particularly buoyant in the pre-preparatory and preparatory ages (4/5 to 13). However, the number of children at boarding school has dropped by about 30,000 during the 1990s. The most recent figures from the Independent Schools Information Service (ISIS)* indicate that in 1996 about 55,000 boys and 34,500 girls were boarders.

Choosing between the state and independent sectors

Choosing the right school for your child is probably one of the most difficult decisions you will have to make as a parent or guardian. One fundamental choice is deciding between state or independent education. These two sectors are distinct, and each has its own subdivisions that do not necessarily coincide (see Chapters 2 and 3). If you select the independent or 'private' sector then it is not only your child who will be affected by this decision, but inevitably your pocket. You will therefore not only be looking for what is best for your child but also seeking value for money.

Your choice will be restricted to some extent. Parents do not have complete freedom of choice to send their child to whatever school they wish within the state sector. In practice the constraints that admission criteria place upon parents, the financial strictures on schools and high levels of over-subscription to popular schools mean that what parents have been granted is only a right to express a preference, not necessarily a right to exercise it. In the independent sector, selection and financial considerations may prohibit choice.

Your background and principles

The financial circumstances and educational backgrounds of parents differ widely and will inevitably have some bearing on their choice of school. Most parents will have had no intimate association with schools since they were on the receiving end of formal education, and will make assumptions based on their own experience.

The majority of parents send their children to state-funded schools, which educate 93 per cent of all pupils. Many are unable to afford to have their children educated privately or have opted for the state sector because of their personal or political beliefs. By contrast, some parents who were educated in the private sector will not consider alternatives to independent schools. Others are prepared to pay for their children's education, regardless of their own background, because they believe that independent schools offer better facilities and higher academic standards. However, increasing numbers of privately educated parents are turning to the state alternative.

Fluidity between sectors

Within the state and independent sectors of education, there is no clear demarcation between the two types of 'customer'. Despite some people's assumptions to the contrary, children at private schools come from varied social and economic backgrounds, demonstrating a degree of social mobility. Many independent schools offer scholarships and foundation awards, as well as bursaries – a form of financial assistance (see Chapter 17). In addition, some parents switch their children between state and private schools to take advantage of opportunities in each system.

Although there are undoubtedly advantages in exposing children to both sectors during their educational careers, they can experience teething problems. You are advised to think carefully about how the pattern of school attendance you are planning for your child might affect him or her beyond the age of seven.

- When children who have been privately educated join the state sector, at whatever age, it is possible that they could be held back or bored in lessons. Independent schools tend to prepare children for academic study at an earlier age and may cover subjects earlier than state schools.
- If your son or daughter is transferring from a state school to an independent school, you might find that his or her new classmates are studying at a more advanced level. Home tutoring could enable your child to catch up (see page 209), and this could in fact be vital if you are aiming for a scholarship or award.

In either case, the exact level of adjustment required to ease the transition will of course depend on the individual child. By no means does the exercise always result in a mismatch: most children weather the change without any problems.

Keeping an open mind

Although you must make your initial selection between the two sectors, it is wise to keep your options open. After having chosen either state or private education (and frequently after completing admissions procedures), many parents have a complete change of heart and end up plumping for the alternative sector. Once you have fixed on your preferred sector, you should then investigate all the options within that area in order to facilitate your choice and reassure yourself that you have made the right decision.

Devising a plan of action

Whether you are determined upon the state or independent system, or just cannot make up your mind, one thing you should do early on is to start formulating a plan of action. If you are interested in the independent sector, it is a good idea to start sorting out your finances and investigating schools soon after your child is born (see Chapter 17). For the state sector, explore the possibilities of local nursery and primary schools when the child is two.

Analysing what you want and what schools have to offer at an early stage will put you in the best position to obtain the most beneficial education for your child (and, in the case of the independent sector, value for money).

Warning

A word of caution about sending your child to your own school, if that is an option. Schools can change considerably over the years and sentimentality should play no part in your choice. What may have been good for you could turn out to be a disaster for your child. It is the staff who matter, more than the bricks and mortar; it is their dedication and ability that will influence your child, and teachers neither stay forever nor live forever. In the state sector, government policies cause schools to evolve constantly, and indeed they may change out of all recognition over time.

Establishing your priorities

It is often said that the main criterion for choosing a school is that it must be suitable for the child. But how do you define suitability? The answer depends entirely upon the individual child's strengths and weaknesses.

Forget the rose-coloured spectacles or your own personal ambitions. The questions you must ask yourself are:

- Does my child show particular academic or practical strengths?
- Is he or she gregarious or shy?
- In what sort of atmosphere will my child flourish?
- Does he or she have any problems such as a disability, dyslexia or behavioural difficulties?
- Does he or she have any particular talents in, say, sport or music?
- If boarding is an option, will he or she be happy to board?

These questions take on varying significance at different age levels within either system and will therefore have to be answered at each stage. How you answer these questions will give you the necessary direction for your next step. Your first task, before any consideration as to whether cost will be involved, is to decide what your essential requirements are in the light of your child's strengths and weaknesses, followed by the facilities you consider indispensable.

Other factors to consider when looking at schools

In addition to establishing what your child's requirements are, the following factors will be important when choosing a school.

Academic performance

The keen interest shown in the league tables by both parents and schools, and the resulting intensity of competition on both sides, clearly demonstrate that academic achievement is generally regarded as a key requirement. It is the reason offered by many parents who are prepared to buy education, and why others fight to attain their preferences in the state system. For information on the league tables, see Chapter 13.

Tip

People tend to assume that private schools are more likely to achieve better academic results than state schools. However, some state schools – comprehensives and sixth-form colleges as well as grammar schools – are outperforming some of the most expensive independent schools. When choosing a school, do not be blind to the fact that the state sector contains many excellent schools that offer superb teaching.

Location

Your requirements will need to be found within a specific geographical area, and your address could have a bearing on whether your child is eligible for the state school of your choice (i.e. you live within the school's catchment area – see page 228).

You may regard as important a school's setting and facilities, the level of local parental involvement in school activities, and how far you want your child to travel every day. If you are not satisfied with the schools in your neighbourhood you should consider whether you are prepared to send your child to boarding school (see page 64), or to move.

When considering geographical areas, be careful not to choose a day school at a distance that is too tiring. A full day at school followed by a long journey home and homework could leave your son or daughter exhausted by the end of term, and may affect the quality of his or her work – which could be significant if you are after a scholarship (see Chapter 17).

Tip

Although you may think you have no alternative than to pay school fees for private education, there may be an option that gives you access to a good state school – by moving house. Many parents now do this, to take advantage of school catchment areas. Indeed, their activities can affect the housing market, sometimes pushing up prices by as much as 20 per cent in the area concerned.

Co-educational vs single-sex schooling

Some parents have the option of choosing between a co-educational or single-sex school; others may have a preference one way or the other. Although studies indicate some differences in the academic performance of boys and girls, it is a mistake to place too much faith in these. Note that schools that are currently single-sex may change – many boys' public schools now take girls in the sixth form, for example – so it is important to adopt a flexible attitude. For more information, see Chapter 4.

Day vs boarding school

The vast majority of schools are day schools, and boarders – most of whom attend independent prep and secondary schools – are in a minority. Some parents feel that it is unkind to send children away from home, while others believe that the atmosphere and discipline at boarding school are beneficial. Other parents may have no alternative if they live and work overseas, or are in the armed forces. For some, a happy compromise is weekly boarding, whereby children come home at the weekend. There is some debate about the age at which it is suitable to send young children away from home – parents' personal feelings will play a part here. For more on boarding, see Chapter 4.

Pastoral care

Pupils' personal and moral welfare, and the curricular and practical arrangements in place to promote this, matter to parents, but are particularly important to those whose child is to attend boarding school. Parents should find out how the pastoral care system is organised, and how problems such as bullying are countered. For more information see Chapters 9 and 11.

Discipline

Another major issue for most parents is the school's attitude towards discipline. They will want to know what line the school takes on drugs, vandalism and theft, and how punishment is exercised. Some parents choose the private system in the belief that discipline will be better. This cannot be guaranteed – independent education does not automatically mean better discipline. This matter is discussed further in Chapter 10.

Special interests

If your child is keen on sport or has a talent for music or drama, this could influence your choice of school. Sporting prowess can count for a great deal within the independent sector, while specialist schools provide an element of opportunity within the state system (see pages 37–9). If a certain activity is important to your child, you might want to look carefully at the relevant facilities when touring different schools. Chapter 4 looks at special interests in greater detail.

Financial considerations

If you are thinking of paying for your child's schooling, you will need to know how much it will cost. Value for money is crucial. If you have set out to buy the best education you can afford for your child, you have every right to expect the school, to which you are paying fees, to deliver what it has promised. *Do not be fooled into thinking that a school with much higher fees will provide a superior education.* This is one area where the expression 'you get what you pay for' does not hold true. Nor are schools within the remit of Trading Standards departments.

The range of school fees, whether in the independent sector or in state boarding, varies quite considerably across the spectrum, even within a given age range. Only you can decide whether you are willing to pay and how much you can afford. You should not

---

Warning

To be successful in today's climate, many head teachers of private schools must be super-salespeople, continually dreaming up fund-raising activities such as barn dances, summer fairs, plant sales and auction evenings. Do not forget that as far as an independent school is concerned, fees from increased numbers are top of the list – which means that you, as a prospective parent, are a prime target. Marketing has become openly aggressive, be it via the media or direct approach. While successful state and independent schools struggle to keep parents at bay, the rest actively set out to attract pupils, and, in the case of private schools they do not select pupils purely on *their* ability, but primarily on their parents' ability to pay.

---

immediately rule out private education because of expense. Some ways of planning to meet the financial commitment of school fees are outlined in Chapter 17.

Stick to your principles

When you have decided upon your main objectives, do not lose sight of them. While researching schools, most of which are competing for pupils, you will be bombarded by generalisations, vague promises and occasionally facts and figures as they attempt to persuade you of their worth. Do not be swayed. You should view all the data you are offered, and that which this book will show you how to obtain, with a critical eye. Avoid making hard-and-fast decisions too early: you may find that circumstances do not allow for their realisation.

How to use this book

Once the major criteria outlined in this chapter have been decided upon, consider the types of schools available to you according to the relevant age level (see Chapters 2 and 3). As there is considerable variation not only between the independent and state sectors, but also within the sectors themselves, this book deals with the state and independent systems separately. However, it is advisable to understand the principles of each system since this will enable you to effect workable crossovers if necessary.

After you have got to grips with the structure of the school system, you can build up a fuller picture of the alternatives. Later chapters in the book investigate the educational and social aspects of school culture in finer detail. They encompass the academic framework – classroom teaching, curriculum, homework, examination performance and league tables – and provide an insight into the internal organisation and personnel, as well as dealing with the issues of discipline and pastoral care.

The facilities on offer at individual schools and practicalities such as school size and school food are all better evaluated at a later stage, during an Open Day or at interview. This guide supplies practical pointers on the basics, while checklists throughout the book suggest what to look out for and suitable questions to ask as you tour a school.

The final section of the book is designed to provide assistance once you have visited and assessed several schools and have arrived at a shortlist. It will help you to make sense of the many impressions you will have received, weigh up the pros and cons and transform negative to positive. This part contains advice on admission criteria, how to evaluate promotional material supplied by schools and how to come to a final decision.

Most of the information in this book is relevant to choosing a school wherever you live in the UK. However, some regional variation exists. Where the educational system of a country differs from that in England, this is highlighted in the text, while Appendices at the back of the book detail the particular arrangements in Scotland, Wales and Northern Ireland. Readers in these countries should refer to the relevant appendix in conjunction with Chapters 1–20.

Chapter 2

Schools in the state sector

The state education system is not always easy for a parent to understand. While at primary level the types of school are relatively uncomplicated, at secondary level you will be faced by a complex array of schools, depending on where you live. You are not alone; even some teachers consider the system confusing.

Local education authorities (LEAs)

A local education authority, or LEA, is a department of a county or borough council set up to provide educational services within its geographical boundaries.

There are 171 LEA areas in England and Wales. In Northern Ireland the five LEAs are called Library and Education Boards and Scotland has 32 education authorities (SLAs). Some LEAs are sub-divided into separate geographical areas for administrative purposes, and some do not offer every type of school.

LEAs manage the provision of nursery, primary and secondary schools and some post-16 education, as well as facilities for special educational needs. They must ensure the supply of sufficient school places of the right type for the children in their area. Included in the education service are school transport and benefits such as free school meals, specialist services such as those provided by welfare officers and educational psychologists, special educational needs assessment and relevant legal, property and financial advice. LEAs also provide staff advice/training and governor training.

LEAs may formulate their own policies within given parameters, although they are ultimately answerable to the Secretary of State for Education and Employment. LEAs regulate admission policies at LEA schools or adopt a consultative role – see 'Categories of school', below, and Chapter 16. They can allocate and distribute funds to schools according to their own criteria (based mainly on the number of children in a school) that must nevertheless meet government requirements. LEAs will retain some funds to administer services provided centrally. Disparities exist in LEA funding throughout the UK: various attempts have been made to produce a common funding formula but because of local circumstances this would not necessarily guarantee the same provision in all areas.

The government expects LEAs to play a strategic role: the Schools Standards and Framework Act 1998 outlines the partnership between LEAs and schools and gives LEAs a specific duty to promote high educational standards. The Fair Funding programme aims to make LEAs more accountable by making their spending arrangements more transparent and requires them to review their spending on education, while Local Management of Schools (LMS) devolves responsibility to schools and awards them control of a larger share of the budget.

Categories of school

The School Standards and Framework Act phased out grant-maintained schools and established five categories of state school which are to operate from 1 September 1999. These are:

- community
- foundation
- voluntary-aided
- voluntary-controlled
- community special and foundation special.

These categories cover all levels of schooling from primary through to secondary schools. They may be comprehensive, selective, co-educational or single-sex. Schools of a religious character may be found in the voluntary-aided, voluntary-controlled or foundation categories, depending largely on their history. In introducing the new categories, the government's ambition is that all state schools should provide an equally high level of education.

Community

Community schools comprise the previous County schools. The LEA owns the school, employs the staff and is the admission authority, determining the catchment boundaries in accordance with local schooling patterns (see page 228). About a third of the governing body will be made up of LEA representatives. Religious schools are not permitted to belong to this category.

Foundation

Foundation schools account for most of the former grant-maintained schools. A few religious schools may fall under this category. The governing body usually owns the school land, employs the staff and is the admission authority in consultation with the LEA – see Chapter 16. Unlike grant-maintained schools, foundation schools must now include some LEA representation on the governing body and they are funded by the LEA rather than centrally.

Voluntary-aided

These schools are owned by a voluntary body, usually a church or other religious authority, rather than by the LEA. In most cases the voluntary body appoints the foundation governors, who must be in the majority: other governors are either appointed or elected. Funds are provided by the LEA, with the exception of building and repair costs, which are shared between the voluntary body, the LEA and the government. The governors employ the staff, determine the admission criteria in consultation with the LEA and decide about admissions in cases of over-subscription. Voluntary-aided schools may give priority to pupils who are practising members of the appropriate religion, and the catchment area tends to play a much less significant role in the case of over-subscription. Religious education at voluntary-aided schools is denominational.

Voluntary-controlled

Voluntary-controlled schools are owned by a voluntary body, normally a church, but are maintained by the LEA. At voluntary-controlled schools the number of foundation governors will not exceed the number of other governors appointed. The LEA determines the admission criteria which the schools may then apply on its behalf if this is delegated. For more information see Chapter 16.

Religious education is non-denominational, although parents may request denominational teaching.

Community special and foundation special

These schools cater for children with complex or severe special educational needs: mainstream schools provide education for most children with special needs with the assistance of external support services. Children attending special schools, some of which are residential, will either have 'statements' of special educational needs or will be undergoing statutory assessment. See Chapter 5 for more information.

Religious schools

Religious or church schools may be voluntary-aided, voluntary-controlled or, in a few cases, foundation schools. They offer education to children of all school ages and tend to be in demand as a result of their showings in the league tables and their perceived good standards of discipline.

The education that religious schools provide is funded by the state and is free, but admission may be open only to families that actively practise the relevant religion. However, some schools have places for children of other denominations or faiths. The majority of religious schools cater for Church of England or Roman Catholic pupils. In rural areas many primary schools are affiliated to the Church of England but accept all local children.

As religious schools in some areas are heavily over-subscribed, families may be subjected to a rigorous selection process based on their history of worship. Where demand is highest, a parish priest or minister may be asked to confirm the family's regular attendance at the church or temple, while in areas where competition is less frenzied the religious qualifications may be more relaxed.

Types of school according to age

The age ranges fall broadly into the following categories, although the structure of individual schools will vary depending on the policy of the LEA.

Age	Type of school
18 months–5 years	Childcare centre (strictly speaking not a school)
3–5	Nursery/nursery class
4/5–11	Primary (or infant and junior)
11–16 or 18	Secondary
16–18	Sixth-form college and further education college

Lower, middle and upper schools

In a few areas, educational provision is divided into three stages, rather than two (primary and secondary), with the addition of the middle school:

- **first school**: ages 4 to 9/10
- **middle school**: ages 9/10 to 12/13
- **upper school**: ages 12/13 to 16/18.

Childcare and education in the early years

Pre-school education is a key to later performance, in that children who have spent the most time in a nursery or playgroup are better prepared for their future school career (see page 46).

Nursery education should have a caring approach, with schools aiming to accommodate each child's particular needs and each child being allowed to develop at his or her own pace. Ideally, the emphasis should be on personal development, and on preparation for the next step up the educational ladder.

Early learning goals for pre-school children

The Qualifications and Curriculum Authority (QCA), a government body, has set down six 'desirable outcomes' – now to be known as 'early learning goals' – which children should attain by the time they move into Year 1 of the National Curriculum at the age of five. Most establishments catering for pre-school children will follow these guidelines (see pages 155–6).

Since many parents organise care for their pre-school children in both the state and private sectors, and some free places are available in the private sector (see page 44), this section should be read in conjunction with Chapter 3, which covers independent nursery care.

The Daycare Trust* can provide the telephone numbers of day care services in your area. You could also ask your LEA and Social Services department whether they produce any leaflets on pre-school facilities. Your local library will also be able to provide information, and publications are available from the National Early Years Network.*

The boom in pre-school places

During the 1990s the number of children attending nurseries in Britain has increased dramatically, with more than 1.1 million children between the ages of two and four attending various forms of nursery provision.

Free places for 4-year-olds

Although there is no legal requirement for a child to attend school before the term following his or her fifth birthday, free part-time education is now offered for every 4-year-old. The Nursery Education Grant Scheme (also known as the Early Years Grant) was introduced to subsidise each child's early education from the age of four until he or she starts school.

- On reaching the age of four, your child is entitled to a free pre-school place for a maximum of five two-and-a-half-hour sessions per week, 33 weeks per year (i.e. three terms of 11 weeks).
- The government provides a flat-rate grant, £1,130 at the time of writing, to the pre-school provider to cover the cost of this provision.
- If parents want more sessions than are covered by the cost of the grant, they must pay whatever fees are required to top up the provision, either with the original provider if this is possible, or elsewhere. Note that there is a considerable variation in fees throughout the UK.

- No more than two sessions may be combined in one day. You do not have to take up all the sessions, but you cannot carry forward unused sessions to another week.

You can take the entitlement up at a nursery school, a playgroup, a day nursery, an independent school, a nursery unit or a reception class in a primary school for 4- and 5-year-olds, depending on the number of places available. The provider does not have to be within LEA boundaries – you can combine different providers free of charge up to the maximum five sessions per week and pay to top up this attendance if you wish. Every provider must comply with the educational standards laid down by the government and will be inspected by a registered nursery inspector. Reports are available from the provider, your local library and Ofsted.* Ofsted is to assume responsibility for the regulation of pre-school facilities in 2001 (see page 44). Checks are also carried out on staff and premises to ensure safety.

To receive funding, your child must be registered and attending the chosen provider by a given date. This may be in September, January or the summer, depending on when his or her fourth birthday falls. If this is:

- between September and December, your child can start the following January
- between January and March, your child can start the following summer term
- between April and August, your child can start the following September.

Every provider must offer at least one place covered by the cost of the grant. Parents do not need to complete any paperwork for this grant. It is claimed by the provider on their behalf. You should ensure that your provider is registered: ask the school or check with your LEA.

Free places for 3-year-olds

The government has underlined its commitment to expanding early-years education by allocating £390 million to provide pre-school places for 3-year-olds. The scheme will be phased in over three years. In the first tranche, £41.5 million was made available from September 1999 to provide 41,500 free nursery places. This will increase to 47,800 in 2000, with a further 190,000 extra places available by 2001–2. This is not a universal entitlement, but the government hopes to attain a participation rate of 66 per cent by April 2002. The driving force for the first year is 'greatest social need', and at the time of writing 57 LEAs in urban areas have been selected to offer this provision, with different targets agreed for different areas in relation to the population.

The structure and type of provision is much the same as that for 4-year-olds, with the exception that places should not be in reception classes and should be appropriate for that age level. As with the existing scheme, LEAs are encouraged to involve the private sector through existing Early Years Development Partnerships (see page 44).

In recognition of the different qualities necessary for working with such young children, a new Standards Fund for the training and development of early-years staff has been established.

Ensuring that your child gets a pre-school place

With demand high, it is advisable to make enquiries and register your interest early to ensure a pre-school place with your chosen provider. In the case of reception classes, being awarded a place will depend on your child satisfying the specific admissions policy for that school (this is because once a child enters a reception class, he or she has effectively gained entry into the school); other providers are more flexible since parents have to apply separately for primary-school places. If you are seeking a reception place, contact your LEA to see what is available and find out about admissions procedures.

When you first enrol your child, you will be asked to produce his or her birth certificate (copies are not acceptable), and must complete a form declaring the number of sessions you wish the child to attend. To prevent possible abuse of the system, you will be required to sign a declaration each term that you are not receiving a grant for more than five sessions a week. You must also confirm at the beginning of each term whether your child is included in the school's claim for that term. In exceptional circumstances some children at LEA schools or nursery units may attend full-time without paying extra.

Childcare centres

These are also known as family centres or early-years nursery centres and are provided and funded by the local LEA and Social Services. Children may attend from as young as 18 months until they reach school age at five years. Extended day care is available outside school hours (9.15 a.m. to 3.15 p.m.) and childcare centres are open for most of the year. Casual visiting during the day may be possible. This can be helpful for parents who work and those with older children of primary school age, who can join in during school holidays.

The adult-to-child ratio tends to be highly advantageous: for children under three, it should be 1:4, while over the age of three the ratio should be 1:8; it is not unusual to find one teacher and three assistants to 30 children.

A charge is made for very young children (usually those under the age of three), and for extended day care hours regardless of age. This fee may be means-tested, so ask if you are in doubt. In the case of Social Services referrals, extended day/holiday places will be paid for.

You can find out about childcare centres via your local Social Services department, which will supply the *Under Eights Directory* listing all the childcare services in your area, or alternatively through your LEA. The Daycare Trust★ will provide details of local centres.

Nursery schools

Nursery provision is either in a nursery school or the nursery unit of a primary school. Some admit children from the age of three and admission arrangements are controlled by the schools themselves. It is important to register your interest sufficiently early – see opposite.

The education provided in the maintained sector is primarily play-based, offering a range of activities designed to promote social and intellectual development. Pre-school children are now expected to achieve certain learning goals by the end of the reception year in primary school (see pages 155–6). If you prefer a formal approach to learning at this stage, you might want to investigate independent nursery and pre-prep schools (see Chapter 3).

The Department for Education and Employment (DfEE) recommends that for every 26 full-time children in nursery classes which belong to primary schools there should be at least one teacher and one full-time qualified assistant. It is a legal requirement in the state, but not the independent, system that teachers at such nursery schools have qualified teacher status (see pages 112–13). The teacher–pupil ratios at stand-alone nursery schools are 1:10 if the head teaches and 1:13 if the head does not teach. These figures are on occasion flouted.

Easing the transition to nursery school

The first experience of nursery school can be traumatic for children parted from their mothers for several hours a day and exposed to strangers and possibly to school food. Some children are ready for these hurdles much earlier than others. Parental attitudes to when is the right stage to introduce children to this environment also vary: some start their children from as young as two in the independent sector, while others keep their children at home until the age of five.

How you introduce your child to the system is up to you but, whatever you choose, it is imperative to plan well ahead and take your child's needs into account.

Some children are very sociable and enjoy being part of an enlarged community; others – although benefiting from social contact and the opportunity to develop their social skills – require a gentler induction. However, do not assume that just because some children are extroverted, they can be launched immediately into a full day at nursery school before their fifth birthday. It may be better to allow your child a probationary period of mornings or afternoons only, followed by an increasing number of full days, as a means of building up to a full week in preparation for his or her fifth birthday.

Private nursery care may offer parents greater flexibility if choice is restricted in the state sector. If a school is unwilling to accommodate your apprehensions or allow a gradual introduction to the world of formal learning, you should question its motives. Do not be bullied into accepting a regime about which you have misgivings.

If you are not happy with what is available, do not try to force the issue. If a nursery school does not meet your basic requirements and falls at the crucial hurdles it might be more beneficial to keep your child at home, provided this is an option.

Primary schools

The primary-school age range extends from 5 to 12 years, although in the majority of cases children will transfer to secondary school at the age of 11 (12 in Scotland). Parents should be aware that primary education may be provided in separate infant and junior schools (infant schools are for ages 5–7, junior schools for ages 7–11). These schools are usually linked or on the same site; the arrangement segregates younger childen so that they are not overwhelmed by the older pupils. Most schools now combine these age groups into primary schools. Some schools are divided into first and middle schools (see page 27). Parents should note the differences in the system and plan accordingly, particularly if they are likely to move into another area.

Starting primary school

Teachers in reception classes at primary schools, some with little early-years training, are having to adjust to an influx of 4-year-olds as LEAs expand primary and infant schools to meet their new responsibility to provide places for this age group. At the same time as children are entering primary school at a younger age, the introduction of the literacy hour and numeracy session (see Chapter 14) has made primary education more formal. However, an improvement will be brought about by new legislation on class size which aims to ensure that by 2001 infant classes, including reception classes, do not exceed 30 pupils to each qualified teacher. In 60 LEAs where social need is greatest, this ratio reduces to 15:1.

Admission to primary school

Your child is more than likely to be four years old at the time of starting school. For details on admission, see Chapter 16. While the transition is likely to be straightforward if your son or daughter attends the nursery class of a primary school, at a new school the staff will be alert and sympathetic to your fears and those of your child. Many schools operate a gentle introduction system, with flexible attendance for part of the first term. As with the independent system (see Chapter 3), some schools may divide classes strictly by age group, others group vertically with pupils from two or more year groups mixed in one class. This depends on school policy and is more common in schools with low pupil numbers.

Feeder schools

Some LEAs link specific secondary schools to 'feeder' primary schools to ensure close co-operation in the development of an educational programme and a smooth transition from the primary to the second-ary school. This can act as a preferential factor when a secondary school becomes over-subscribed and admission criteria have to be applied.

Matt

Matt's parents wanted him to attend a particular secondary school. The family lived outside both the secondary school's catchment area and that of his primary school, and Matt did not have an elder brother or sister attending the secondary school. His chances of gaining a place therefore seemed slim, but a factor in his favour was that his primary school was 'linked' to the secondary school his parents liked. When it came to applying for a place, the special status of the primary school and his parents' expressed preference helped him to secure a place.

Secondary schools

Children receive secondary education between the ages of 11 and 16. Most secondary schools are comprehensive and co-educational (i.e. they are non-selective and boys and girls are taught together). A minority are selective. Single-sex secondary schools also exist – some LEAs have a much higher proportion of single-sex schools than the national average. Single-sex schools are examined in Chapter 4.

Some schools have mixed-ability classes, although children are increasingly set, or grouped according to their ability in different subjects. The advantages and disadvantages of teaching children in different ways are discussed on pages 194–5.

For information on admission procedures, see Chapter 16.

Easing the transition to secondary school

The move up to secondary school can be traumatic. The children are leaving a familiar community and need to adjust to a new environment and a different system of classes. They may be overwhelmed by the surroundings and older pupils. With this in mind many secondary schools organise introduction or 'taster' days whereby pupils from their traditional feeder schools can spend the day finding their way around the facilities. Independent schools use these as a sales vehicle and entertainment is laid on to make sure the 'visitors' are sold on the idea.

Grammar schools

These schools have been retained in a few LEA areas. They select pupils by academic ability and achieve good examination results. In England at the time of writing there are just over 160 grammar schools. In Northern Ireland the tradition of grammar schools is entrenched, with 72 grammar schools alongside 165 non-selective schools. Scotland has no grammar schools. Several state boarding schools (see pages 39–40) are grammar schools.

To gain entry, pupils sit an entrance exam, the '11-plus' or equivalent, at the age of 11 or 12 depending on local arrangements (see page 241). This selection process has been a contentious issue in England and Wales for many years (see below).

The future of grammar schools

The future of grammar schools is once again the subject of political debate. Those in favour argue that grammar schools have a long tradition of providing academic education to children who can benefit from it, and point to the many children from less well-off backgrounds who have been given a 'leg up' by grammar schools. The opposition, including parents whose children have not succeeded in gaining a grammar-school place, believe that segregating children at 11 is wrong and argue that selection fails to identify late developers and bright children who perform badly on the test day. Over-subscribed grammar schools in areas with otherwise poor state schools are particularly at risk.

The government has indicated that grammar schools may continue unless local parents vote against them. The machinery to enable this will be in place from September 2001. Campaigners must get 20 per cent of eligible parents to sign a petition demanding a ballot. In those LEAs where at least 25 per cent of secondary places are selective there will be area ballots in which all parents of school-age children can vote. In other LEA areas which contain grammar schools, only parents whose children attend the feeder schools (see page 34) can vote. All the signs are that the respective campaigns to save or end selection will be fiercely fought.

City technology colleges

These schools are partly funded by the government, but the DfEE classifies them as being outside the maintained sector. They provide free education. The capital funding they receive per pupil from the government is topped up by a minimum of 20 per cent from outside sponsorship.

City technology colleges (CTCs) were originally set up to provide education to inner-city areas and are therefore mostly found in urban centres. There are 15 in all: 14 CTCs and one CCTA (City College for the Technology of the Arts). All 15 operate within a fixed catchment area and, although they can apply to the DfEE to have their catchment area changed, alterations are very unlikely in practice. With the introduction of the technology colleges in the Specialist Schools Programme (see opposite), their number will not be expanded.

CTCs are popular due to their good exam performance and there can be as many as 1,500 applicants for 200 places. The intake is essentially comprehensive, but in an effort to ensure that those children who can benefit most from what they have to offer are awarded a place, CTCs look for aptitude in mathematics, science and technology. All pupils are tested and grouped into ability bands, and from these bands a cross-section is selected to reflect the catchment area. This testing process is loosely defined and varies in different colleges. For example, some may use an open discussion, others a series of questions based on viewing a video – there are no hard-and-fast rules.

Parents interested in CTCs are advised to contact individual colleges to obtain current details of the admission process and other information. Your LEA should be able to provide the necessary addresses and telephone numbers.

Specialist schools

Superimposed upon the maintained secondary schools system in England is the Specialist Schools Programme, which has been designed to provide centres of excellence in the community in four main categories:

- technology colleges
- sports colleges
- language colleges
- art colleges.

Specialist schools are existing secondary schools which have been granted specialist status in one of the four disciplines listed above as a result of a national competition which is held twice yearly. Special schools (see page 26) can also apply for specialist school designation. At the time of writing there are over 300 specialist schools, with technology colleges much the largest group as these have been in existence for a longer period. The government has revised the original target figure of 450 and is now aiming for 800 designations by 2002–3. Nearly all specialist schools are comprehensive, admitting pupils of all abilities, with 10 per cent of places being reserved for children with an aptitude in the specialist area.

Priority is given to applications from schools in Education Action Zones (see pages 215–6) and deprived areas. Schools competing for specialist status must satisfy a rigorous procedure and raise private sponsorship before the government will determine which to designate, depending on available funding. The special status ensures financial support from the government over and above the normal level of funding to allow the school to improve its facilities and employ specialist staff. The private sponsors also play their part and become closely involved with the schools, providing business and work experience and careers advice. See Chapter 15 for more information on business involvement in schools.

While specialist status does not significantly affect the fundamental character of the school, a responsibility to the community accompanies the conferred advantages. A condition of the award is that a school must share its expertise and facilities with other schools in the area and the local community, thus maximising government resources and extending their impact.

Schools in all four categories teach the full National Curriculum (see Chapter 12). In addition, they must develop their specialist field – in terms of skills and numbers of pupils – and seek to improve examination results in that area. They must also provide courses for children over the age of 16 which lead to relevant academic or vocational qualifications, and prepare students effectively for an adult working life through methods such as work experience. Further provisions exist for the different disciplines. To comply with these requirements many schools extend the school day, use information technology where relevant and ensure that teachers receive appropriate training.

Technology colleges

The government has responded to the demand from the manufacturing and service industries for workers with better technical knowledge by expanding the number of technology colleges. They concentrate their energies on teaching technology, science and mathematics, providing full courses to GCSE-level or equivalent, followed by courses leading to vocational or academic qualifications for those over 16.

Sports colleges

The remit of these colleges is to improve standards in physical education and community sport across a wide range of disciplines, both team and individual, through first-class coaching and facilities and by forging links with various sports bodies. The colleges must encourage talented students to fulfil their potential and prepare them for careers requiring relevant qualifications, for example those of professional player or coach.

The intention is that these colleges will enable local communities to tap into their resources and possibly boost national sporting performance.

Language colleges

The increasing realisation among businesses and employers that skill in at least one modern foreign language is necessary in order to compete commercially outside the UK has fuelled moves to address the sorry state of the UK's foreign language base. Specialist language schools aim to answer this challenge.

In addition to teaching linguistic skills in a broad selection of languages, they also teach cultural awareness in relation to those languages, aiming to immerse students in the learning process as much as possible. Pupils must study two languages in Key Stage 4 (see Chapter 12) and are expected to attain a qualification in at least one. After the age of 16, they are required to add a third modern foreign language. The schools organise exchange or study visits, as well as work experience abroad.

Arts colleges

These schools have been set up to maximise the growing career opportunities available in the media industry. They aim to do this by providing a solid foundation, and raising teaching standards, in the relevant disciplines. With just a handful in existence, they are the smallest category of specialist school.

Colleges must choose one of three areas in which to specialise:

- **the performing arts** (music, drama, dance and related technical disciplines)
- **the visual arts** (for example, painting, computer-assisted design, textiles, jewellery design)
- **the media arts** (film, television, advertising, journalism and related technical aspects).

Financial and advisory support is supplied by the relevant industries.

For more information on all types of college, contact the DfEE Specialist Schools Division.★

State boarding schools

An increasing number of parents are showing an interest in these schools, which are one of the state system's best-kept secrets – many members of the teaching profession are not even aware of their existence.

These local authority schools take day pupils and boarders, and range from mixed-ability and co-educational to selective and single-sex. Most are secondary schools, although one or two cater for the very young and several take siblings of primary-school age who will attend the local day school. Two are sixth-form colleges (see below).

In summer 1999 the 36 schools throughout England and Wales provided over 4,000 boarding places. However, Wales and the north-east of England are badly served. Pupils can apply from anywhere in the UK and the European Union, and some schools admit children from outside the EU provided they have UK resident status in order to board.

Admission requirements vary according to the type of school. Entry may be by interview, selection tests, school reports or, in the sixth form, GCSE performance.

Tuition is free as in all state schools; parents pay only for boarding and there is usually a reduction for weekly boarding and for siblings. The cost varies from just under £1,000 to just over £2,000 per term. Bursaries and scholarships may also be available (see Chapter 17).

All schools follow the National Curriculum (see Chapter 12) and some have specialist school status (see pages 37–9). Pupil–teacher ratios are advantageous and facilities tend to be good, offering a wide range of extra-curricular activities.

To find out about state boarding schools, contact the State Boarding Information Service (STABIS)★ to obtain a free booklet, *Parents' Guide to Maintained Boarding Schools*, or ask your LEA for information. The Boarding Education Alliance★ provides advice on both state and independent schools. Members of HM Forces can obtain details from Service Children's Education (UK).★

Sixth-form and further-education colleges

Not all secondary schools have a sixth form for 16- to 18-year-olds, so it may be necessary for your child to continue his or her education at another secondary school with a sixth form, or at a sixth-form college or further education college. Some teenagers choose to switch to a sixth-form or further education college at 16 because they prefer the company of other young adults.

Sixth-form colleges and further education colleges teach GCSE courses, A-levels, AS-levels and vocational GNVQ courses. They can make provision for students to re-sit GCSE subjects where necessary. Some colleges require a minimum level of achievement at GCSE-level to gain entry and stipulate minimum GCSE grades for certain A-level courses. For more information on courses see Chapter 12.

LEA sixth-form colleges are not necessarily restricted to those living within the LEA boundaries. Further education colleges are independent corporations funded directly by the Further Education Funding Council (FEFC)★ – see box. These colleges have links with local LEAs for the provision of special education, vocational and non-vocational adult education and courses for pupils aged 14–16 who are at risk of disaffection from school.

Replacement of the FEFC

The 450 colleges under FEFC control have suffered from poor standards and low staying-on rates. The government intends to raise standards and improve quality by replacing the FEFC with the Learning and Skills Council, which will be the responsibility of the Chief Inspector of Schools. These proposals will come into effect in 2001.

Parents who require general information and advice on all types of state school should contact the DfEE Public Enquiry Unit.★ Staff will put callers in touch with specialist advisers.

Chapter 3

Schools in the independent sector

The Independent Schools Council (ISC),★ formerly the Independent Schools Joint Council, is a national body that represents the collective interests of eight independent schools' associations, by whom it was formed. These are:

- the Girls' Schools Association (GSA)★
- the Governing Bodies Association (GBA)★
- the Governing Bodies of Girls' Schools Association (GBGSA)★
- the Headmasters' and Headmistresses' Conference (HMC)★
- the Incorporated Association of Preparatory Schools (IAPS)★
- the Independent Schools Association (ISA)★
- the Independent Schools' Bursars Association (ISBA)★
- the Society of Headmasters and Headmistresses of Independent Schools (SHMIS)★

Also included is representation from the Scottish Council of Independent Schools (SCIS).★

The ISC does not cover all private schools. For example, nursery schools will not belong to the ISC unless they are part of an independent school. Over 1,300 independent schools belong to one of the ISC associations listed above, together accounting for 80 per cent of all pupils in private schools.

The press and communications office of the ISC is the Independent Schools Information Service (ISIS),★ which helps to advance the aims of the ISC in marketing independent schools.

Categories of school

Independent schools do not display the same variation in categories as state schools (see Chapter 2). The majority of independent schools are selective.

Types of school according to age

The types of school fall broadly into the following categories, dependent on the age of the pupil:

Age	Type of school
2–5	Nursery/playgroup
4/5–7	Pre-preparatory
7–11 or 13	Preparatory
11 or 13–18	Independent secondary schools (including public schools)
16–18	Sixth-form tutorial colleges

Apart from the variations that exist amongst the schools themselves, parents may make certain modifications within the age framework. For example, a child might go to a pre-preparatory (pre-prep) school at the age of four, or to a preparatory (prep) school at the age of eight or more.

Parents should note that the age of entry to secondary school varies. Most independent secondary schools have their major intake at 11 or 12, and fill only a few leftover places at 13. Others – including some public schools (see page 54) – recruit most of their intake at 13, and some have a lower or middle school for children aged 10/11 (see page 53). Parents are advised not to rely on second-hand information, but to find out what the policy is at each school under consideration.

Childcare and education in the early years

Childcare and education in the private sector can be expensive and the younger the child the more costly this is, as the ratio of staff to children is higher. With the increasing tendency among women to delay parenthood until their careers are well established and to return to work following the birth of their children, childcare has become big business and organisations catering for this have burgeoned, taking advantage of an expanding market.

Unless you are going to employ a live-in nanny or an au pair, you may wish to consider some of the following options:

- day nursery
- registered childminder
- playgroup
- crèche.

Kindergartens

You may come across institutions called kindergartens (German for 'children's garden'). The term does not signify any special type of provision – they operate along similar lines to the providers listed here. Ask for details at each kindergarten.

Many childcare providers now offer education following the introduction of the Nursery Education Grant Scheme. This provides free places for all 4-year-olds (see pages 28–9) and some places for 3-year-olds (see pages 29–30). The extension of this scheme into the private sector was brought about by the Early Years Development Partnership, set up by each LEA to administer early-years education in each area. This produced the Early Years Development Plan, under which providers must register to become eligible for funding from the Nursery Education Grant Scheme.

Each provider must comply with the educational standards laid down by the government (see box, page 27), and will be inspected by a registered Ofsted nursery inspector. Reports are available from the provider and the local library. From September 1999 it became a requirement that a qualified teacher must be present wherever the scheme operates. Parents must also be given information about the number of early-years workers and their qualifications.

In 2001 new proposals will come into effect whereby a new branch of Ofsted★ will co-ordinate the regulation of early-years education and childcare and be responsible for registration, inspection and enforcement.

The Daycare Trust★ can provide the phone numbers of local private day-care services. As all pre-schools and playgroups must currently register with Social Services, a phone call to your local department will provide you with a list of services in your area, while the Pre-school Learning Alliance★ can supply a list of its members and put you in touch with your local group. The National Early Years Network★ provides a range of useful publications.

Day nurseries

These are childminding operations open virtually all year apart from Christmas and bank holidays. They cater specifically for working parents and provide care for babies and children up to five years old throughout the day.

Fees are charged on a weekly or per-session basis and may be up to £180 per week. However, if the day nursery participates in the free places scheme (see opposite) it must provide free education for 4-year-olds for two-and-a-half hours daily.

Day nurseries must adhere to the following adult–child ratios: 1:3 for children under two; 1:4 for children over two and under three; 1:8 for children over three and under five. Meals are included and a broad range of activities should be on offer. All day nurseries are inspected and registered by Social Services. For advice on starting your child at nursery, see 'Easing the transition to nursery school', page 32.

Following the government's introduction of learning goals for pre-school children (see pages 155–6), private day nurseries may move away from play-based activities towards more structured education where appropriate.

Registered childminders

Childminders who care for children under the age of eight must be registered with Social Services if they look after children for two hours or more, and their homes are inspected regularly. The Children Act restricts the number of children a childminder may care for. Most childminders have public liability insurance, and some local authorities insist upon this.

Childminders provide children with a normal daily routine both in and outside the house, and may visit parks and playgrounds. You should check whether the childminder can drive if you want your child to be transported during the day. Logistical problems might occur if your holidays do not coincide.

Weekly rates vary from £50 to £300, depending on location (Greater London is the most expensive). Childminders can register for the Nursery Grant Scheme under the Early Years Development Plan. For more information, contact the National Childminding Association.*

Crèches

These are regulated in the same way as day nurseries. Some nurseries run by employers are called crèches, but the term is generally used of any establishment that only takes children under the age of three.

Parents with children at workplace crèches do not have to pay tax on childcare costs, provided the care is wholly or partly subsidised by the employer and does not constitute educational supervision. The Daycare Trust* can provide information on workplace crèches and how to organise one.

Pre-schools and playgroups

These schemes are organised by the local community, with parent volunteers helping out, and tend to provide a relaxed family atmosphere. Usually, care is provided for only a few hours in the morning or afternoon each day during term time, which may not suit parents who work full-time.

The benefits of pre-school attendance

In spring 1999 an American study undertaken by the National Institute of Child Health and Human Development, which followed 1,200 children from one month old to the age of seven, reported that children who attended crèches and nurseries made greater leaps in their development, both in learning and social skills, than those who remained at home with their mothers. It is thought that nursery teaching provides intellectual stimulation at an important stage of brain development. However, this does not mean that children kept at home do not benefit from the parental support and care they receive there.

The cost ranges from £2.50 to £6 per session. If the pre-school offers free places to 4-year-olds (see page 28) and your child qualifies for a place, you will only have to pay if he or she attends for more than two-and-a-half hours each day or more than 33 weeks per year.

Nursery schools

Not to be confused with day nurseries, private nursery schools are primarily concerned with children's development and education, in preparation for full-time attendance at a pre-prep school. Hours coincide with normal school hours and holidays. Fees, payable a term in advance, start at about £400 per term. However, two-and-a-half hours of education per day may be free if the school belongs to the free places scheme (see page 28).

Increased demand has led to private day nurseries incorporating nursery schools into their system, and *vice versa*, in order to cater for children from the age of a few months upwards. Some of these schools have conveniently geared their hours to working parents.

Free-standing nursery schools (i.e. those which are not part of a pre-prep school) recognised as efficient are staffed by certified teachers with special nursery-school training, assistants with National Nursery Examination Board (NNEB) certificates and often students in training. At least half the teachers in the school must have a teaching qualification. The permitted adult–child ratio is 1:13, so classes supervised by a qualified teacher and one assistant may contain up to 26 children, or 1:10 if the head teaches. If the children are supervised by an unqualified adult the ratio is much stricter, namely 1:8.

Warning

Nursery units attached to independent schools are not obliged to meet legal requirements on pupil–teacher ratios and staff qualifications, although ISC members are expected to ensure that staff are suitably qualified. In a worst-case scenario, you could find yourself paying through the nose while a school deliberately milks the lack of legal controls (see case history overleaf).

Jenny

Jenny had recently qualified with her NNEB Diploma in Nursery Nursing when she went to work at a new pre-prep department in an independent school whose headmistress had just been appointed. Either through the headmistress's incompetence or cost-cutting, Jenny was put in sole charge of a reception class of 18 children with no assistance whatsoever. Unsurprisingly, her workload led to chaos and confusion with little learning being achieved. Jenny left shortly afterwards.

The element of choice among private nursery schools or units will be limited by where you live, although you are unlikely to be restricted to just one school unless you live in a rural area. Some parents will be able and willing to travel further than others.

Children normally enter their chosen nursery or pre-prep school in the company of others of the same age. They join a specific class or form and remain there for a full year. Exceptions to this may occur if a single class covers the age span of say, two to four years, or if an exceptionally bright child is moved a year ahead of his or her age band. The section entitled 'Easing the transition to nursery school' on page 32 explains how to ensure that your child's experience is as trouble-free as possible.

ISIS* can inform you about private schools with nurseries in your area.

Selection tests

Some nurseries and pre-prep departments (see pages 51–2) apply selection tests. These may range from verbal skills and reasoning to basic arithmetic tests. The pressure on parents and children can be considerable (see page 188). You may or may not feel comfortable about your son or daughter being exposed to this kind of stress at a young age.

The use of IQ tests alone has been questioned, as they can be unreliable – results in the same child can vary greatly and are seemingly wholly dependent on the type of test and the mood of the child on a given day. The contrasting concept of 'emotional intelligence' has also been advanced as a measure of ability. It is suggested that academic intelligence, which may be discerned from IQ tests, does not guarantee success in later life, whereas those with emotional and social competence, which can be measured at an early age (even as young as four), display more academic competence in the long run. Testing for emotional intelligence involves the child being observed while undertaking exercises such as puzzles; the child should not be aware that he or she is being assessed. The hallmarks of emotional intelligence are said to be self-motivation, self-reliance, determination and the ability to empathise with others.

IQ and emotional intelligence are not mutually exclusive, as we all have both to varying degrees. Good pre-school education should aim to improve both.

Montessori schools

The Association Montessori Internationale was established in 1929 to maintain and propagate the principles of Dr Maria Montessori, the first woman to qualify as a doctor in Italy. She developed her approach to education as the result of her work with young disadvantaged children in Rome.

The overriding aim in the Montessori classroom is the development of the child's whole personality. There are three stages:

- **Infant and toddler communities** (2 months–3 years) provide the opportunity for very young children to develop their social skills through contact with other children.
- **Children's house** (3–6 years) As well as learning the skills of reading, writing and mathematics, children are encouraged to observe their surroundings and individual development is fostered through an appreciation of the environment.
- **Elementary level** (6–12 years) The major curriculum subjects are introduced. Children work in small groups, developing reasoning skills which are honed by excursions outside the classroom.

Montessori teachers are more actively involved with the younger children and will provide individual instruction to this age group; as the children grow and develop they will adopt the role of guide and observer.

Montessori practitioners claim that confidence, self-discipline and esteem result from children being given a certain freedom to make their own discoveries. To obtain a list of local Montessori nurseries, contact the Montessori Society.*

Rudolf Steiner Waldorf education

The Steiner Waldorf School Movement was founded in 1919 by Rudolf Steiner, an Austrian philosopher and educationalist whose ideas were embraced on a global scale. The 62 kindergartens and 27 schools in the United Kingdom are all co-educational. Boarding is arranged at some schools while others educate those with special needs.

The educational philosophy aims to develop and nurture the child's artistic, intellectual and practical faculties as part of the spiritual whole. Most teaching is experiential. Teaching techniques encourage imagination and creativity as a means to establishing a sound foundation and enthusiasm for learning, not just within the school environment but in adolescence and adulthood.

Apart from the parenting group and the nursery, there are three distinct age groups:

- **Kindergarten** (4–6+ years) Within a secure atmosphere, creative play is encouraged alongside practical activities such as handicrafts, baking and painting. Seasonal rhythms and festivals provide themes for activities.
- **Lower school** (6–14 years) Children normally remain with one class teacher throughout the entire period and are taught and inspired by that person across a wide variety of subjects. Writing and reading are introduced later than in most British schools, at the age of seven. At this point, additional teachers introduce foreign languages and eurythmics. By the age of 14, pupils will have reached the equivalent of the end of Key Stage 3 of the National Curriculum (see Chapter 12).
- **Upper school** (14–16 years) Subjects are taught by specialist teachers, with mentoring provided by a guardian teacher. Emphasis is placed on balancing academic worth with practical problem-solving, social and personal skills and artistic expression.

Steiner schools do not adhere to the National Curriculum, regarding it as too prescriptive, but share an international curriculum, adjusted and developed according to local conditions. Although each school is self-governing, a national Code of Practice is in place to ensure accountability and continuity. Qualified teacher status is not a requirement, but is recommended. Teachers receive training in Steiner educational methods.

Fees are either fixed or may be negotiable, usually based upon income. For more information and a list of schools, contact the Steiner Waldorf Schools Fellowship.★

Pre-prep schools

These establishments, for 5- to 7-year-olds, range from those with only one or two classes of mixed ages, to several quite large organisations with separate year structures. Most are mixed, but a small number are single-sex. Many pre-prep schools are accommodated in large private houses, although some have been purpose-built to meet recent demands for improved facilities, or have constructed extensions. Admission to pre-prep school is usually by interview. Fees per term range from £400 to £2,000.

By and large, pre-prep schools concentrate more on formal teaching than state schools, preparing children for entrance exams to their chosen prep school. Most also prepare pupils for the relevant scholarship exams. Pre-prep classes normally have the same teacher covering all academic subjects, but may also bring in on occasion specialist teachers in, for example, French, Latin, science or design and technology (subjects which, if taught at all, will be taught at a very elementary level).

Tip

Do not be over-impressed by pre-prep schools which use the existence of additional instructors as a selling point (see 'Laura and William', overleaf). If you have any knowledge of the subjects offered, be inquisitive and critical; if not, use common sense.

The boom in private pre-school provision

Parents who wish to start their children early on the educational ladder, but find restricted or unsuitable provision in the state sector,

Laura and William

The couple's daughter attended a pre-prep school which Laura and William had chosen for its specialist French teacher, an asset much hyped by the school. Naturally, they expected that their child would benefit from the extra tuition. However, the teacher spent most of her time teaching the pupils well-known French songs and archaic vocabulary from out-of-date books. As a consequence, the children could translate 'shepherd' and 'shepherdess', but were quite incapable of voicing any greeting or saying their name.

are swelling numbers in private nursery and pre-prep schools. However, many prep schools that offer facilities for younger children complain of decreasing numbers at the top end due to pupils moving on prematurely (before the age of 13) to state schools or private schools which take pupils at 11. The top end is more costly to run due to increased teaching demands and, as a result of an insufficient number of older pupils to pay their way, some of these establishments have had to close down, despite having a surplus of younger children.

Prep schools

Although several preparatory departments are run as separate parts of public schools, the majority are wholly independent organisations run as educational trusts. A few are still to be found in the ownership of the head teacher (see 'Proprietor heads', page 103).

Heads of prep schools are eligible for membership of the Independent Schools Association (ISA)★ and the Incorporated Association of Preparatory Schools (IAPS).★ The head must be a qualified teacher and the school must be accredited by the Independent Schools Council (ISC)★ after an inspection under a framework agreed with and monitored by Ofsted (see Chapter 6).

The theoretical aim of these schools is to prepare pupils for secondary school, which means coaching them for the Common Entrance exam at the appropriate age (11+ or 13+). Teaching is much more formal than in the pre-prep classroom, with children embarking upon preparation towards Common Entrance as soon as they join at the age of seven or eight. A scholarship stream is singled out in the last two years.

Prep schools are generally organised within a structured framework. They offer children the opportunity to assume responsibility as school officers as they move up the school, and badges of office and sports colours promote a sense of duty and achievement.

Most prep schools with boarding facilities are co-educational, although there are some single-sex boys' boarding schools. Prep school fees range from £2,700 to £11,000 per year, depending on whether the school provides boarding.

Some prep and secondary schools are under the same management structure. Often these are on different sites, but it is not necessarily an advantage when they share a site. Many children reach a stage where they welcome a change of scenery when it is time to enter secondary school. ISIS* can provide details of prep schools in your area.

A springboard to the state system

A child who benefits from the academic grounding a prep school offers and goes on to win a place at a grammar school or a good comprehensive could save his or her parents thousands of pounds on private school fees.

Middle/lower schools

An increasing number of private secondary schools, aiming to capture the market at 13, have opened up a middle (or lower) school for children aged 10 to 11. This means pupils do not experience membership of the top form in prep school; however, middle schools can offer a valuable service to parents who are dissatisfied with their child's prep school but do not want to remove him or her to another prep school.

A middle school's organisation within the framework of the main school is important. Be wary if school authorities play down the significance of this. Age is the main concern: sixth-formers aged 17 and 18 will have different needs from 10- and 11-year-olds; equally, 13-year-olds who have left prep school will not want to mix with younger children again.

Public schools

The oldest public schools were independent grammar schools, some dating from the Middle Ages, which were founded by the Church, the monarch, city companies and guilds, or wealthy patrons. In 1861 nine boarding schools – Eton, Winchester, Westminster, Charterhouse, Harrow, Rugby, Shrewsbury, St Paul's and Merchant Taylors – were recognised as 'public' by the Clarendon Commission because they took in boys from all over the country. Also accorded this status were schools run by governing bodies created as non-profit making organisations for the greater good, as opposed to those run by private proprietors for financial gain. Today public schools are recognised as members of the Headmasters' and Headmistresses' Conference (HMC),* the Governing Bodies Association (GBA)* or the Governing Bodies of Girls' Schools Association (GBGSA).* In addition, several other associations to which independent schools belong are loosely considered to confer 'public school status' upon their members (see page 42). Some people make distinctions between 'major' and 'minor' public schools or do not accept as 'real' public schools those which have day pupils only. This has no bearing on the suitability of an individual school.

Secondary schools

Independent secondary schools are sometimes described as 'public schools'. However, this definition is misleading since entry is not open to all and the schools charge fees ranging from £1,000 to £5,000 per term. In addition, not all independent schools are public schools, which is a title reserved for a minority of schools.

Owing to market pressures, many boys' independent schools have either become fully co-educational or are co-educational in the sixth form.

This shift has enabled parents to treat the sixth form as a separate entity and there is now considerable pupil movement between schools at sixth-form level, facilitated by the natural break between GCSEs and A-levels. Girls may join boys' schools, or pupils may come in from the state sector and *vice versa*. Note that some schools only take pupils up to GCSE-level, making a move at this stage necessary.

The prospect of attending secondary school can be daunting for some children. Moves adopted by schools to introduce pupils to this new environment are described on page 35.

The aims of secondary independent education

Pupils are prepared for GCSE exams at the age of 16, although certain subjects are taken earlier depending on ability. The GCE A-level and AS-level exams are taken in both lower and upper sixth. Some schools offer GNVQs for the older pupils as well as the International Baccalaureate. (See Chapter 12 for more information on courses.)

Outside the confines of the core curriculum subjects, schools may place a different emphasis on different subjects, or may specialise in a specific field.

Tutorial colleges

These colleges, sometimes known as 'crammers', teach GCSE, A-level and AS-level courses. Many offer a competitive alternative to school, and in selected subjects the standard of tuition may surpass that at school. They are a popular choice if exams have to be retaken and some allow pupils to take exam courses within one year. When choosing a college, check which examination board is used and the results in individual subjects, especially those your son or daughter wishes to take. The college's choice of examination board may affect exam results – see page 180.

Students enjoy a great degree of independence and some seize the opportunity to have a good time before university. Tutorial colleges can be very expensive – up to £3,000 a year – and most are selective. For more information, contact the Conference for Independent Further Education (CIFE).★

Chapter 4

Key concerns for parents

As well as deciding on the preferred educational sector and a suitable type of school (see Chapters 2 and 3), parents may have additional options open to them. These include choices between mixed and single-sex education and day and boarding schooling. Parents may also be in a position to choose establishments that place particular emphasis on sport or other activities such as music.

Co-educational *vs* single-sex schooling

The choice between co-educational and single-sex schooling raises some complex issues. Some differences between boys' and girls' academic performance are apparent, and gender issues become significant at adolescence when children start to get interested in the opposite sex. Some parents prefer the idea of one system rather than the other. However, it is important not to attach too much weight to this issue, as this section will demonstrate.

School statistics

There is more choice in the independent sector than in the state sector, but it is not as pronounced as some parents think. The figures vary slightly from year to year.

- **England** In 1998 there were 3,146 mixed state secondary schools and 193 boys' and 228 girls' schools. All primary schools were mixed apart from one boys' and one girls' school. Of the 2,242 independent prep and secondary schools, 282 were essentially boys-only, while 322 were essentially girls-only (these statistics are blurred because some private girls' schools allow boys in the younger age groups and some boys' schools admit girls in the sixth form).

- **Wales** All primary schools were mixed in 1998. There were 220 state secondary schools including 4 boys' and 4 girls' single-sex schools, while the independent secondary schools included 3 boys' and 4 girls' schools.

- **Scotland** Reliable figures are not available for Scotland, particularly for primary schools, as information is collated differently from elsewhere in the UK. However, it is possible to establish that in 1998 the 400 state secondary schools included 1 girls' school, while out of 176 independent schools 14 were single sex (4 boys' and 10 girls').

- **Northern Ireland**, in comparison, has a large proportion of single-sex schools. In 1998, out of a total of over 900 primary schools, over 40 were single-sex (at the time of writing 19 boys' and 23 girls'), while there were over 70 single-sex secondary schools (35 boys' and 38 girls') as against 164 mixed schools.

Many single-sex schools feel they are fighting a rearguard action while others, playing on examination results that appear to demonstrate the academic success of single-sex schools, have taken the opportunity to develop a niche market.

Parental preference

One survey carried out among parents on the issue of co-education *vs* single-sex showed that they preferred co-educational schooling for their sons and single-sex schooling for their daughters. This seems to beg the question, with whom should the boys be co-educated?

Co-educational schooling

As the figures above demonstrate, the vast majority of schools – particularly those in the state sector – are co-educational. The main argument propounded by those advocating co-education is that it reflects the real world. The sexes must co-exist in adulthood and sound emotional and social relationships are dependent on a mixed social structure developed in childhood. Proponents of co-education argue that interaction between boys and girls at an early age promotes a better understanding of each other in later life. This interaction starts at school, where it enriches classroom life. Those in favour of mixed education claim that segregation, or sexual apartheid, can distort the scheme of things, cause unnecessary problems in adolescence for children deprived of contact with the opposite sex and later lie at the root of unsatisfactory relationships.

In both educational sectors, the provision of science, technology and arts facilities can vary. The majority of mixed schools will provide across the board whereas some single-sex schools find themselves in difficulties in science and technology for girls, and arts for boys.

It is recognised that girls in co-educational schools are sometimes challenged by the presence of boys. Teenage boys tend be rowdy, dominate the classroom environment and demand more of the teachers' attention. In PE lessons, boys can be aggressive and may remark that girls are lazy and have little hand/eye co-ordination. Girls not only have to learn to cope with this behaviour but may also have to fight gender stereotyping when choosing subjects such as science and technology, which are traditionally male-dominated. In spite of this, girls in co-educational schools tend to outperform boys up to A-level (see page 186).

Making mixed classes a success

Teachers find that the most efffective lessons are those where the numbers of boys and girls are equally balanced. Many schools are now assessing classroom management techniques and teaching materials to ensure that they appeal equally to boys and girls. Some mixed schools are experimenting with single-sex classes in certain subjects, with some success.

Boys' academic performance

There is evidence that boys may not be as well equipped as girls when starting formal education, as boys and girls develop at different rates. A 1994 study of 3,200 children by the Educational Psychology

Service of Surrey County Council found that at the age of five, girls were ahead of boys in almost all areas of learning. This lead is consolidated when pupils take examinations. Psychologists believe that these figures may be due to gender stereotyping at an early age and the fact that reading tends to be seen as a female activity. In spring 1999 the government accordingly requested the introduction of literature likely to appeal specifically to boys – such as thrillers and action stories – to the curriculum, as well as recommending the inclusion of more non-fiction. The issue of boys' underperformance is contentious. Of course, individual children can become high achievers with the right encouragement and support.

Boys' lack of role models

Although the balance between the sexes within the staffroom is relatively even at secondary level, the number of male teachers at primary-school level is low and decreasing. It is believed that the lack of male role models could be linked to the slower improvement in boys' achievement.

Single-sex schooling

Single-sex schools offer an environment where learning can take place without the possible distraction of the opposite sex. Some parents prefer single-sex schooling for cultural or religious reasons. League-table results suggest that pupils achieve more academically in such schools (see Chapter 13).

Supporters of single-sex education argue that the presence of the opposite sex can change the atmosphere in a school, and that those who would otherwise be friends could become rivals, particularly among the girls. Girls mature earlier than boys both physically and emotionally. They also tend to be more conscientious, studious and desirous of praise in the classroom. Female pupils can struggle in a mixed environment, and it is argued that girls' schools allow pupils to reach their full potential because they can use school facilities and take all available subjects without competition from boys. Supporters of single-sex schooling cite as evidence the excellent exam results girls obtain, particularly in science and maths, when boys are absent.

In addition to promoting academic success, many schools emphasise the confidence-building propensity of a single-sex environment.

External factors affecting single-sex schools

Choosing a single-sex school will not guarantee a superior education for your child. A school's success ultimately depends greatly on the social and economic circumstances of the school and the quality of the intake.

Girls' schools

The first girls' schools in the private sector were founded in the mid-nineteenth century to provide social accomplishments together with a limited education. Later, organisations such as the Girls' Day School Trust (GDST)★ promulgated the spread of independent girls' schools that provided an academic grounding. The decline of girls' schools in the state sector began during the 1960s with the phasing-out of grammar schools. In recent years the number has been declining in the private sector, despite opposition.

In both the state and independent sectors, many mainly selective girls' schools achieve high GCSE and A-level pass rates and regularly send a large number of applicants to university. However, parents should not make the mistake of thinking that they are inherently superior. There is no conclusive evidence that single-sex schooling is better than co-education.

Girls' schools are said to engender the self-assurance required for adulthood and to equip young women for pursuing careers in male-dominated spheres. However, this does not take personality into account. If a girl is naturally shy in a mixed class, transferring her to a girls' school is not going to transform her into an extrovert.

Boys' schools

The first boys' establishments to be founded were the grammar schools (see box, page 54), some now private, some in the state sector where they survive as comprehensive schools. The number that have remained strictly all-male has fallen considerably since the 1960s.

Going mixed at 16

Now that it has become popular to change schools after GCSE, many girls take the opportunity to escape all-female surroundings and enter a co-educational sixth form. Integration may be smoother if classes at the new school have been mixed at lower age levels. At a public school, a girl might be viewed as an interloper by boys not taught with girls prior to A-level, and could be branded as 'bossy' or 'feminist' if she is assertive. Female pupils at boys' public schools may be vastly outnumbered, which makes it more important that a girl gets on with her female companions, especially if she is boarding.

Then, nearly all the schools belonging to the Headmasters' Conference were single-sex; now 75 per cent take girls either all the way through or in the sixth-form. Today, boys' schools are found in both the state and independent sectors, and some are among the highest academic achievers in the league tables (see Chapter 13).

It is suggested that teaching methods geared towards boys may be the basis for some single-sex schools' success. Boys tend to be more easily distracted, less good at organising themselves and more in need of stimulation than girls in class. However, there is proof that teachers who can capitalise on boys' enthusiasm and curiosity will achieve good results when mutual respect exists between pupils and teacher. A 1988 survey of French teachers of the La Jolie Ronde organisation found that boys do best at foreign languages when taught in an all-male class.

Boys' schools can allow boys to develop their interests in subjects like art, music and drama which are sometimes seen as 'girly' in mixed schools. As many teachers at boys' schools are male, this may also be a factor – it is thought that boys do better when taught by a man (see page 59).

For many boys' schools, the move to co-education has been via the introduction of girls into the sixth form. The opinion is often voiced that girls have a civilising effect. However, they may also be a distraction. Boys may change their behaviour when girls are present – acting in a more macho manner, for example – and the development of sexual relationships could affect pupils' studies.

Significance of the teacher's sex

Some people presume that in segregated schools, boys and girls do not get the chance to be taught by the opposite sex. However, there are few single-sex schools where the entire staff is male or female, and even if they were this should not matter. Individual children react in quite different ways to a particular teacher's technique (see pages 109–110), which could be a far more important factor than whether the teacher is male or female. The best teachers meet the needs of children as individuals, while trying to satisfy boys' and girls' specific requirements.

Boarding arrangements

In some co-educational schools, you may find that classrooms are mixed, but boarding facilities are provided only for one sex or the other, not both. This arrangement is common in state boarding schools (see pages 39–40).

Choosing between co-educational and single-sex schooling

When a child is young it is difficult to judge whether he or she is in need of one particular type of education rather than another. Despite the good results of some single-sex schools, it is clear that children do not need to be in single-sex schools in order to achieve. A good mixed school can be just as successful as a good single-sex institution. The real answer lies with your son or daughter's personality. His or her academic inclinations and social competence will determine which sort of school is most suitable, if the choice is available.

In the independent sector, financial pressure may dictate that a school opens its doors to the opposite sex as a means of survival. Therefore, even if you have decided on segregated education, bear in mind that the situation could change, and the opposite sex might be admitted during your child's time at the school.

Children's preferences

When young children are faced with a choice, they do not generally show an overwhelming preference for either co-educational or single-sex schooling. However, once territories have been established in single-sex environments, a 'club' mentality takes over and the prospect of intrusion by the opposite sex may be viewed with dismay. Generally, young boys and girls segregate themselves into single-sex groups both in and outside the classroom. As they develop physically and mentally, this invisible dividing line gradually disappears; usually at a time when the social values of co-education are sought.

Checklist for co-educational schools

(1) Find out the ratio of boys to girls. Is it equally balanced?

(2) Establish the ratio of boys to girls in science and arts subjects. There are still too few girls in science-related subjects; conversely, boys often consider arts subjects to be 'sissy'. Your child should receive full exposure to a wide variety of opportunities, which must by law be on an equal footing.

(3) If the school is partly single-sex, at what age is co-education introduced? If it is at sixth-form level, are there plans to change this?

(4) In boarding schools, ask how much socialising is permitted outside the classroom, particularly with regard to boarding-house visiting.

(5) At a boarding-school interview, try to judge accurately whether you think the head can enforce the rules. As your meeting will usually be brief, your judgement could well rest on a gut reaction. The head's personal viewpoint on fraternisation and how he or she controls this within the school community may give you a clue, but could be hot air.

(6) On a school visit, can you see older boys and girls overtly walking around holding hands? This is an indication of what they think they can get away with on school premises.

(7) If it is your intention to move your daughter into the sixth form of a boys' school, check on places and entry procedure well in advance to avoid disappointment.

Checklist for single-sex schools

(1) Remember that a school can change its policy. It pays to keep an open mind and recall the benefits of co-education.

(2) If there is no single-sex school within commuting distance, your child may have to board and you will be faced with the expense.

(3) If you are considering a single-sex girls' school, check what science subjects are taught and how they are taught.

Boarding school

The decision between day school and boarding will have an impact not only on family life (and the fees), but will also affect the number of schools available to you. The majority of people in the UK send their children to day schools. The following section contains specific information on boarding, including local, 'twilight' and weekly boarding.

People choose boarding for various reasons. Some prefer this method of schooling, perhaps having experienced it themselves, while others, including those who live abroad or have to move frequently, may opt for boarding because it suits their circumstances. The choice is a personal one and you will want to discuss the issue with your son or daughter, to establish his or her views and tackle any anxieties. Organisations that can provide advice include the Boarding Education Alliance★ and ISIS.★ Members of HM Forces can obtain details from Service Children's Education (UK).★

Boarding: pros and cons

Boarding has both advantages and disadvantages. On the positive side, boarding:

- offers more choice in that it expands your catchment area, making schools available nationwide (provided you can afford the fees)
- can provide a valuable stabilising influence where, for example, parents are separated or frequently on the move

- eliminates the wear and tear, and cost, of the daily school run
- may not be as expensive as you think (see 'State boarding schools', overleaf).

However, there can be a downside:

- boarding removes children from the immediate support of their parents and the home environment
- young children in particular may find it hard to adapt
- children may have to keep problems pent up until they can be aired with parents
- boredom may be a problem, despite schools' attempts to organise out-of-class activities.

Other potential problems are outlined on page 68.

Tip

It is wrong to feel uncomfortable or guilty about sending your child away from home to a boarding establishment. Boarding can promote self-confidence and independence in children.

Boarding schools are no longer exclusively single-sex institutions – the balance is swinging towards co-education. Life at boarding school is neither as pampered nor as strict as is commonly assumed. Some children prefer to board because they enjoy independence from their parents and the social life at school. As they progress through the school, pupils may take on the running of a dormitory and become responsible for the care and discipline of a group of younger children (see Chapter 10 for more on discipline).

An increasing number of parents are selecting local boarding schools. This enables them to see their children at weekends and to support mid-week matches and events: another benefit is that 'leave weekends' (exeats) and half-term holidays do not involve long journeys.

If you are flirting with the idea of boarding, one solution is to start your child off as a day pupil at a boarding school. You can then change to full boarding as and when your child is ready and willing to do so. Many independent schools are a mixture of boarding and day and will be happy to accommodate such a schedule. 'Twilight boarding' is an option at some schools in both sectors: in this case, children eat supper at the school and are collected after the meal.

State boarding schools

These schools operate along the same lines as those in the independent sector and offer the same benefits. There are no tuition fees; parents are required to pay only for board and any extras (see Chapter 17). Such schools could be of interest to parents obliged to dismiss boarding on the grounds of cost. See pages 39–40 for more on state boarding schools.

Some state boarding schools offer boarding facilities to younger siblings of secondary-level children so that they may attend the local primary school. Parents pay only for the boarding.

Weekly boarding

This relatively new concept is growing rapidly in popularity. Weekly boarding, or flexi-boarding as it is sometimes called, can offer a good compromise for families that find the long estrangements of full boarding too disruptive, since children can go home at the weekend. Many schools reduce the fees for weekly boarders. One advantage is that parents are well placed to keep track of any problems arising in the academic, social or domestic sphere.

If you do not wish to full-board your child and are unhappy with the local day schools on offer, weekly boarding could extend your catchment area – a long journey at weekends may be preferable to a daily trek to a distant school for your child. Some schools accommodate this by having a system of flexible leave weekends, without going so far as to admit to weekly boarding.

Welfare at boarding school

The housemaster or -mistress and school matrons are responsible for children's personal welfare. Boarders and weekly boarders must register with the school doctor, who should know any special factors relating to your child's health. Chapter 9 covers the topic of pastoral care in detail.

Parents should make a conscious effort to remain in contact with children – frequent letters or emails can enable children to stay in touch with events at home, however trivial, and many pupils now have mobile phones and pagers. Most schools allow children to phone home from a public phone box within the school (check whether this affords an adequate amount of privacy). You should be suspicious of schools that do not permit contact by telephone.

Tip

Before being thrown into a boarding environment, a young child should be given instruction in small everyday tasks, to ease the settling-in period. Knowing how to make your bed, clean your shoes and tie your tie can provide an enormous boost to confidence when everything else seems strange.

Boy–girl relationships

Naturally, relationships between pupils develop in day and boarding schools but the situation can be compounded under boarding conditions. At mixed boarding schools, separate boarding houses are provided for boys and girls, while work in the classroom is co-educational.

However strict a school's rules, the chances are that pupils will indulge in some form of sexual activity. At some schools, pupils having sexual intercourse may be suspended or excluded. Schools approach the subject in different ways. Some require the prescription of oral contraceptives to the girls, others advocate a relaxed atmosphere and supply counselling.

The emotional and social development of a child should be the subject of a three-way partnership of the student, staff and parents, with the last shouldering ultimate responsibility. At your initial interview, you should ask the head what his or her stance on boy–girl relationships is, if this is not mentioned.

Potential problems at boarding school

Hazards you should watch out for once your child has started boarding are listed below.

- If a school has predominantly day pupils, with only a small number of boarders, and prep or homework is taken home, pupils who board in that group will be left to complete the prep in isolation. This is more likely occur at prep-school level, although it can happen in public school where a child is the only one in his house in a particular set. Find out how many boarding pupils are in your child's group and whether prep is completed at school before the children go home each day. This may suit boarders better.
- If there is an exodus at the weekend, there could be only a very small group of boarders left in school. Check the likelihood of this happening and find out what arrangements are made in those circumstances – e.g. changing dormitories, weekend activities.
- Rarely, a head teacher may decide to change the boarding arrangements on offer at short notice – for example, scrapping boarding for certain classes but not others. This could cause considerable inconvenience, particularly for parents with children in different year groups who might be picking one child up at weekends but leaving the other behind.
- Parents could choose a boarding school just a little too far away for commuting comfort only to discover after the first term that boarding is to cease and the school is to become exclusively a day school. This can happen due to lack of finance – an insufficient number of boarders will not support the enormous expense involved in providing proper boarding facilities. In such a situation parents have no power of dissent, so it is advisable to calculate how you might be affected should this happen at the school of your choice.

The right age at which to board

The age at which a child should board is a contentious issue. Most boarders are aged seven or older, although a few boarding schools cater for those with special family circumstances and take children from as young as five. It is widely believed that sending children away at a very tender age is unkind. Seven is felt by many parents to be too young, but generally 8- and 9-year-olds are able to cope. Success will obviously depend on a child's individual development and on whether he or she is happy to board.

Boarding prep schools unsurprisingly extol the benefits of boarding between the ages of seven and 13, and claim that the experience is a good preparation for public-school life. However, many independent secondary schools suggest that it is sufficient to send children to day school (prep or primary) prior to boarding, ignoring pressures on new pupils that could be increased if a child is new to boarding.

Checklist for boarding schools

(1) Establish whether the school is single-sex or co-educational (remember, this can change).

(2) Ask if children are freely permitted to telephone home.

(3) Find out the ratio of day children to boarders. If there is only a small number of boarders, how this will affect your child in the dormitory and at prep times? Does this mean that there is a likelihood of the school closing the boarding side?

(4) If weekly boarders outnumber full boarders, will the full boarders be alone in the dormitory at weekends?

(5) Find out about weekend and after-school activities for boarders. Are school facilities readily available outside classroom hours (just because they are there this does not mean they are used)?

(6) If a certain mode of attendance – for example, single-sex boarding – is fundamental to your choice of school, make sure the school is made aware of this in writing, so that it has the opportunity to respond, and ensure that you confirm the school's future intentions. Agreement on this point will then become a fundamental term of your contract and can be acted upon, if necessary, at a later date.

The performing arts

If your child has a particular talent for music, dance or drama you might want to choose a school that will enable that ability to be developed. To find out about suitable establishments, ask your local

LEA about state schools. For details on independent schools, contact ISIS★ or look in your local library for *The Independent Schools Yearbook*, which includes schools that are not members of ISIS.

Music

The teaching of music and music appreciation is an integral part of the school curriculum (see Chapter 12). It is recognised as a powerful form of communication that can improve perception and creativity, enhance other areas of experience and learning, and stimulate aural memory, concentration, self-discipline and emotional well-being.

Mainstream schools

Depending on the degree of emphasis placed on music and available funds, schools in both educational sectors usually encourage some form of musical activity such as a choir, orchestra, brass band or jazz group (see page 210). In the state system, a small number of specialist schools provide intensive tuition in the performing arts (see pages 37–9). Many independent schools place strong emphasis on music and may employ a large contingent of permanent and visiting staff with music qualifications.

Music schools

These independent schools provide expert tuition for gifted young-sters who are likely to continue to music college or a music degree and become professional musicians. You may find that these schools are more limited in the choice of their academic curriculum, although good results are still achieved in national public exams. Composition, singing, counterpoint, harmony and aural skills are taught and pupils normally study one first-choice instrument (or voice or composition) and one second instrument. There are strong links to the national youth orchestras. Admission to these schools is via an audition.

Choir schools

These independent schools are linked to, and provide choristers for, the cathedrals. While it is an honour to be selected for the choir (by audition), parents should be aware that the extra workload for the pupil is considerable. Choir duties are imposed over and above those of the normal school curriculum; choristers may be required to rise early for choir practice before breakfast and much of their spare time will be given up to the choir. They will be particularly busy at Christmas, and tours may be organised at this time, as well as other times of the year. Chorister scholarships are available; contact the school for information.

Dance and drama schools

In the state system, specialist schools may concentrate on dance and drama while following the academic curriculum (see pages 37–9). Classical ballet, modern and contemporary dance, jazz and tap dancing may be taught. Admission will include an audition to demonstrate special skills.

Checklist for the performing arts

(1) If you are interested in the music facilities at school, check what opportunities exist for your child to join orchestras or other music groups and investigate the practice rooms.

(2) Ask how many staff have music/dance/drama qualifications, and whether individual lessons are available.

(3) Ask whether a school with a strong focus on the performing arts has links with national or local arts organisations.

(4) At an independent school specialising in music, dance or drama, check that academic choice is not unduly restricted and that your son or daughter can take other subjects that are of particular interest.

Sport

The quality and type of sport played matters a good deal to some parents when choosing a school, particularly in the independent sector, which tends to set great store by effort on the playing field.

Sport in the state sector

The state sector is emerging from a decline brought about by opposition in some schools to competitive games, overcrowded timetables and the withdrawal of after-hours support by teachers, amid recognition that sport and physical education have an important role to play in children's development.

PE staff in the state system are specialist teachers, unlike many in private schools. State schools frequently make use of local council facilities, such as sports halls and swimming-pools, the quality of which can vary. Some schools which sold off their land for development in the years when sport was not encouraged lack a wide range of facilities. LEAs are seeking to address this problem; one solution has been the construction of shared council facilities near school premises.

Specialist sports schools, designed to help gifted children attain their sporting goals (see pages 37–8), share their facilities and expertise with the community, including primary schools, although only certain neighbourhoods have the benefit of a sports college.

Sport in the National Curriculum

The teaching of physical education is compulsory in the National Curriculum up to the age of 16. Following revisions announced in May 1999, greater flexibility has been introduced at all stages, and from the age of 14 pupils can give up competitive team games in favour of more individual sports. The requirements for each stage differ to some extent:

- **Key stage 1** Dance, games and gymnastics must be included; swimming and water safety are optional.
- **Key stage 2** Dance, games and gymnastics must be included, plus two of the following options: swimming and water safety, athletics, outdoor and adventurous activities. If a full programme of swimming was not completed during Key Stage 1, swimming must be included.
- **Key stage 3** Games must be included, plus three of the following options: dance, gymnastics, swimming and water safety, athletics, outdoor and adventurous activities.
- **Key stage 4** Two of the following options must be included: dance, gymnastics, swimming and water safety, athletics, outdoor and adventurous activities. Games become optional. It is hoped that as a result of this increased choice, 14- to 16-year-olds will be encouraged towards greater participation.

These changes have resulted in logistical difficulties: in some schools there may be large numbers of pupils taking part in individual activities and not enough staff to supervise them. On top of the requirements of the National Curriculum, some schools also provide extra-curricular exercise.

Sports co-ordinators

In June 1999 the government announced that it would appoint 600 sports co-ordinators in an attempt to raise standards. Their brief is to ease pressure on teachers by helping to arrange competitive sports fixtures, encourage links between schools and sports clubs and increase the amount of after-school sports. In addition to raising sporting standards, it is hoped that achievement will be encouraged on a wider level (physical activity is known to stimulate motivation and improved attitudes in the classroom), as well as helping to combat disaffection and encouraging links with the wider community.

Sporting success for state schools

The government states that two periods a week should be devoted to PE, but many state schools do not fulfil this. Generally, schools in the independent sector devote more time to sports coaching than state schools. Nevertheless, despite a more limited timetable and less available time after lessons, state schools have been known to beat private schools in sporting competition.

Sport in the independent sector

Sport can assume great importance in the independent sector, to the extent that some parents will ignore a school's academic failings if it produces outstanding sports results.

Children with pronounced sporting ability at state or prep schools may be 'headhunted' by independent schools; or, if parents mention a child's talent at interview, this may sharpen a school's interest. Some talented children virtually have the power to dictate terms to private schools, many of which have built a reputation on sport. If your child is particularly talented you might be able to turn this to your financial advantage when seeking an award (see 'Scholarships and other awards', pages 255–61). The practice of using financial persuasion to enrol outstanding athletes is widespread, depending on the school funds available.

In most independent schools, the academic staff fill the roles of sports teachers at different levels and for different sports throughout the school. The head of sport is invariably a sportsperson first, with an academic subject as a supplementary. There is usually some form of physical activity every day.

The benefits of sport

Research has shown that out of school hours, children are failing to take sufficient exercise. The popularity of television, videos and computer games is proving detrimental to their health: inactivity, exacerbated by unhealthy eating habits, is producing a flabby and overweight generation of young people. Medical evidence indicates that children are becoming predisposed to the problems of coronary disease – the biggest cause of death in the UK – later in life. Girls are at greater risk than boys of being unfit.

Sport or other physical activity in school, across all ages, is therefore required to play an even greater role in countering the effects of our children's increasingly sedentary lifestyle, and fortunately the choice of different sports is now so varied that even 'non-sporty' children are bound to find an activity to enjoy. Among the benefits of sport are improved mental as well as physical abilities – PE advisers acknowledge that those who indulge in some form of physical activity are better equipped to deal with academic work. An Aberdeen University study found that children who were active in competitive sport at school tended to be more stable and extroverted as students. This supports the view that parents should not expect their children to focus on academic studies at the expense of exercise – in fact, sport is beneficial at times of stress, such as during exams.

Sport and its effect on children

The sports provision could affect your child's happiness and ability to settle at a school. The following elements are significant at both state and private schools.

Sports culture

Try to discover how much emphasis a school places on competitive games. If it is a great deal and there is a lot of pressure on children to participate, think about how the regime will suit your child. If he or she is not inclined towards sports, misery, or at least a sense of alienation, could develop.

Some drawbacks of school sport

Surveys of pupils and physical education teachers have consistently found that in schools which place heavy emphasis on sport, sports teachers are under pressure to maintain their position in the school hierarchy by consistently achieving good results, thereby promoting the prestige of the school. Teachers consequently tend to opt for selective competitive games, with the negative result that pupils see them as 'competitive, aggressive and giving greater attention to more highly skilled pupils', according to one survey. Further drawbacks of school sport are that pupils who are not considered good enough at games may be relegated to the sidelines if no alternative to team sport is provided, while the morale of children in a team that is repeatedly trounced could suffer.

Sports teachers

Sports teachers provide added value to a school's academic role by involving children in physical activity and promoting interest and enjoyment in sports. Most sports teachers are balanced and understanding but, as with any subject teacher, be on the lookout for difficult personalities.

Ideally, staff should take the trouble to channel children who have little interest in or aptitude for sport into alternative forms of physical activity, and they should ensure that children who are highly success-ful at a particular activity are physically challenged in other areas.

The teacher's ability will determine how well he or she can motivate pupils, and may affect sporting performance and morale at a school. Try to find out what sporting qualifications the teacher has. At a private school, PE lessons may be taken by subject teachers with more enthusiasm than expertise.

From farce to fighting fit

A small private school experienced a run of failure on the hockey field. The reason for its disappointing performance was that the games teacher had been seconded to hockey coaching on the strength of his knowledge as to which end of the stick should be held – he had never actually played the game. When the head appointed a hockey teacher with serious credentials, the team became a force to be reckoned with.

Extra-curricular sporting activities

Depending on the school facilities, these may take the form of lunch-hour activities and/or after-school clubs.

Apart from the official sport in the timetable, physical activities outside classroom hours are usually given a high profile in the prospectus. However, do not lay great store on them being carried out to the letter. Long lists of interesting and exciting activities,

Sport as a stepping stone to success

Skilled coaching at school can provide an excellent grounding for pupils who become professional sportsmen and -women, and specialist sports schools exist to further such ambitions (see pages 37–8). Some football clubs have formed partnerships with state schools, which enables them to talent-spot young pupils. Meanwhile, outstanding sporting talent may augment moderate academic achievements in applications to those universities where sporting competition is intense.

designed to whet the appetite, often have a habit of being seriously limited in reality. If there is a specific activity your child is keen to pursue, make enquiries to determine whether this is really on offer or just a sales gimmick. For example, if your child wishes to learn the golf or squash mentioned in the prospectus, check that the activity is not granted only to those already proficient in the sport.

How to assess a school from the sports angle

If you have a child with obvious sporting ability, or want your child to have the best opportunities to achieve in sport, you will want to find out what a school really has to offer. Note that some schools will overrate their sports facilities – be sceptical and inquisitive.

You will find diverse facilities in different schools – one school may have a state-of-the-art sports hall, another a structure more like a large shed. Do not be misled by appearances. The question is whether these facilities are fully utilised. More importantly, are those offered likely to be relevant to your child? For example, perhaps he or she does not like swimming but enjoys squash, which is unavailable.

If your child has a preference for a particular sport, find out whether this is played. Do not take it for granted that all schools offer all the major sports; for example, you may come across an option of football or rugby. In addition, some schools may concentrate on one sport to the detriment of another. Try to ascertain the situation first to avoid any disappointment.

If you are investigating the state sector, you may find that your choice of school is limited. In these circumstances, ask the school and PE adviser about opportunities both within the school and through the LEA. Do not stop there: the local professional and amateur teams in football, cricket, rugby, hockey, swimming, tennis – or whatever your child is interested in – may offer coaching, or run youth teams, and there should be county or borough teams and competitions.

If you do have a choice of schools (state, independent or both) and want to make a comparison, ask what sports are available and request a list of each school's sporting records for the last three years (looking at three years will give you a clearer picture – a single year could be an aberration). Make sure that you are given the records for all ages, not just the first and second teams. From these, you will discover how well the teams perform and whether there is strength all the way through the school. You will also see any patterns that emerge during competition between the local schools – some schools may consistently beat others, for example. Studying the fixture lists will also indicate how far your child will have to travel for away matches.

Distortion of results by talented pupil intake

At a private school, successful results in the first year may reflect the strength of the prep-school intake, rather than the strength of coaching. However, if a high success rate in a certain activity at the top end of the school contrasts with poor results at the bottom end this may denote more expert coaching of that sport at that particular school.

Checklist for sport

(1) If you are limited to one particular state school, do your homework on the opportunities at that school and within the local area; otherwise ask for the sports results for the last three years at the schools you are interested in.

(2) Ask to meet the head of sport. A conversation may introduce a new perspective and will give you the chance to assess his/her character.

(3) Ask what qualifications the sports teachers have.

(4) Find out whether members of staff pursue their own sport on Saturdays – they will not be available for weekend matches.

(5) Check what sports are available. Ask if any are compulsory and whether there are any alternatives – for example, a school may arrange tennis for those who do not play cricket, or hockey for those who dislike rugby. If you are told that something is compulsory and you do not like the idea, say so. Many head teachers will be reasonable on the subject.

(6) Confirm the existence and status of any extra-curricular activities which interest you – do not rely on the prospectus.

(7) Ask for a copy of the school magazine and study the sports results. As well as listing all the results of which the school is proud, you should be able to determine if problems exist. Bear in mind that there may be a good deal of literary licence, and that in a disastrous year the results may be conveniently missing. Where this occurs, ask for details.

(8) Insist on seeing the facilities on offer for yourself. If you are told, for example, that it is too long a walk to the rugby field or hockey pitch, it would be advisable to make that trip in case you do not like what you see when you get there.

(9) Take into account any health considerations – for example, if your child has asthma, will the fumes in the school swimming-pool exacerbate the condition?

(10) Confirm whether transport arrangements might curtail your child's participation in extra-curricular sporting activities.

Chapter 5

Children with special requirements

Some children may have special educational needs, which could require extra help at either a mainstream or special school. Parents of other children may decide to educate them at home, if they feel their needs are not being met by the existing system.

Special educational needs

A child with special educational needs (SEN) is defined as having learning difficulties and being in need of special help. The child with a learning difficulty may find it harder to learn than others of the same age, or have a disability that makes the use of normal educational facilities impractical. The help required is referred to as 'special educational provision'. Learning difficulties can range from a relatively minor affliction, requiring a period of correction, to very serious disabilities, and may include:

- a physical disability
- a mental disability
- difficulty with sight, hearing or speech
- emotional and behavioural problems
- a medical or health problem
- difficulties specifically related to aspects of language – for example, problems with reading, writing, speaking or mathematical work
- general difficulties with school work.

According to the Warnock Committee, which carried out a major study of special needs in the UK, some 20 per cent of children may need extra help at some time during their school careers.

The severity and duration of problems vary. The most complex are dealt with by special schools dedicated to, for example, the education of visually- or hearing-impaired children or those with severe learning difficulties. Special schools cater for just under two per cent of the child population and are mostly state-funded, although some independent schools also deal with special needs.

Parents of children with special needs often assume that they have the fewest options in finding the best education for their child. Selective schools by their very nature exclude children with learning difficulties. In the state system, mainstream schools sometimes struggle to cope with SEN children, although that is where parents often prefer their children to be educated. Parents for Inclusion★ is a group offering support to such parents. Despite national guidelines, parents can find that policy on SEN education varies in terms of policy and funding from one LEA area to another.

Most special educational needs are satisfied through mainstream schools in the state system, with outside specialists being used where necessary. In most cases, statutory assessment is not considered necessary. Where the LEA finds it necessary to make a statutory assessment (see page 84) and to draw up a 'statement of special educational needs' (see pages 85–6), it is the mainstream school that is initially expected to provide the help required. It is thought to be beneficial for these children, whether 'statemented' or not, to be educated with others of the same age. Special schools are regarded only as a last resort. The ideal is a working partnership of the parents, school and LEA. Parents can express their concerns by talking to their child's teacher or to a professional working with their child.

A booklet entitled *Special Educational Needs* is available from DfEE Publications.★ You can also contact your LEA and your local Citizens' Advice Bureau★ or Council of Voluntary Service.★ State-school parents can consult the Advisory Centre for Education (ACE),★ an independent advice centre with expertise in special educational needs, while parents of children with reading difficulties can contact the Reach National Advice Centre.★

Pre-school learning difficulties

You may be aware of a problem before your child starts school. If so, the health service must inform the LEA and provide you with information about any voluntary organisations which may be able to give you advice. Your LEA should be able to provide help from a very early age by offering home-based learning schemes, if necessary, while teachers can make home visits to children with, for example, hearing or sight problems or other severe learning difficulties. You can ask the LEA to assess your child's needs if your child is under two years of age; if he or she is over two, you may ask for a statutory assessment (see page 84). It will be up to the LEA to decide whether this is necessary, and the decision on whether to make a statement also rests with the LEA. When your child starts school, any difficulties and/or special provisions by the National Health Service and Social Services must be brought to the school's attention: a special form will be provided by your LEA for this purpose. It is a requirement that all state schools publish information about their policies for children with special educational needs. Most schools will have a staff member and a governor with responsibility for SEN.

Learning difficulties at school

Special educational needs may not always become apparent before a child starts school, and it may be the teacher who brings the matter to your attention. If you identify a problem, you should speak to the head and to the teacher with specific responsibility for SEN, usually called the special educational needs co-ordinator, as well as to your child's teacher. Persevere if you feel you are not being listened to.

Ask the school for a copy of its SEN policy, if you do not already have one. The school's annual report will include a report on the policy. This will tell you the name of the SEN co-ordinator, arrange-

---

SEN Code of Practice

A Code of Practice, issued under the 1993 Education Act, gives practical guidance on identifying and assessing special educational needs. All LEAs and schools must refer to this Code, as must the health service and Social Services when advising the LEAs. The Code gives guidance to schools, but does not set down what must be done in every case. How the provision is tailored to your child's needs is up to the school and the LEA, if a child has a statement (see pages 85–6).

---

ments for special provisions and how the school will work with you to tackle your child's problems. The school should be able to make an assessment of specific learning difficulties, such as dyslexia, and parents may request an assessment by an educational psychologist.

Stages of approach

Assessment is carried out in stages, matching the level of help to the child's needs. There may be instances where the school will miss out the first two stages and go straight to Stage 3. Satisfactory progress may result in a reverse move from Stage 3 to Stage 2.

Stage 1

After a full discussion between you and the school, your child will be monitored. Targets will be set and help given where this is judged necessary. This will often entail extra help in class from the teacher and a classroom helper. Where the problems are mild, this usually proves to be sufficient.

Stage 2

If satisfactory progress is not made, an individual education plan will be drawn up by the SEN co-ordinator. New targets will be set along with a reviewing process.

Stage 3

The school may decide that outside specialist help or advice is necessary and may call on the assistance of an educational psychologist or a specialist teacher. Taking your child's case history into account, the SEN co-ordinator and external specialist will then draw up a new individual education plan with review meetings. After careful monitoring, if your child is not achieving the progress expected, the head will then decide whether to request a statutory assessment from the LEA.

Support for parents

You will be involved in the programme of treatment and kept informed of any action taken. If you do not understand or you have misgivings, talk to the school. The school should provide details of local voluntary organisations and parents' groups and you may take along a 'named person' to any meetings who may express views on your behalf. This person may be from a voluntary organisation, a parents' support group, a professional or a friend or relative.

Parents who are unhappy with their child's treatment should use the school's complaints procedure first (this will be detailed in the policy document). If not reassured, they should contact the LEA and, if still not satisfied, the Secretary of State for Education.

Statutory assessment

A request for a statutory assessment may be made either by the parents or the school. This is a detailed examination of a child's needs, based on progress reports and special help that has already been provided. Parents will be given 29 days' notice to agree to an assessment, while the LEA has six weeks in which to inform parents of a statutory assessment. If this time limit is exceeded and you are not happy with the explanation given, you may complain to the Secretary of State. Details of how to do this must be provided by the LEA.

The LEA may ultimately decide that a statutory assessment is not required and may continue to rely on external specialists. If you do not agree with this decision, you have a right of appeal to the special educational needs tribunal (see page 86).

If the LEA decides to make a statutory assessment, it will advise how you can take part, and will inform you of the different educational provisions in the mainstream schools and the special schools in your area. You may then visit those schools and choose the one you consider most suitable for your child. Some will cater for specific disabilities, such as hearing and sight difficulties, while others will have good wheelchair access. The LEA will also provide you with a list of non-maintained special schools and suitable independent schools approved by the Secretary of State for Education.

Having collected all the evidence, the LEA will then decide whether to make a 'statement of special educational needs' for your child. From the initial consideration to an assessment to the final decision, the process should take no longer than 26 weeks.

Statement of special educational needs

This is a document that sets out your child's needs and the special help required to meet those needs. It is created when the LEA decides that your child's needs are beyond the resources normally available at school. It is set out in six parts:

Part 1 parents' name and address
Part 2 child's learning difficulties and disabilities identified during the assessment
Part 3 special help required; long-term objectives; short-term targets and reviewing
Part 4 details of the special school or alternative arrangements
Part 5 details of non-educational needs, such as transport
Part 6 details of how the help will be provided for part 5.

You have a right to express a preference regarding the school that you would like your child to attend (in part 4). The LEA must respect your wishes, if that school is a state school, provided:

- the school is suitable for your child's age, ability and SEN
- your child's presence will not detrimentally affect the efficient education of other children already at the school
- this will be an efficient use of resources.

If you wish your child to attend a school in the non-maintained sector, although the LEA will carefully consider your wishes, it has no legal duty to comply with them if there is what it considers a suitable state school.

Once the statement is made, the LEA must provide your child's school with any extra resources required and the school governors must ensure that your child receives the special educational help described in the statement. This may include the assistance of a classroom helper or physiotherapist and access to word-processing facilities.

If, after all this, the LEA decides not to make a statement, it may draw up what is called a 'note in lieu of a statement', which must set out its reasons for not doing so. Copies of all the professional advice it obtained must be sent to you. Should you disagree with this, or with the statement if it is made, you may appeal (see 'Special educational needs tribunal', overleaf).

Annual review

Your child's statement must be reviewed at least once a year, to ensure that it continues to meet your child's needs and that targets are being met. Changes may be made to accommodate a change in requirements or a move to another school, in particular from primary to secondary school. Should you move to another LEA area, the new area will be supplied with your child's statement, to ensure continuity. The new LEA must also pay any private fees in line with the provision of your old LEA, unless it changes the statement – in which case you can appeal.

A statement may last for the whole of your child's school career, or for only part of it. After the age of 14, your child's annual reviews will also include the careers service and the local Social Services department. A 'transition plan' will be drawn up to facilitate your child's move to adult life and to further education.

Special educational needs tribunal

This is an independent body, made up of three people, which hears parents' appeals against LEA decisions with regard to statutory assessments and statements. An appeal must be made within two months of a decision. In exceptional cases, this may be extended.

You can appeal to the tribunal if:

- the LEA refuses to make a statutory assessment following your request
- the LEA refuses to make a statement after an assessment
- you disagree with parts 2, 3, or 4 of the statement, either when it is first made or after is has been changed
- your child already has a statement and the LEA refuses to reassess your child or change the named school in that statement
- the LEA decides to stop maintaining your child's statement.

In areas in which the tribunal has no jurisdiction – for example, where an LEA fails to keep to time limits – you may complain to the Local Government Ombudsman.*

Special schools

These schools come under the community special and foundation special category (see page 26). The scanty provision of special schools very often means that parents have to travel further to obtain this service. Some LEAs provide residential schools within their area which accept children with social as well as educational needs. This service constitutes an essential part of the children's educational development.

Pupil referral units

There are also special off-site units which provide education to children whose continued attendance at a mainstream school has proved inappropriate for them and detrimental to other pupils. These units deal in particular with those who have behavioural problems and children for whom work experience is not suitable. They are sometimes known as behavioural support service units.

In many cases these children will have been excluded permanently from school and a move to another school is not feasible. Referral units provide a more suitable environment since they offer skilled and understanding staff who have been trained to help youngsters with severe problems achieve meaningful objectives and gain self-respect.

State boarding schools

Most SEN care is provided in local mainstream day schools, with provision in special schools for more serious disabilities. State boarding schools (see pages 39–40) offer an alternative for parents who do not consider the local provision suitable, although this is limited by the number of places available. The SEN provision in these schools will depend upon the individual school and the facilities available, and the regulations described earlier will apply.

Independent schools

The majority of schools in this sector restrict their SEN provision to the needs of the dyslexic child (see overleaf) and, in the majority of cases, only to those with mild dyslexia. Schools often refer to 'special units' and special coaching, but parents may not find these live up to expectations. There can be no doubt that the league tables (see Chapter 13) have distracted schools from paying attention to dyslexic children, and parents have reported a tendency in some schools to pay lip service to children's needs. As far as the school is concerned, a dyslexic child will not produce the results necessary for its league-table ambitions.

However, some independent schools devote their attention to children with mild or severe learning difficulties. Specially trained staff cater for children with physical disabilities and buildings may be adapted for wheelchair access. Teaching is done in small groups, with advantageous pupil–teacher ratios – even on a one-to-one basis in some cases. Since the whole curriculum is geared to the needs of these children, a mainstream school cannot match this level of provision. Some of these schools provide 'special school' facilities for LEAs, which pay for the boarding and tuition. A limited number of taxi journeys between home and school are also paid for by the LEA.

ISIS★ can advise parents whose children have disabilities.

Dyslexia

This is a learning difficulty, ranging from mild to severe, that hinders the learning of both literacy and mathematical skills, as well as musical notation. It is neurologically based and tends to run in families. Despite the attention paid to the subject, not enough is being done to cater for the growing numbers of children diagnosed with the condition. According to the Dyslexia Institute, over 350,000 pupils – some 10 per cent of the school-age population – are currently identified as dyslexic. Three times more boys than girls are affected, and up to 15 per cent of all boys. Normal intelligence is not impaired.

Recognising the condition may not be straightforward, particularly in mild cases. Although dyslexic children can excel beyond their years in areas unaffected by their condition, many are dismissed as slow or lazy by teaching staff who do not understand the nature of dyslexia. The following criteria may be applied to establish whether a child is dyslexic:

- bright children who show significant under-achievement in any of the following: reading, spelling and writing, written number skills (putting letters or figures the wrong way round can be a symptom)
- poor concentration
- difficulty carrying out three instructions in sequence
- difficulty understanding time and tense
- confusion between left and right
- answers questions orally, but has difficulty writing the answer
- unusual clumsiness
- trouble with the sounds in words.

If your child displays most of these symptoms, you should seek advice. The condition, mild or severe, can be helped by skilled specialist teaching and may provide the grounds for a statutory assessment process (see page 84). Your child may also be eligible for additional grants for extra training and equipment (such as tape recorders or word-processing facilities). If your child needs to be assessed, either the school or the LEA may make arrangements. Alternatively, you can arrange a private assessment. If your GP refers you for assessment and you have private medical insurance, this may cover the assessment fee. Alternatively, some GP practices may pay the costs.

For more information, contact your child's school. The Dyslexia Institute★ and the British Dyslexia Association★ can also offer advice. ISIS★ publishes a booklet listing independent schools which provide for dyslexic children, but as this is compiled from information supplied by the schools, without inspection, parents are advised to visit the schools themselves and to interview the teacher in charge of special needs provision.

Gifted children

Gifted children are those with an unusually advanced intellectual or performance ability. They make up about five per cent of the child population and may have specific requirements. The educational system has previously failed to address fully the needs of this group, although their predicament is slowly being recognised.

Some schools do not know how to stretch a gifted pupil to the full, with the result that the child starts to mark time and then switches off. The child may then develop behavioural difficulties. This state of affairs exists in both the state and the independent sectors and is not helped by the fact that special needs are recognised in law only if there is a learning difficulty.

Special measures have been introduced in an attempt to close this gap in educational provision. A pilot scheme has been set up which allows selected primary- and secondary-school children to have access to master classes at their local specialist school. These classes may be in the arts, languages, mathematics or sciences. At the time of writing, only 10 schools have been selected out of over 300 specialist schools, restricting general access to the scheme. For more on specialist schools, see pages 37–9. Another government programme targets inner-city schools (see pages 219–20), giving the brightest children access to accelerated learning via extra classes at local specialist schools, and a review of the exam system could allow pupils to take GCSEs when they are ready rather than when the system dictates. Many parents are resorting either to teaching themselves or to hiring extra help (see page 209). It may often make more sense to broaden a child's education in areas not covered by the school curriculum than to push too hard over a very narrow academic front.

Warning

Parents should be aware that hot-housing children and accelerating their educational development can have adverse effects – including emotional immaturity – which will affect their social interactions and could cause burn-out. Children who take GCSE and A-level examinations years ahead of their peers or attend university in their early teens make headline news. However, enjoyment of university life may be severely limited if a child is too young to take advantage of the opportunities available.

There have been an increasing number of studies into the 'child prodigy'. It was once thought that ability was genetically transmitted, but opinion is now growing that talent is a matter of 'practice makes perfect' – i.e. that opportunity and dedication will accelerate a particular skill. Whether or not this is the case, research has found that there has been an increase in IQ levels over the past 100 years, since they were devised. Parents are understandably anxious that their children be given every opportunity to capitalise on their recognised abilities.

Many schools set great store by IQ test results as a means of determining entrance. However, there is increasing recognition of the concept of emotional and practical intelligence (see pages 48–9).

The Mensa Foundation for Gifted Children★ runs courses for talented pupils. The National Association for Gifted Children (NAGC)★ is a national charity supporting gifted children, their families and professionals. It has a network of local branches providing specific support for the top two per cent of children, who are particularly vulnerable. The NAGC can also supply details should tests be required to convince a school of a child's high ability.

Children who miss out through illness

LEAs are required to make provision for sick pupils who are away from school for significant periods. Parents of children suffering long-term illness can contact the National Association for the Education of Sick Children (PRESENT)★ for advice and support.

Home education

In the event that formal education does not suit your requirements, you are unable to find a school that meets your criteria or your child is seriously unhappy at school, you could consider educating your child at home. You are entitled to educate your child at home provided you can satisfy the education authorities that the education you supply is adequate and suited to the child's age, ability and aptitude – you do not need to hold any specific qualifications or to give formal lessons. Similarly, there is no need to follow the National Curriculum (see Chapter 12) or adopt school hours. Home inspections by LEA representatives are not compulsory; instead, parents may write reports and supply examples of their child's work. An increasing number of families is taking this action, which could be interpreted as an indictment of parts of the current education system.

Research has found that children educated informally benefit from the individual attention they receive and are more confident as a result of not being continually graded and compared to other children. However, the move towards coursework at GCSE level and the necessity for it to be authenticated by an independent scrutineer is making it difficult for home-educated children to receive recognised GCSE qualifications.

If you intend to educate your children at home, you should research carefully any possible future consequences of your actions. Educating a child in isolation is a serious decision and may only be appropriate in the early years. The social skills a child needs can be developed only as a member of a larger group, and teenagers in particular need contact with others of the same age.

If it is your intention to educate your child at home, contact your LEA to discuss your plans. You will have to register with the LEA. In addition, you will receive support from an education officer who will provide consultancy. Education Otherwise★ is a national organisation which has set up local branches to assist parents educating their children at home. The Advisory Centre for Education (ACE)★ can also provide help.

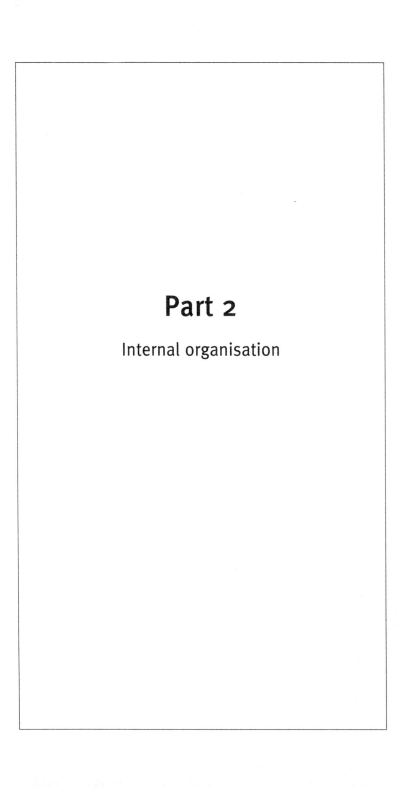

Part 2

Internal organisation

Chapter 6

School regulation and inspection

Now that you have worked out your essential requirements for your child's school (see Chapters 1–5), it will help you to understand how schools are organised and regulated. This chapter offers a brief survey of schools' legal obligations in both the state and the independent sectors.

Finding out about the internal structure will assist you in interpreting information provided by schools and give you a more informed insight when visiting schools (see Chapter 19). The results of school inspections may be quoted in admission information supplied by LEAs, so it is useful to understand on what basis these are carried out.

Although the administration differs from one school to another, there are some basic ground rules of which you should be aware.

The regulation of schools

The state system is wholly governed by Acts of Parliament, while the independent system is only loosely affected by Acts and regulations. Nevertheless, all independent schools have been brought under the umbrella of the Department for Education and Employment (DfEE), and must be registered. The DfEE can refuse registration if the proprietor, staff, buildings, accommodation or instruction are not suitable. Boarding schools must comply with duties imposed under the Children Act 1989.

Before registration, all schools are inspected by Her Majesty's Inspectors (HMI) and are liable to periodic inspection thereafter. The following section examines the role of school inspectors and their input into improving overall results.

School inspections

Until the beginning of the 1990s, parents had little or no knowledge of what was happening in schools and not much information about whether or not their child was making proper progress. Parents' right to know about such affairs has been extended through the publication of inspection reports and by the election of parent governors in state schools (see pages 104–5).

State school inspections

All state schools in England are routinely inspected by the Office for Standards in Education (Ofsted),★ headed by Her Majesty's Chief Inspector of Schools, which is independent from the DfEE. For details of the inspection procedure in Scotland, Northern Ireland and Wales see pages 290, 301 and 299.

Ofsted's purpose is to improve standards of education and achievement in schools and provide independent advice where necessary. The results of Ofsted inspections are supplied to the school and to the LEA and the school must send a summary to the parents of each pupil. Full copies should also be sent to the media and to local libraries.

Inspections normally take place every six years, but schools in difficulty are inspected more frequently.

A 'Framework for Inspection' lays out the principles and procedures to be followed and the four major elements that must be examined, which are:

- quality of education
- educational standards achieved
- management of financial resources
- spiritual, moral, social and cultural development of the pupils.

Although HM Inspectors are permanent staff of Ofsted and monitor the inspection system, inspection teams are allocated to schools by competitive tender. Teams include from three to eight Ofsted-accredited independent inspectors led by a registered inspector, and include one lay member who is not a teacher or educationalist.

Parental involvement is deliberately encouraged and parents are invited to express their views directly to the inspectors, either in writing or at a meeting before an inspection takes place.

In addition to schools, Ofsted also inspects teacher-training facilities, LEA central services, LEA-funded further education and independent schools on behalf of the DfEE. From 2001, Ofsted will also assume responsibility for the regulation and inspection of early-years education and childcare.

Inspection results

Inspectors may decide that some schools are performing poorly enough to be in need of 'special measures'. These failing schools will be placed under close scrutiny and speedy improvement will be demanded. Schools that reach an acceptable standard overall but fail in certain departments will be identified as having 'serious weaknesses'.

Schools with faults and those that are required to take 'special measures' must react to the inspectors' report within 40 days with an 'Action Plan' demonstrating how the school intends to address the key issues identified in the report. Schools in need of special measures must submit this for approval by the Secretary of State for Education. HM inspectors will monitor the Plan, submitting reports to the Secretary of State on the school's progress. Schools in need of special measures will be expected to improve their performance significantly within two years. All schools must make Action Plans available to parents.

Reaction to inspections among schools and society varies but is generally positive. Many schools consider that inspections provide useful indicators for future improvement and development. Inspections highlight schools' accountability, certainly, but they have also proved that with inspired teaching and raised expectations schools in traditionally disadvantaged areas are capable of reaching high standards.

Inspections in independent schools

A sweeping new system of inspection has been established to bring independent schools into line with those in the state sector. Until spring 1999, the associations listed on page 42 carried out their own inspections yet despite being available to parents of current pupils, reports were not made available to the public except in summary form. Following consultation with the DfEE and Ofsted, the 1,300 member schools of the Independent Schools Council (ISC)★ now submit to ISC and Headmasters' and Headmistresses' Conference (HMC)★ inspection schemes. In 2000 these two schemes will be unified as the Independent Schools Inspectorate (ISI). Inspection teams will be made up of head teachers from independent schools and led by former HM inspectors. Inspections will be carried out on a six-year cycle and their contents will be published for all parents to read for the first time. Ofsted will retain the right to inspect if a particular school gives cause for concern. Schools that are *not* within ISC membership (about 1,100) will be inspected by Ofsted on a six-year cycle, and reports will be made public.

Some independent-school heads have criticised the practice of publishing inspection reports on the grounds that, as these are in the public domain, individual staff and departments will not be denounced. However, it could be argued that competent heads should not need to be told who is failing among their staff. The situation whereby prospective parents were locked out from knowing what they were buying was untenable and this innovation can, on balance, only be an improvement. Parents will be able to enjoy a degree of confidence in knowing that a school is 'accredited by the ISC' and that it meets legislative requirements.

Tip

At schools in both sectors, ask for a copy of the most recent inspection report if you have not already been given one. These will be available from your local library, while state-school reports can also be found on the Internet at: *www.ofsted.gov.uk/reports/index.htm*

In the case of independent schools, reports available for inspection by all parents will be restricted until the new system has come into operation (see above).

Chapter 7

Head teachers and governors

Having looked at the organisational structure and external regulations to which schools are subject (Chapter 6), you will want to consider the people who are responsible for making policy decisions and running the school: the head teacher and governors. Their roles are dealt with in this chapter, while Chapter 8 discusses teaching staff.

Head teachers

The head is responsible for managing the day-to-day affairs of the school, while at the same time administering the policies and aims laid down by the governors (see pages 104–6). As chief executive and figurehead, he or she also sets the tone of the school.

Most heads belong to the National Association of Head Teachers.* At the time of writing there is little specific training for the job. However, headship is increasingly being professionalised and the founding of the National College for School Leadership reflects this. Starting in 2000, courses will lead to the National Professional Qualification for Head Teachers (NPQH), which will be mandatory for all teachers newly appointed to the post. It will be some years before all heads have this recognised professional qualification.

All teachers are in the business of people management, but the qualities of a successful head – strength, patience, tact, tolerance, common sense and especially a strong sense of humour – are seldom found in one person, and an excellent teacher or deputy head will not necessarily make a good head. The best heads are popular with parents and children, continually strive to improve standards and deal with complaints rapidly and without rancour.

How to assess the head teacher

The head is usually your first point of contact with a school, apart from the school secretary, and the impression he or she makes on you will be a major factor in your ultimate decision. Meeting the head allows you to evaluate his or her personal qualities and educational ideals, both of which will impact on your child. Do not be swayed by presentation skills or charm. As well as being aware of your gut reaction, try to judge whether this individual will:

- **be available and approachable** Be wary of heads who are often absent or have little contact with the school community – poor communication with staff and students signals poor communication with parents. If you are being given a tour by the head, watch for the interaction with pupils and whether names are used: this will indicate how much he or she is in touch at ground level. Obviously, the larger the school the more limited contact will be and you must make allowances for this

- **act swiftly and effectively** Be cautious if there are signs that a head fails to follow up assurances with prompt action. This is of course hard to establish in the context of a brief school visit and/or interview. However, you could gain insights by asking the head how he or she intends to implement goals for the school in the near future, and, if you know any parents of current pupils, asking them whether the head deals with problems effectively

- **acknowledge accountability to parents** Heads who appear keen to deny accountability or complain that parents make excessive demands should be avoided since they are unlikely to be receptive in the event of any difficulties

- **know how the staff are performing** – without such knowledge, the head cannot do the job properly. Heads' relationships with staff vary depending on the size of the school and the head's commitments. Those in control at ground level make frequent visits to classrooms and do not need an external report to pinpoint the poor teachers. Heads who teach are usually the most involved, although in a large secondary school the amount of paperwork may preclude active participation in the classroom.

In state schools, the head generally leads Open Days/Evenings for prospective parents. An individual meeting would be rare, but an

> **The head: determining factor in whether a school sinks or swims**
>
> The performance of a school depends to a great extent upon who is at the helm, and a failing institution may improve beyond recognition under a talented head. Needless to say, the reverse is also true: a top-rated school could spiral downwards through weak management. However, it takes longer to pull a school up than it does for one to crash if the wrong person is sitting in the driving seat.

option if parents felt the need. In the independent sector, particularly at a boarding school, a meeting, however brief, is of paramount importance as this person will have a direct influence on the immediate future of your child.

Once your child starts school, the frequency of your contact with the head may have a direct bearing on your level of satisfaction with the school, especially in the case of secondary schools in both sectors. While things are running smoothly there should be little need for contact, but if problems arise the ability of the head to listen and act effectively becomes crucial. In most secondary schools problems are initially raised with form tutors or heads of departments or year. The head should however be ready to intervene and be accessible to parents in the case of a serious matter.

Availability following publication of A-level results

Ask who is on-hand at the school when A-level results are published in August. Schools with a responsible attitude will not be staffed just by a secretary handing out results – the head or head of sixth form and a careers officer will be on hand to offer advice to students who have not achieved the grades required for university entrance. Some schools display a disturbingly casual attitude towards A-level students who do not pass or obtain the grades expected, and fail to offer distraught youngsters guidance or support (regardless of money spent on fees, in the case of independent schools). The sort of head you are looking for is someone who will make a point of being available, or ensure that other senior staff are present, to console as well as to congratulate, to offer advice and encourage a new assault on the A-level exams or plan a change of direction.

Popular opinion

The reputation of a head is often the subject of gossip. Use your own judgement, but if you are at all unhappy about the personality of a head – above all if this uneasiness is backed up by reliable sources – be extremely wary of committing your child (and, if fees are involved, your wallet) to such a person.

Taking the head's advice

The head might make pronouncements about other schools in the area, or recommend another local school to you if his or her lists are full. By all means add the head's advice to the list of factors by which you intend to make your decision, but do not allow it to override the rest. The head's representation of other schools might be based on what he or she has heard within the educational community, where rumours about different schools are likely to be circulating, or vested interests. In the independent sector, relationships between schools may lead to your being steered in a particular direction, regardless of a school's suitability for your child. In the

---

Schools with head shortages

Filling the post of head seems to be difficult for some schools. The shortage of applicants in the state system is a serious concern: some schools start the school year with no one in the pivotal position. In the independent system, some schools flounder through three or four heads in the space of ten years. Constant changes can destabilise an institution, even though each new head may not introduce revolutionary changes. It is worth taking a more critical look at a school where this pattern is in evidence, as it could indicate that all is not well. Possible reasons for rapid turnover might be an inability on the part of the governors to interview and select a suitable person, or an indication that a succession of heads have encountered with governors and/or staff.

---

state sector, 'feeder' primary schools may be linked to secondary schools (see page 34).

For reliable, objective information, contact your LEA. To obtain an indication of a school's academic performance, check the league tables (see Chapter 13). Chapter 18 contains advice on how to interpret the prospectus and other information issued by the school. ISIS★ deals with enquiries about schools in the independent sector.

Proprietor heads

In any school the personality of the head is crucial. In schools that have a board of governors, the freedom of the head is restricted to some extent (see overleaf). In the independent sector, a sole proprietor (a head teacher who owns the school) is responsible for making all the decisions.

One of the arguments in favour of the proprietor head is that the survival of the school, and therefore the head's bank balance, will suffer if a dispute gets out of hand and is not settled amicably. For such heads, repercussions can be unremitting: bad publicity could result in damage to the school and the threat of a depleted school roll. This does not mean, however, that parents can take advantage of this susceptibility by trying forcibly to override reasonable school rules and regulations, even if they have been newly imposed to parents' annoyance.

Nevertheless, difficult situations do occur and you may have to argue your case. As there is no governing body, the outcome will hinge upon the personality of the proprietor head. Tread very carefully, since hackles may rise if it is thought, mistakenly or not, that criticism is being levelled at his or her ability as a head teacher. If agreement cannot be reached and the school belongs to ISIS, parents can complain to this organisation.

Deputy heads

Deputy heads may be in charge of managing budgets and staff, curriculum development, pastoral care, the day-to-day running of the school and liaison between governors, parents and the LEA, depending on the structure of the senior management. In the state and independent systems, parents may not meet a deputy head when being shown round the school, but may encounter this person at parents' meetings if he or she teaches their child, or if there are problems relating to the deputy's area of responsibility.

School governors

The role of governors at state and independent schools varies (see below). At the time of writing, a parliamentary select committee on education has undertaken to review school governors' powers.

Governors in both sectors share some general aims. These include the obligation to:

- formulate the policies and aims of the school in agreement with the head, and decide how these will operate in practical terms
- approve the school budget and development plan
- appoint the head and, generally, most senior staff
- examine any complaints by parents which it is felt the head has not resolved satisfactorily.

Most parents' contact with this body tends to occur only in the event of a dispute or complaint which has not been resolved. In such circumstances, your best recourse is to approach a parent governor informally, or, if the situation is serious, write to the chair of the governors, who will be in a position to raise the matter with the head or at the next meeting of governors.

Governors at state schools

The governing body and the head are responsible for fulfilling the policies of the LEA and its duty of providing a proper educational service to parents and children. The School Standards and Framework Act 1998 empowers governors to do 'anything which appears to them to be necessary or expedient for the purposes of, or in connection with, the conduct of the school'.

The governing body is more democratic than its equivalent in the independent system in that it must include parents elected by other parents of children at the school, teachers elected by their colleagues and representatives from the LEA. Further members may also include the head and representatives from the parish council, church or local businesses and the community. The constitution of the governing body and the number of governors will depend on the type and size of school – see also 'Categories of school', pages 24–6.

In addition to appointing the head, state school governors may take an active role in the appointment of staff. They will convene appeals to determine whether a head is justified in excluding a pupil (see page 138). Governing bodies of state schools have a statutory duty to publish an annual report for parents and to hold a meeting to discuss any issues that parents wish to raise (whether included in the report or not).

Governors at independent schools

The majority of governors at independent schools hail from non-academic backgrounds and consequently may have little understanding of school life. It can be advantageous for a governor to have some business acumen, although not all do. Many governing bodies contain no representation from parents with children either at, or recently at, the school who could properly represent the views of their peers. When it comes to appointing teachers (which frequently involves governors in the state system), the head is often left a free hand.

Parent governors

Under this system, parents make up the full complement of governors and elect all new governors. This is a different scenario from mere

---

Head hoodwinks governors

At a school operating the parent governor system, the head persuaded parents to rely on her superior knowledge for the selection of new candidates. With the governors in her pocket, she permitted the whole ethos and structure of the school to change. Against the wishes of most parents, she decided to double the size of the school, breaching her promise that it would remain a small, exclusive unit. A vast building programme was instigated. It was no coincidence that the parent insinuated on to the board of governors was a builder, who was handed the contract on a plate.

---

parent representation on the board of governors. The arrangement, not commonly encountered, is used at pre-prep level. Although the idea of parents having sole responsibility may be an attractive prospect, it may not be as straightforward as it appears.

Taking a dispute to the governors

Head teachers are answerable to the board of governors for the outcomes of their decisions and actions. If a dispute arises and the head is unwilling to alter his or her position, parents have recourse to the governors as a court of appeal. Do not assume, however, that the governors will automatically take your side in a dispute. Note that a common line of defence heads and governors adopt is to protest that you are the only one to find fault, and all the other parents are satisfied. Do not let this deter you from proceeding with your complaint.

Checklist for head teachers and school governors

(1) Find out for how long the head has been at the school and if necessary enquire about his or her previous position and its duration.

(2) Ask the head for details of the annual staff turnover. This can indicate the relationship a head has with members of staff. A figure above 10 per cent (excluding retirements) may require an explanation. The reasons for a high turnover may of course be perfectly innocent, but in some cases could signify a problem with the head's personality. The way in which your query is answered may reveal whether there is any cause for suspicion.

(3) Ask the head about what he or she is actively achieving, or hopes reasonably to achieve, and enquire about the ability of the intake and recent exam or test results. Remember that a selective school ought to be able to achieve more than a non-selective one.

(4) Useful questions to ask the head include: 'Do you still teach? Do you make a point of visiting classrooms in session to keep an eye on things? Do you frequently watch sporting fixtures? When A-level results are announced, are you or senior staff in school to advise students who have not achieved their targets?' Avoid questions likely to elicit meaningless answers, such as 'What do others think of your school?' which could encourage economy with the truth. The answers to your enquiries will indicate whether the head is closely in touch with what is happening in the school.

(5) Ask for a list of governors, and at an independent school discover whether the head teacher is a sole proprietor. Find out whether there are any academics or business people among the governors and how many parents are present.

Chapter 8

Teaching staff

An experienced teacher, himself a father, was asked what he considered the single most important factor in choosing a school. He replied: 'The teachers – but unfortunately they are hidden away and you don't get to meet them.'

This is particularly true of secondary schools. You should therefore take any opportunity that arises to get to know the people who will be responsible for your child's education.

Each member of staff fulfils an independent and a collective function, both of which affect a parent's relationship with the school. This chapter outlines the role of teachers and explains how to judge their performance and qualfications.

Tip

Do not be so impressed by new facilities at a school that you forgo making a thorough appraisal of the staff. They, not the bricks and mortar, are the essential ingredient for any school. A school with poor or average facilities that is staffed by excellent teachers will rise head and shoulders above those with inadequate teachers but the latest in technology and impressive buildings. If schools you are considering hold open days or evenings for prospective parents, make a point of talking to as many staff as you can.

In both state and independent schools, teachers are officially appointed by the governing body, although selection is often delegated to the head. Parents are likely to have a greater degree of contact with teaching staff than with the head, except at nursery level, where the head will take a more active role with the pupils. Most parents see their child's teachers only at parents' meetings (see pages 211–12).

How to assess teaching staff

The calibre of the teachers with whom you come into contact will vary. Excellent teachers are to be found in both educational sectors. While it should not be assumed that teachers at private schools are superior to their counterparts in state schools, or *vice versa*, one practical difference is that teachers at private schools tend to take on more responsibility for extra-curricular activities.

The significance of qualifications differs according to whether you have opted for the state or private sector, and the age of your child. Teachers' qualifications are discussed on pages 112–15.

In order for a teacher to be effective in the classroom, personal qualities are also important. A good teacher has the professional skills and character to engender respect. He or she will capture the children's attention and inspire enthusiasm for the subject. Success is dependent upon the relationship between student and teacher and the latter's expectations of the former. High expectations are a major factor: if a teacher raises expectations, he or she will raise standards. If they are not challenged, pupils will not achieve; but inspired teaching can empower children of all abilities to meet goals and gain confidence and self-esteem. Poor teaching, however, can undermine a pupil's self-esteem and turn him or her against academic work and school in general.

Teachers are human too

As well as being professionals, teachers are also individuals, with personal quirks and preferences. You should not expect them to be free of human frailties.

Teaching method

The best teachers present information in more than one way. The principles of neuro-linguistic programming (NLP) have been employed to explain why a child might get on better with one teacher than another. Practitioners of NLP divide communication into visual, auditory and kinaesthetic modes (sight, sound and touch). They argue that the way a subject is taught has a direct bearing on a child's ability to learn. Teachers tend to prefer certain methods. If a teacher uses predominantly visual stimuli, such as diagrams or slides, a child attuned to this mode will thrive while others who favour sound (the spoken word) or touch (practical examples) will struggle – at which point problems with that teacher could arise. Ideally, all three methods should be adopted in the classroom, particularly for younger age groups. For example, children who have problems looking at sums written down may benefit from handling counters or an abacus because they are more attuned to touch than to sight. It is important to realise that this could be a factor if your child is experiencing difficulties. For information on NLP, contact the Association for Neuro-Linguistic Programming.*

It is not easy to assess teachers' methods while being briefly ushered through their classrooms. You will probably find it much easier to strike up conversations with primary, pre-prep and prep teachers than with those at secondary level, whom you may not have the opportunity to meet unless the school organises an Open Day. Ask whether they support the spoken word with diagrams and practical examples – their answers will indicate how attuned they are to the fact that children learn in different ways. A keen and skilled teacher will enthuse about teaching methods and how he or she recognises and adjusts to a child's difficulties.

If serious problems arise, particularly with reading and writing, staff should be aware of diagnostic procedures and know when to request expert help for a child.

Classroom behaviour

The body language and general demeanour of the teachers and pupils can strongly influence visitors' impressions of a school. When touring classes, try to assess the atmosphere. Is the mood pleasant and friendly? Does the teacher's tone of voice sound strained or relaxed? Do the pupils respond willingly to questions, or are they suspiciously quiet? Are students slouching at their desks, or do they seem alert and industrious? Chapter 19 offers more suggestions on what to look out for when touring a school. If not given the opportunity to see classes in action, you could ask current or former pupils, or their parents, for their opinions of members of staff. This can often be a useful source of information – former pupils in particular can be remarkably forthcoming.

Pressures on teachers

Teaching staff can come under immense pressure. They may be anxious – even desperate – to produce glowing results to impress the school, the parents or the inspectors. Some, including head teachers, have become so ill from the strain of undergoing an Ofsted report (see pages 96–8) that, although skilled and capable, they have left the profession.

Education has changed following the introduction of the league tables (see Chapter 13). Schools are now pushing children to produce better exam results, while anxious parents are demanding more of both children and schools. Many teachers and parents do not stop to think whether they are simply asking too much of children. Pressure will only make things worse if a child is genuinely making an effort with schoolwork.

Other roles played by teachers

Some teachers have additional responsibilities within the staffroom hierarchy. It is unlikely that you will meet these individuals while investigating schools, but it is useful to be aware of their function.

Heads of department

Among various duties, heads of department organise the curriculum, prepare the exam syllabus for their particular subject, oversee the teachers within the department and liaise with the head, the director of studies and the teachers.

Heads of year

These teachers cater for the needs of the year group assigned to them in an administrative capacity and supervise the form tutors.

Form tutors

Form tutors supervise the classes into which children are grouped for administrative purposes, which includes taking the daily register, and are responsible for pastoral care (see Chapter 9). They may not actually teach any of the children in their care.

Academic tutors

Secondary schools operate this mentoring system to help guide a pupil's exam attempts. Under it, a member of staff is assigned as an academic counsellor to every student preparing for NVQ, GNVQ, GCSE, AS- and A-level exams. The aim is to provide encouragement and pressure, defining goals appropriate to the pupil using a target timetable. Regular meetings where progress and problems can be discussed are organised on a one-to-one basis, and the tutor will establish close contact with the parents where possible. In some schools pupils can choose their academic tutor, which should avoid clashes of personality.

Supply teachers

Teacher shortages have reached crisis levels in an unacceptable number of state schools (see page 116). Many schools are forced to draft in supply teachers to fill the gap. Some schools try to use the same personnel each time, so that they become familiar to the pupils (and the pupils familiar to the teachers), but if many are used continuity cannot be maintained. Parents should ask what proportion of supply teachers are used alongside the permanent instructors.

Teachers' qualifications

Teachers enter the school system via a number of routes. The following sections look at teachers' qualifications and training.

Teachers in state schools

It is a legal requirement that all teachers in state schools have qualified teacher status (QTS). An exemption exists whereby in the absence of someone with QTS an unqualified person may be employed. All teachers are given a reference number by the DfEE, although this does not in itself denote QTS (a common misunderstanding). QTS is achieved by gaining a degree followed by either a Diploma in Education (DipEd – now phased out) or a Postgraduate Certificate in Education (PGCE), or a BEd degree. Special arrangements exist for approving overseas graduates for QTS.

Most state-school teachers are graduates, although a few older ones may still be teaching on the basis of the two-year Certificate of Education, awarded by colleges of education until 1976. The BEd and PGCE qualifications prepare teachers to offer specific subjects and/or to teach specific age groups, i.e. children up to seven, children between five and 11 (primary phase) or secondary pupils. The Graduate Teaching Programme allows a small number of graduates to achieve QTS while in a teaching post.

The specific requirements for different types of school vary:

- **Nursery school** State nursery schools and classes are staffed by qualified teachers assisted by nursery nurses.
- **Primary school** Teachers must have a primary PGCE or BEd, specialising in any subject. GCSE science is a requirement if the candidate is born after 1 September 1979.
- **Secondary school** Teachers must have a PGCE or BEd in any subject to secondary level (i.e. covering ages 11–18).

Primary and secondary teachers are excepted if they have attended a registered teacher programme consisting of English and maths to grade 'C' GCSE and have completed not less than two years' full-time higher education; this confers QTS.

Because the academic range is broad at primary level but subject-specific at secondary level, it would be hard for most primary teachers to teach at secondary level. However, teachers wanting to cross over can take a conversion course.

Teachers in independent schools

It may come as a shock to some parents, but paying for your child's education does not guarantee that the teachers will be either well trained or well educated. While in the state system qualified teacher status is a legal requirement, this ruling does not apply in the independent system.

Teachers in independent schools are not required by law to have QTS, although increasingly the schools with the highest academic standards do require their staff to have a PGCE as well as a first degree. However, some schools still employ graduates without teacher training, or completely unqualified staff.

Qualifications vary in the different strata of schools.

Pre-prep schools

Impressive qualifications do not carry the same weight as in prep and public schools: ability with small children is more important. However, although in the minority, honours graduates are in demand.

Prep schools

Prep schools that wish to persuade parents to pay substantial fees must be able to offer teaching staff with good qualifications. At this level, teachers are generally better qualified than at pre-prep level, with as many as half the staff having degrees. Nevertheless, some prep schools employ teachers who have only had the benefit of a short training course. The number of the degrees listed (particularly honours degrees) should indicate whether the school is competent, academically speaking. It is an advantage for the head and/or deputy head to hold a university degree if the school is to achieve an academic reputation.

Independent secondary schools

Secondary schools must naturally be able to provide a list of teaching staff with even stronger credentials than prep schools. Without proof of the teachers' attainments, parents cannot be assured that the staff will be capable of instructing pupils effectively at an advanced level.

Icing on a school's cake

An attractive bonus for a secondary school is to have external examiners on its staff list. These people will be well versed in examination technique, and in what is required not only to pass exams but also to attain good grades. The more a school can name, the better.

How to assess teachers' degrees

The staff list will detail teachers' qualifications, and it can be useful to know how to decipher the nomenclature of degrees. Generally, a BA (Bachelor of Arts) or a BSc (Bachelor of Science) is a first degree, although in Scotland some first arts degree courses award an MA (Master of Arts). Oxford and Cambridge (Oxbridge) follow a different pattern. At these universities, a BA is awarded regardless of whether the course is an arts or science subject. There is no BSc at Cambridge, while at Oxford a BSc is a postgraduate degree. A Masters degree at Oxbridge will be labelled MPhil, BPhil, BLitt or other variations. An MA from an English university is a higher degree which has involved further study, except at Oxbridge where graduates can obtain an MA simply by paying for it. A PhD (Doctorate in Philosophy) is awarded usually after three years' additional study following a master's degree, whatever the subject. Senior doctorates – for example DLitt, DSc or LLD (the nomenclature depends on the individual subject) – are awarded on the basis of outstanding published contributions to knowledge in that particular sphere. The degree BEd (Bachelor of Education) is awarded after a first degree course at a university or college of education linked to a university, and combines study of a specialist subject and education.

This is merely a very broad outline of the types of degree you will see listed after the names on a staff list. Added to this are a myriad of other certificates and diplomas, either university-based or professional.

You should now be able to run a more critical eye over any seemingly impressive staff list.

Potential problems with the teaching staff

The teaching profession is often embroiled in controversy. Some of the ramifications may affect your child's education.

In line with the focus on standards, colleges and university departments of education have come under greater scrutiny. One criticism voiced is that they fail to weed out those individuals who are obviously unsuited to a career in the profession, thereby doing a disservice to the student teachers as well as to their future pupils. Students themselves complain that the system concentrates too much on abstract theories and that they are not being given practical guidance on how to teach. Although they serve a useful purpose, courses are no substitute for experience.

Some people suggest that standards in education cannot be improved until teaching is accorded the esteem it gains abroad and more graduates with top degrees are attracted to the profession (the majority of graduate teachers currently hold ordinary or third-class degrees). However, it is argued that high-fliers will stay away until teachers' pay, prospects and workload equate to opportunities in the commercial sector.

In the classroom, your child may be directly affected by the following:

- **teacher shortages** In spring 1999, the Secondary Heads Association voiced fears that some schools may no longer be able to teach the full National Curriculum because of shortages in some areas, particularly modern languages. At schools afflicted by shortages, supply teachers are brought in to fill the gaps and some teachers are being recruited from abroad – although that does not necessarily indicate poor quality. As a result of shortages, teachers who are well qualified in their own subject may be assigned to teach other subjects they know little about – for example, you may find teachers who are teaching science without proper knowledge of that subject. Children should not suffer unduly in the short term, but may experience adverse effects if the absence of a fully qualified teacher is prolonged
- **budget constraints** in some state schools encourage governors to appoint cheaper young teachers rather than more experienced applicants at the top of the pay scale. Funding differs from LEA to LEA. Smaller schools have less money and therefore less flexibility in appointing staff
- **schools employing new graduates** In the independent system, where parents are paying high fees with the belief that these will ensure experienced and competent teachers, the untried capabilities of a graduate without teacher training or experience (and a track record you can check upon) could be a cause for concern, particularly if he or she carries sole responsibility for a subject. The individual may have left school, studied at university or college and gone straight back on to the school campus without acquiring experience or insights from the outside world

- **schools with large numbers of old teachers** At the other extreme, you may find too many teachers nearing retirement. There is a tendency for teachers who have held a position for many years to become stale. Such people may not be up to date with current thinking, and their age could conceivably hinder their teaching abilities.

Children teaching children

The father of a pupil at an independent secondary school was concerned by the high proportion of young staff, and asked the head why he was employing staff little older than the sixth form. He was told that the school could only afford to employ raw graduates, leading the parent to wonder just where his money was going.

Overleaf, a checklist for teaching staff lists useful questions to ask.

Checklist for teaching staff

(1) During a school tour or open day, particularly at primary, pre-prep and prep stage, try to involve teaching staff in conversation. Ask them about their teaching methods and find out whether they endeavour to engage children on different levels.

(2) Ask whether all the teachers are qualified to teach their subjects.

(3) Request a current list of teaching staff, if this has not been provided with the prospectus, and try to assess the quality of the qualifications listed. Do not allow letters after names to distract you from all other indicators.

(4) Enquire whether your child will be affected by teacher short-ages, and whether the school relies on supply teachers. If this is the case, find out what percentage of staff they represent.

(5) Ask the ages of the relevant staff. At an independent school, you may be surprised by the proportion of inexperienced youngsters amongst the older, more experienced (and more expensive) teachers.

(6) Ask whether pupils are assigned to an academic tutor and if they are allowed to choose.

(7) Find out whether there any external examiners for GCSE or A-level examinations among the staff, and how many are present.

(8) Bullying by staff is not unknown (see pages 145−7). If you have a gut reaction against any teacher when visiting a school, ask the head about him or her.

Chapter 9

Pastoral and domestic care

How your child is cared for as a human being, as opposed to a pupil being educated, matters a great deal in the context of school life, particularly if the child is boarding. However, this aspect of education tends to take a back seat in favour of academic issues. This chapter examines how schools cater for children's personal and social welfare. It also looks at the issue of school food.

State schools

The provisions for pastoral care vary from school to school. Some common systems are outlined below. The system in state boarding schools resembles that in independent schools (see pages 121–5).

The pastoral care framework

One LEA pastoral care officer advises parents to look for 'a school with a planned provision for personal and social development, together with well organised pastoral support'. The extent to which schools are able to fulfil this varies. There is considerable flexibility beyond the statutory requirements, and the type of arrangements a school has in place can provide significant clues to its general ethos.

Common pastoral arrangements

Pastoral support is organised in numerous ways, starting in the classroom:

- **support from teachers** All teachers have a contractual duty towards nurturing the personal and social development of their pupils, and a child's first contact is usually his or her class teacher, or possibly a tutor at secondary school who is responsible for the welfare of the class. In some schools, the class teacher/tutor changes each year. In others, one teacher remains responsible for a class group for several years, or from the first form through to GCSE. Parental approaches to the school will be through the class teacher/tutor in the first instance

- **confidential meetings with tutors** Some schools allocate time for pupils to have a confidential chat with their form tutor on a rota basis as an integral part of the timetable. Any problems, academic or personal, can be discussed behind a closed door, and as the session is compulsory there is no need for the pupil specifically to request a teacher's attention. The tutors are supervised by the heads of year. Academic tutors at secondary school help children preparing for examinations and provide support on a one-to-one basis (see page 112)

- **homework supervision** Many schools provide children with an 'academic planner' or 'homework organiser' – a timetable or schedule in booklet form which the parent must see and initial. This enables teachers and parents to keep up with a child's progress and allows teachers to flag up any areas of difficulty. This booklet may contain helpline numbers, such as that of Childline.* Under the new home–school agreements, homework is considered an area of joint responsibility between school and parents (see Chapter 15)

- **staff briefings** Many schools hold staff briefings each morning, which provide a forum for teachers to discuss any problems faced by particular children

- **pupil counsellors** Under this initiative, prompted by concerns about playground culture, teams of children trained in supervision, social interaction and behaviour keep an eye on their less confident fellow pupils. With staff supervision, the counsellors organise games during break time and help shy children to integrate – no one is allowed to feel neglected or isolated, and the counsellors are on the alert to intervene if necessary in the event of bullying problems (most bullying occurs in the playground). At secondary school, pupil counsellors help younger children to settle in and may run confidential advice sessions for students in difficulties

- **external counsellors** Professional counsellors are sometimes used by schools to provide extra support to staff and hold sessions for individual pupils
- **vertical groups** The norm in primary schools is to change form or class teacher each year, but with this system children of various ages are vertically grouped together with a form teacher to whom they will be attached throughout the school, except for specialist subjects. Changing form teachers each year can be a lottery but this method potentially offers greater continuity and security. The downside can be that children get stuck with a form teacher they dislike.

The curriculum: non-compulsory subjects

Secondary schools are legally obliged to provide sex education, although this is discretionary in primary schools. Religious education must also be taught in both types of school. Parents can withdraw their children from either or both of these subjects if they wish. Secondary schools also offer careers education.

PSHE lessons

Personal, social and health education (PSHE) is not compulsory within the National Curriculum, although it is part of the non-statutory framework (see Chapter 12). It is however expected to be taught and some schools take the subject rather more seriously than others. Lessons cover topics such as alcohol, smoking, drugs and child abuse and may involve speakers from the police and other organisations. The PSHE syllabus also includes lessons incorporating role play in social situations – to show, for example, how to discourage bullying.

PSHE is not a substitute for an integrated pastoral care system. In some schools it is treated purely as an academic subject, although it is not assessed. 'Citizenship' is to be included in the National Curriculum from 2000 (see page 158).

Independent schools

The tendency to stress academic achievement over pastoral care is a risk in private schools, particularly those that set great store by examination results.

In the independent sector, too, pastoral arrangements vary from school to school, and you should ask each establishment for specific details. You may find that a number of the measures adopted in state schools are in place, such as homework planners and counselling services (see 'Common pastoral arrangements', pages 119–21). Note that if the school has not adopted the house system, the form teacher/ tutor or head is likely to be the first point of contact for children and parents in the event of a problem.

The house system

Both day and boarding schools may be split up into houses for organisational purposes. Sometimes this is a purely nominal arrange- ment – for example, divisions are not pronounced at prep-school level – while other houses are run as self-contained units. At boarding school, children will return to the house each evening to see their friends, do their homework, relax and sleep. Older pupils will be appointed as house monitors under a head of house. They will assist the housemaster or -mistress and supervise younger children.

The character of a house can be a strong formative influence on a pupil, so it is important to make the right decision for your child. Often, different houses in the same school concentrate on separate activities – one might favour sports while another promotes drama, for example. House spirit and rivalry are very much part of school life, as evidenced by the loudly enthusiastic displays at house matches, and being part of one can instil a reassuring sense of belonging in children.

Avoiding the prep-school mafia

When choosing a house, check whether the school takes large numbers of children from the same prep school every year. There is a tendency for these pupils, thrown together in a strange environment, to club together for mutual support and gang up on 'outsiders' joining the year group. By the second and third year, friendships will have been forged outside the gang but in the meantime your child could possibly find it difficult to fit in with this clique.

Choosing a boarding house can be difficult if you lack insider knowledge. Always ask to see more than one house when touring a school. The housemaster or -mistress is a key player and you should trust your instincts when introduced to him or her.

Housemasters and -mistresses

At secondary school, these staff administer the school houses and look after pupils' general welfare in addition to teaching. They should be readily available in case of any problems. After the head, the housemaster or -mistress is the most influential figure in authority.

If the school is large, find out how it is administered. Houseparents sometimes operate independently of the head and it is not unknown for individual houses to be effectively a law unto themselves.

Some schools stipulate that housemasters must be married or add a requirement that they should have families of their own. If a housemaster is married, his wife plays an important role and is expected to ease children's homesickness and general worries. Husbands of housemistresses in girls' establishments do not generally assume the same prominence, although male housemistresses (as it were) have been employed in some girls' schools.

In prep schools, housemasters and -mistresses do not have such far-reaching responsibilities and generally work in conjunction with the senior matron.

Tip

A housemaster's wife at secondary school often has relatively intimate contact with the children and will bring influence to bear on her husband. Ask to meet her.

Tutors

The pastoral tutor system is becoming more widespread in prep schools. Despite being made much of by schools, in practical terms tutors may simply perform a similar role to that of class teacher or housemaster. Some parents have voiced concerns about intrusive behaviour on the part of tutors at boarding schools, such as asking to see children's letters home, which is unacceptable.

Biggest is not necessarily best

The size of independent schools varies dramatically: while one might have fewer than 300 pupils, another could take as many as 1,500. For some children the prospect of a large school could be overwhelming, especially in the first year at boarding school. If you have doubts about your son or daughter's ability to adapt, a smaller school might be more user-friendly. It will allow greater contact with the housemaster or -mistress, which should enable your child to settle in more quickly.

Matrons

Matrons look after the health and personal needs of children of all ages at boarding school, and perform general domestic duties. They can provide support and a sympathetic ear for children to confide in, but mothers and fathers should not expect matrons to be parent substitutes. Their job is demanding and requires organisational skills, efficiency and discretion. Prep-school matrons without nursing qualifications will be assisted by qualified staff.

At prep school, the senior matron will assume overall responsibility for pastoral care, if the headmaster's wife does not take this role. Not all senior schools employ matrons in each house. Where they do, the matron will assist the housemaster or -mistress.

Restricted finances have caused a large proportion of prep schools to employ young and inexperienced school leavers as matrons. It is arguable whether this could affect children's welfare.

The sick bay (or sanatorium) and the dormitories are both in the matron's domain at prep school; in senior schools the sick bay comes under the control of qualified medical staff. When visiting a boarding school, look at these areas carefully.

Sick bay

The matron will attend to children's day-to-day medical needs; many have nursing qualifications. School doctors at prep and senior boarding schools hold morning surgeries and are on call in case of emergencies. The school should have an established procedure for coping with illnesses and accidents of varying degrees of severity. If emergency treatment is required but a child's parents cannot be reached, the head, housemaster or -mistress will act *in loco parentis*. Questions to ask at prep school include:

- Does the matron have SRN (state registered nurse), RNS (registered nursing sister) status, or other medical qualifications?
- What qualifications do the assistant matrons hold and are any new to the job?
- How near is the sick bay to the overnight duty matron's quarters? (Ideally, they should be next door to each other)
- Has an alarm system been installed in the sick bay?

Dormitories

When touring dormitories, check that they are safe and clean. Try not to take offence at posters that may not be to your taste – these allow children to express their individuality.

- Be on the lookout for any potential dangers – for example, the upper tiers of bunk beds should be securely fitted with sides to prevent occupants falling out.
- Is ventilation adequate? Crowded dormitories can become stuffy.
- Are sleeping quarters clean and neat? Bear in mind that teenagers can be extremely untidy (think of your own child's bedroom).

Living arrangements at boarding school

At a boarding school, find out about the day-to-day practical arrangements relating to comfort and security. Ask the following questions.

- Are there cooking and laundry facilities on site for seniors?
- What other facilities are provided (e.g. snack machines)?
- Do leisure facilities, such as televisions, work?
- Can personal possessions be stored securely?
- How is pocket money controlled?
- At a full boarding school, how often may parents visit?
- At prep school, are letters home censored?
- Are secondary-school boarders allowed off the premises and how is this regulated in terms of security?
- How does the school guard against unauthorised access to the boarding houses and students' rooms?

Checklist for pastoral care

(1) Establish what pastoral care arrangements are in place and the extent of support systems such as counselling services. At an independent school, ask to meet the relevant personnel such as the housemaster or -mistress and matron.

(2) At a state school, how is the subject of PHSE viewed and what form do PHSE lessons take?

(3) Do children take on any responsibilities within the pastoral care framework – for example, at a state school are pupil counsellors employed? At an independent school, do senior pupils supervise or guide younger pupils?

(4) At an independent school that operates the house system, find out how the houses differ and ask to see more than one to provide a comparison. Ask what policy is adopted when allocating pupils to houses, and discover whether the school takes a disproportionately large intake from one school.

(5) At boarding schools, be sure to visit the sick bay and dormitories and ask about the security and living arrangements.

(6) At a prep boarding school, ask whether the matron or headmaster's wife reads to the younger children or involves them in extra-curricular games and activities.

School food

Although this is sometimes not fully appreciated by parents, the quality and quantity of school food are extremely important to children, particularly boarding pupils.

The 1970s were the heyday of subsidised school dinners in state schools, when 66 per cent of pupils tucked in. Following this period, services were downgraded or contracted-out and the number of students eating school meals fell to 40 per cent. However, in part due to new concerns about healthy eating, there has been a resurgence of interest in the quality of school food. In recognition of the contribution of school meals to raising educational standards, the government has placed a legal obligation upon schools to ensure that the food offered is nutritious. Recipe suggestions have been drafted along with the regulations, coming into force in April 2000.

The introduction of nutrition regulations will mean that head teachers must address issues of food hygiene and safety. Where schools lack resources, there is a risk that heads might cut corners with the meals budget. Parents touring a school prior to deciding where to send their child should therefore try to look closely at the school kitchens and the food emerging from them.

Ensuring a balanced diet

Many children do not eat properly. Given the choice, most teen-agers opt for junk food with a high fat and salt content. Figures show that worrying numbers of young people are obese and facing attendant health risks (see box, page 74). Meanwhile, some children suffer so-called 'muesli malnutrition' – calcium and iron deficiency – as a result of dieting. This condition, affecting mostly girls, has been proven to impair a child's IQ level in the short term. Scientists stress that where possible a child's diet should include energy-dense foods containing vital nutrients such as iron, calcium and zinc. Many parents give their children vitamin and mineral supplements in the belief (not supported by evidence) that they enhance academic ability.

Parents should check that the school menu supplies adequate amounts of protein, carbohydrate and fat, together with vitamins and minerals, and contains sufficient portions of fresh fruit and vegetables. With such a diet there should be no need whatsoever for dietary supplements.

State schools

Children in the state system are entitled to free meals if their parents receive income support or income-based job seekers' allowance. Application forms should be obtainable from the school, or alterna-tively contact your LEA. Milk is available in some schools at the discretion of the head and must be paid for.

Breakfast: the best start to the day

More than 40,000 British children go to school every day on an empty stomach. Children from disadvantaged backgrounds are more likely to leave their homes hungry. However, scientists have proved that high-calorie breakfasts improve children's creativity and physical endurance. As a result, 'breakfast clubs' have been set up in some state schools. The food is free and the scheme boasts a number of advantages: children tempted into school will be less inclined to play truant, and working parents can drop their children off early knowing their needs will be looked after. It is expected that the scheme will expand as the benefits are recognised.

Independent schools

Parents should examine the kitchen facilities and the food on offer at interview stage (see Chapter 19). This will provide an opportunity to find out whether there are menu options, what proportion consists of junk food high in salt and fat, and how meals are supervised.

Boarding schools

Unlike day pupils, boarders are almost entirely reliant upon the school kitchens. The school diet can dictate pupils' general welfare to the extent of affecting academic and sporting performance. Some schools scrimp on nutrition to save money, and it is not uncommon for children to lose weight during term time. Food may be sent from home and senior boarders may have their own cooking facilities.

Warning

Beware a trick played by some schools: serving visitors food that is of superior quality to that served to the pupils. It has also been known for children to be photographed for a prospectus enjoying delicacies totally alien to the school menus.

How to assess the school food

Whatever the type of school, you can check on the menus, but food preparation and cooking methods are variables which you cannot control. Cooks come and go regularly and there may be little consistency from term to term. While checking out the kitchen facilities:

- ask to see some typical summer and winter menus, if these are available. From this you should be able to gauge the amount of fresh and seasonal fruit and vegetables served, and the proportion of hot meals. If your child is to board, pay attention to breakfasts and evening menus
- discuss the availability of alternative arrangements if your child has any food allergies or specific dietary requirements. Schools usually offer a vegetarian option each day and will cater for alternative diets
- find out whether the staff, including the head, eat with the children, and ask whether teachers have a different menu
- if the menus appear inadequate to you, be nosey. Say you would love to see some of the food prepared there. If you do not like the look of what is provided, it is unlikely that your child will
- ask if milk is available for younger children.

Chapter 10

Discipline

A reliable and respected system of discipline is essential to the smooth running and academic success of a school. Discipline is often a key concern of parents, too. However, the subject may be skated over at an open day or interview, with parents left unclear as to what measures are in place. This is likely to be the case both in schools that openly admit to problems and those that claim to exercise an effective regime.

Bad press for certain state schools has led some parents to choose the independent system in the belief that they will find stronger discipline here. However, an independent school does not necessarily deliver good discipline. This chapter outlines common problems facing schools and the methods of enforcing discipline.

The role of discipline

The operation of a fair disciplinary code in a school is a complex issue. At school, children must live within a closed community and abide by its rules. They must learn to be governed while also learning self-government and the government of others. This process continues throughout nursery, primary and secondary school. Plato outlined this progression when he wrote in the *Laws*: 'We are not speaking of education in this narrower sense, but of that other education in virtue from youth upwards, which makes a man eagerly pursue the ideal perfection of citizenship and teaches him how rightly to rule and how to obey. This is the only education which, upon our view, deserves the name.'

Children need parents and teachers to set boundaries and provide structure and order in their development. They are uncomfortable

Finding the right balance

It is natural for children to question authority and challenge rules and commands as they grow up. The energy with which they do this needs to be controlled and channelled to the greatest benefit of the child. Children who have no consideration for others or are disruptive in the classroom are denying their peers their right to enjoy an education. Their classmates may think they are amusing, but the disruption of teaching has potentially serious consequences. Of course, children should enjoy a certain amount of freedom in which to indulge high spirits. There is nothing to be said for the unreasonable quelling of a high-spirited child in the supposed interests of turning out a polite, well-behaved adult – this may result in a repressed, unhappy individual. If it is necessary to exercise punishment, the school authorities should take care not to inflict physical or mental damage.

with anarchy and require an environment of mutual respect in which anti-social behaviour is outlawed and where a code of reasonable rules and regulations provides stability. Only by experiencing discipline can the child learn self-discipline. The prime factor in self-discipline, and an invaluable part of the survival kit for living within any community, is consideration towards others. Many parents regard self-discipline and good manners as important, and will look for schools that share this view.

Reports in the press suggest that discipline is breaking down in some schools. Endless debate has endeavoured to uncover the reasons for this, and an answer. Partnership between schools and parents could provide a solution. One the one hand, schools must set standards and police them effectively, while the new Home–school agreements require parents to ensure good behaviour on the part of their children (see page 206).

'Liberal' schools

Unlike the vast majority of schools, some independent schools are consciously liberal in their outlook. They promote the concept of individual freedom rather than obedience to authority, impose few

> **Tip**
>
> When looking around schools, you may encounter behaviour in some pupils that does not meet your personal definition of good manners. You are advised to adopt a philosophical attitude, particularly if you find your other criteria fulfilled, but be sure to ask questions about attitudes to discipline and the encouragement of consideration for others.

rules and allow informality between pupils and teachers. Adults and children are regarded as equals, regulations are devised by both parties in accordance with the principle of mutual respect and thereafter the regulations are policed by the pupils themselves. Smoking, swearing and non-attendance in class may all be permitted. It is argued that once the compulsion to attend classes is removed, students will turn to lessons and learn because they really want to. Some students report that this system prepares them admirably for university life, where they have to study without close supervision.

It may not be apparent from the prospectus whether a school regards itself as 'liberal': parents who are unsure on this question should ask about the school's attitude at an open day or interview. (Note that an establishment with a liberal policy is quite different from one where anarchy reigns because the head is ineffective.)

The administration of discipline

The day-to-day operation of effective discipline is the responsibility of the head teacher and teaching staff, who administer the general policies laid down by the governors.

The head's style and tone will filter down through the teaching staff to the pupils. The head must also manage the staff, who need to command the children's respect in order to control and guide their charges effectively. Needless to say, the head must command the respect of all parties – it does not augur well if staff are openly disdainful of the head's opinion.

Most state schools have a code of conduct, drawn up in many cases following consultation with parents, pupils, staff and governors. Apart from containing obvious prohibitions against violence, drink and drugs, these generally codify behaviour which respects the rights to order and respect of all the groups in the school and the means for dealing with infringements of the rules.

To be effective, discipline must be clear-cut, easily understood, consistent and fair. One of the fundamental problems in administering discipline is that some staff may not willingly admit that a breach has occurred. They may feign ignorance at first, taking action only after complaints from parents or children. Some schools make exaggerated claims about what will be done to enforce discipline, but fail to follow through.

It is possible to glean some impression of how effectively order is exercised by observing pupils' demeanour when visiting schools. Some pointers are the amount of noise and boisterous behaviour in the corridors and dining room, and the neatness and consistency of the uniform, if one is worn.

Each school has different codes for dealing with disruptive behaviour, and you should try to ascertain the ground rules – for example, does the school send pupils home if they are involved in fights? And at what stage are parents called in if, say, bullying is discovered?

Some powers may be delegated to pupils who assume positions of authority. At:

- **state schools** prefects or monitors are rare and where appointed they do not normally exercise discipline themselves but play a supporting role for teaching staff and act as mentors for the younger children, if required (see 'Pupil counsellors', page 120)
- **prep schools** prefects chosen from the top form may be responsible for ensuring tidiness and good behaviour, particularly in dormitories and changing rooms
- **independent secondary schools** most daily discipline is in the hands of the school or house monitors, or prefects. If most of the policing has been handed over to prefects without proper supervision, this could create problems due to partiality among pupils – for example, a house captain in charge of discipline might be reluctant to rebuke rowdy students who were his friends.

At independent school, a system of privileges for the older children may require younger pupils to perform not-too-onerous domestic duties. 'Fagging' has generally been phased out.

The exercise of discipline inevitably involves punishment. The school's attitude to punishment and the methods it employs will give you an insight into its general philosophy and underlying strategy. Questions to consider are: Is the penalty imposed positive – in other words, does it turn the punishment into an opportunity for added education, for example by requiring the pupil to undertake an academic exercise? Alternatively, is discipline exercised indiscriminately or over-severe?

Punishment should be rational: firm but fair. This requires astute judgement on the part of the teacher. If punishment is inconsistent or ineptly administered, it could lead to insubordination, enmity and distrust.

The different forms of punishment used in schools are considered below. Terminology varies between the state and independent systems, and between individual independent schools, as do the ways in which punishments are carried out. Independent schools determine their own policy.

Corporal punishment

The use of an instrument for admonishment – such as a cane – is outlawed in all schools, and in state schools corporal punishment has been banned since the 1980s. The European Court of Human Rights has ruled that moderate corporal punishment is not unlawful, provided it does not amount to degrading punishment – which means that at independent schools striking with the hand is permitted, in theory. However, many private schools have been compelled to devise other methods of punishment, such as detention, lines, domestic duties or withdrawal of privileges.

The issue of corporal punishment is frequently raised at interview in the independent sector. Some people have blamed the lack of discipline in schools on the effective banning of corporal punishment. One school of thought favours the short, sharp punishment that, provided it fits the crime and is not disproportionate or inappropriate, can end the matter there and then. Some children have expressed a preference for this method of discipline, rather than, for example, detention – better to get it over with than lose any precious leisure time. As a compromise, it has been suggested that children should choose between corporal punishment and the other forms of punishment available for a particular offence.

Detention

Detention is the most common punishment in the state system. It may not be a one-off punishment but could occur on a daily basis for, say, a week: the severity of the offence will dictate the duration and whether or not it is entered on the pupil's record. State schools must give pupils 24 hours' written notice of detention, on the assumption that they will inform their parents. An independent school is not required to give parents prior notice of a detention, which could be inappropriate if it is to take place after school and a parent is not informed that his or her child will be detained.

Monitoring of pupils

In the state system, pupils or entire classes may be put on daily report at the request of parents or staff (supervised children must ask staff/ parents to sign a form after lessons/homework). 'Gating' is adopted at independent and boarding schools. 'Close gating' confines the offender to his or her house, while 'gating' generally means the pupil will not be allowed into town. A teacher or monitor may be required to sign a pupil's gating card every few hours to confirm that he or she is still in school.

Lines and essays

Lines, or 'sides' (written exercises) are of little use unless improved handwriting is the desired result. The point of the punishment is lost if a younger pupil is paid to do it for the offender, as has been known to happen. Essays or exercises are instructive, and can prove much more of a deterrent since they require extra mental exertion. This method could be employed to enforce classroom discipline and control noise and over-exuberance in the dormitories at boarding school. A common alternative, making a child stand in the corridor as a punishment for chattering, has little point and does not encourage learning.

Domestic duties

These can be imposed on children at independent schools. 'Charring' usually takes the form of school cleaning duties such as sweeping, vacuuming and dusting. It can be a viable alternative to other punishments, particularly for those children to whom the idea of exerting themselves is anathema.

Some schools place a little too much emphasis on this form of punishment, to the extent that some parents question whether they are paying for domestic rather than academic instruction. The schools offer the excuse that it makes the children more helpful at home; however, the real reason they favour this measure may be to save on school cleaning bills.

Withholding of privileges

This is often employed at independent schools, most commonly for vandalism and petty theft. However, the measure is effective only if directed against the offender. Some schools sanction all pupils for the offence of one child, often while making little effort to track down the culprit. This is counterproductive and the procedure can become meaningless if repeated.

Disturbed behaviour: a signal for the need for attention

Mild tendencies towards theft and vandalism in a child may be a cry for help. Excessive pressure on pupils to produce high grades or jealousy amongst peers or siblings can result in a child showing symptoms of withdrawal, rudeness and aggression, and perhaps indulging in theft. This can be further exacerbated by the application of petty disciplinary rules without forethought on the part of a school (see below).

School policy encourages sweet snatchers

At a school where pilfering is a considerable problem prefects are permitted to eat sweets in front of younger children denied this privilege, while staff keep confectionery in unlocked desks. The chances are that the spate of stealing should come to an end once temptation is no longer put in children's way.

The forms of punishment listed above are used to enforce everyday codes of discipline. However, certain types of behaviour may deserve more serious punishment.

Exclusion/expulsion

This is the most severe measure a school can invoke. Published guidelines suggest that exclusion should be invoked only in response to major breaches of discipline, when other approaches have failed and it would be prejudicial to the well-being of other pupils for the offending child to remain at school.

- **Permanent exclusion** (**expulsion** in the independent sector) means that the pupil is permanently banned from school. It is invoked only for serious offences – for example, those involving drugs, alcohol, serious theft and vandalism. In the 1997–8 school year, there were 12,300 exclusions from state schools. If the exclusion is permanent, parents have an automatic right of appeal to the governors.
- In the case of a **fixed exclusion** (**rustication** in independent schools) the child is barred for a set number of days. By law this period must not total more than 45 days in any one year. A parent may, depending on the duration, appeal to the governors in writing.
- At an independent school, **suspension** means that a child is excluded for an unspecified period of time until someone decides what action to take.

As the government has a legal responsibility to educate excluded children, it may be necessary to send youngsters to a pupil referral unit (see page 87) or to provide home education (see pages 91–2) if they cannot attend school. Exclusion may affect a child's chances when making an application to other schools (see page 235). If your child has been excluded by a state school and you need advice, contact the helpline run by ACE.★

Some schools appear to be using exclusion as an excuse to get rid of unacademic pupils in a drive to improve their examination record or to remove potential troublemakers before an Ofsted inspection (see pages 96–8). These schools may exercise a 'zero tolerance' policy on relatively minor misdemeanours. Consequently, a growing number of parents are challenging expulsion through litigation, which involves both parents and schools in court cases and legal bills.

Appealing against exclusion

Parents should appeal first to the governing body (see Chapter 7), and if that fails they can consider taking their case to an independent appeal committee. Parents are advised to seek advice on exclusion law and to attend the hearings in person, preferably with someone else to support them. Parents who have appealed against an exclusion will not be able to enrol their child at another school until the appeal procedure is over. To obtain legal advice, contact the Children's Legal Centre.*

Tip

When visiting schools, ask about their stance on exclusion. (You are unlikely to uncover any local knowledge of the subject because any incidents will be confidential.) Try enquiring about the number of permanent or fixed exclusions over the last two or three years to discern how effectively the school exercises authority. Your opinion of the head's capabilities will also inform your decision (see Chapter 7).

Common disciplinary problems

The following problems will be present at most schools, and may incur the penalties described above.

Drugs

At school interviews, parents often tread warily around the question of drugs. You are unlikely to be told that a school has a drugs problem, but drugs are ubiquitous. Adolescents are heavily influenced by peer-group pressure to try illegal substances, and the age of first experimentation with drugs is thought to be getting younger. Statistics indicate that drug abuse is widespread and all schools – both state and independent – are implicated.

Drug use among teenagers

Among 14- to 15-year-old boys, 40 per cent have tried cannabis, 11 per cent LSD and 5 per cent Ecstasy: these figures have increased eightfold since 1987. Among young adults aged 16–24, 29 per cent are thought to have tried drugs. Cannabis is the most widely used drug; however, concern is growing about the increased use of cocaine and heroin.

School policy may vary according to each individual case and the seriousness of the crime. In April 1999 the government's Standing Conference on Drug Abuse (SCODA)* established that only 88 per cent of secondary schools and 40 per cent of primaries have a written policy on drugs.

In the state system, exclusion from school for either possessing or supplying drugs on school premises is not automatic, although highly likely if supplying is suspected. The decision rests with the head, who in turn should seek advice from the LEA. Most schools inform the police if drugs are found.

All independent schools expel pupils for supplying drugs. However, expulsion is no longer inevitable for possession of drugs. Instead, the offender may undergo constant monitoring.

Try to establish what rules are laid down and what policing methods are in place. One positive move by schools has been the introduction of urine tests to confirm suspected drug-taking.

Exclusion may not be the answer to drugs offences

SCODA suggests that no single strategy on exclusion is correct owing to the complex nature of the problem and the circumstances of each individual case. It advises schools to forgo heavy-handed exclusion policies in favour of counselling and behaviour 'contracts' in order to keep pupils in the mainstream school system wherever possible.

Alcohol and smoking

- **Alcohol** is a socially acceptable drug, but worrying figures show that a large number of under-age children, both boys and girls, drink excessively – above the recommended adult limit. To enable 18-year-olds to develop a responsible approach to alcohol within a social environment, some boarding schools have introduced 'sixth-form clubs'. This is a sound idea, often improved upon by the presence of staff socialising with pupils and keeping an eye on proceedings. Parents could check what limits are imposed (for example, one pint of beer or lager per pupil, or one glass of wine). The drawbacks are that where boarding is mixed, the taking of alcohol could encourage intimacy between the sexes, while day pupils could be precluded from joining the club due to transport problems.
- **Smoking** is commonplace in all schools, even though it may be outlawed on the premises. Peer pressure plays a large part in pupils starting smoking, and adolescents have little regard for health warnings focusing on the long-term effects. More than one in four 15-year-olds smokes, and the proportion of smokers among 11- to 15-year-olds is higher among girls than boys: 12 per cent of girls smoke regularly compared to 9 per cent of boys. In addition, pupils with lower educational expectations are more likely to smoke than other pupils.

With regard to both these issues, ask yourself whether you think the head is realistically able to control these problems. No head will ever be able to stamp them out.

Theft and vandalism

As with alcohol problems, theft and vandalism may be denied if a direct question is posed. However, it is not a question of *whether* they exist or not, it is a question of degree. If the school comes clean, admits to a problem from time to time and is prepared to discuss its methods of dealing with it, carry on talking. If you receive a denial, warning lights should start flashing. Schools that flatly deny the existence of theft or attempt to hide it under the guise of items 'borrowed', 'gone missing' or 'mislaid' are being economical with the truth. As a result, the problem can become unmanageable and the atmosphere in the school tense and unpleasant. A few schools may be too frightened to confront the perpetrator because they fear the parents' reaction or, at a private school, worry that the child will be removed, with the resultant loss of fees.

Vandalism is a problem in some schools, although it is not always perpetrated by its own pupils. If there is evidence of graffiti or damage ask about school security and how long it takes for repairs to be effected. You are advised to insure your child's personal belongings at school (see pages 267–8).

Truancy and other absences from school

The level of unauthorised absences from school is causing concern, and criminal activities are being attributed to truants at an increasing rate. Police officers have been joined by truancy officers employed by some LEAs to patrol the streets looking for non-compliant youngsters.

Parents can be prosecuted if they are indifferent to their duty to ensure that their child receives an efficient full-time education. Alternatively, an LEA can apply for an Education Supervision Order to ensure a child attends regularly. Before these measures are taken, however, the local Education Welfare Officer will attempt to give help and support to overcome any difficulties.

Non-attendance figures for schools are published in both the government performance tables and their league table spin-offs (see Chapters 12–13). Despite political pressure, not all schools have the resources to check on every single pupil who is missing from class. In the case of illness or some other valid reason for absence, it is a responsible action for parents to inform the school immediately and indicate when their child is likely to return. Ask schools how they follow up an unauthorised absence – do they automatically contact the parents on the first day, for example?

Time off during term time

Schools may grant children leave of absence to go on holiday during term time, but this must not generally exceed two weeks in any one school year.

Checklist for discipline

(1) Do not be over-impressed by a school's long list of rules and regulations; they may not be adequately enforced. Fewer rules may be more successful.

(2) Ask who is entitled to set punishments and what punishments are permitted. What is the school's philosophy towards punishment? Is it positive or negative (punishment for punishment's sake)?

(3) Find out how any monitor or prefect system works and how the library, classroom, dormitory and homework sessions are supervised.

(4) Ask whether younger children have to carry out duties for older pupils, and whether there is a system of privileges.

(5) At an independent school, ask the head about his/her attitude to corporal punishment. You deserve an honest answer: be suspicious if you sense that the head is prevaricating or dissembling.

(6) Do not waste time enquiring about the existence of drugs, alcohol, smoking, theft or vandalism. More to the point, ask: 'How are these dealt with?' and 'What steps are taken to investigate and recover stolen objects?'

(7) Ask how many pupils have been expelled or suspended recently, and why.

Chapter 11

Bullying and racism

These are serious matters and either form of behaviour is potentially very damaging to the school community. It is vital for all schools to have an effective policy and to be willing and able to deal swiftly with incidents.

Bullying

Bullying is a major issue and a potential tragedy. It can be exacerbated under boarding conditions. Children can suffer intensely from bullying, and it is important for parents and teachers to take heed of what children say and accommodate their fears.

Schools have become increasingly aware of this problem and concerned to find ways to prevent it. However, some schools may deny its existence in their own establishment, particularly to a parent. No matter how difficult is seems, you should probe for information. As with discipline problems (see Chapter 10), teachers are often reluctant to notice bullying, let alone admit to it. Heads and teachers who argue that bullying is a part of growing up and accuse parents of being over-fussy and protective do not run child-friendly establishments.

Whether physical or emotional, bullying is rarely a 'one-off'. Prolonged and severe bullying can have detrimental effects on health, causing psychosomatic illness in the victim. The unhappiness and misery caused by bullying at school could affect a child for the rest of his or her life, possibly leading to him or her being victimised in adult life, or becoming a bully, and has been known to lead to suicide.

The signs of bullying

Most victims of bullying try to keep their misery a secret. However, various changes in demeanour may signal a problem. Some warning signs are a reluctance to go to school, behavioural changes, frequent headaches, a deterioration in the standard of work and lost books or other items. Do not dismiss these signs. A quiet word with your child may reveal the underlying problem.

Bullying is widespread, but it should be controllable if a school takes sufficient action to combat it. Most state schools have written policies on racial and sexual harrassment and on bullying generally. Ask to see these.

Examining the two major sources of abuse in schools – other pupils and teachers – can help pinpoint potential danger areas.

Bullying by other pupils

There can be many reasons for bullying. Children may pick on others because of their race or nationality, their appearance, gender or sexual orientation, because of how they speak, behave or dress, or because of who their parents are. Some children may be bullied if they produce outstanding work.

Pupil counsellors are used in some state schools to deter bullying by other children. These playground support teams of children discourage potential troublemakers and encourage others to play together (see page 120). In other schools, senior pupils act as academic mentors but have a remit that extends to problems outside the classroom. The advantage of this scheme is that bullied children are more likely to talk to older pupils than adults. Arrangements may be made for a local counsellor to be available on certain days, so that pupils can 'drop in' on a casual basis, and each state school must have a designated Child Protection Co-ordinator. This is a specially trained teacher who can call on external agencies for support.

Ideally, the school, the teachers and the parents should act together to combat bullying. However, to some extent parents must rely on their own resolve and determination to guide their child through the problem. Sources of help and advice include ACE,* and Childline,* the number for which may be displayed on the public phone at the school so children can call in confidence.

Tip

If your child is being bullied, do not blame yourself. You should not be afraid that a situation may worsen if you step in; it will deteriorate if you do nothing. You can take positive action by encouraging your child to become more assertive and to challenge the bully. This should deter most bullies, who usually prey on weakness.

Bullying by staff

Bullying or aggressive behaviour on the part of teachers also occurs, although it is seldom acknowledged. It can take a wide variety of forms ranging from physical to mental abuse and is more difficult to deal with given the teacher's status.

As with any institution, schools contain diverse characters, some of whom may be colourful or eccentric. However, any undue harshness or vindictiveness on the part of members of staff should be apparent to other teachers and the head. It is the head's duty to take action immediately when a problem arises.

Inappropriate, unkind behaviour by teachers is sometimes confused with discipline, and has been excused as such. Heads may be unwilling to upset the status quo if the individual is long-serving and well established in the school hierarchy. You could therefore face an uphill struggle for your child's story to gain any credence, or to compel the head to take action.

Physical bullying is easiest to prove. Extreme cases have included children being pushed, pulled by the hair and having their mouths taped up to prevent chattering.

Emotional abuse in the form of sarcasm, intimidation and taunting directed at a child can have a knock-on effect upon the quality of the child's academic work and personal relationships. Signs are the same as for bullying by other children (see box, opposite). If a child is repeatedly denigrated in front of a class by a teacher, the example set

145

by the adult may be picked up and copied by other children, further exacerbating the victim's suffering.

Teacher's terror tactics

A certain teacher used the threat of expulsion to exercise his will over small children. Although this was the prerogative of the head, the children naturally tended to believe the word of an adult, and were much frightened.

Excessive shouting in class could be construed as emotional abuse and fall foul of the Children Act. Other violations of a child's rights might include verbal insults and derision directed at a child in front of his or her peers; or at boarding school, the unnecessary intrusion of a teacher who displayed such behaviour into the dormitories.

Just one bad teacher can infect the atmosphere and colour a parent's perception of a school; external condemnation of an establishment often follows. Lack of action is bad PR. If your knowledge of a school alerts you to a problem teacher, about whom nothing continues to be done, take a hard look at that school. If you suspect the head is unobservant and/or ineffectual, he or she may not be able to control any bullying. You must ask yourself whether the head instils confidence when meeting this individual (see Chapter 7).

Bullying by the head

Some heads are guilty of bullying themselves. In such circumstances, when the truth is discovered, parents are sometimes too intimidated to act. They may fear reprisals or that they will be labelled trouble-makers and have difficulty obtaining a place for their children elsewhere. Teachers may also suffer indignities through fear of losing their jobs. Staff turnover can reflect the head's relationship with members of staff (see page 107).

Sexual abuse by staff

The media highlight occasional cases of child abuse by staff and instances of teachers found with incriminating material such as child pornography. Such coverage has ensured that this anxiety is prominent in the minds of parents and schools alike. When sexual abuse is discovered, it generally elicits prompt action and the police are called in automatically. It has been known for this serious and damaging behaviour to be hushed up by schools. However, the vast majority of cases are dealt with swiftly. Counselling is available to help victims. Sex offenders are listed on a register and may not work with children again. You may come across wild rumours about this or that teacher being a child abuser, but without hard evidence this is a dangerous accusation that could lead to court action if unfounded.

How to assess how a school copes with bullying

As a parent, you are faced with the problem of how to recognise the signs of bullying, which tend to be concealed. The staff and children will probably all be on their best behaviour as you tour the school – your main weapons will be observation and instinct. However, body language can provide pointers (see page 280).

You should ask what pastoral procedures are in place to deal with bullying, and what sanctions are imposed. The form tutor or head of year may play a key role at secondary school. For more information on pastoral care and disciplinary procedures, see Chapters 9–10.

Tip

Parents whose children attend a particular school can usually provide valuable insights into the extent of bullying problems at that establishment. They will probably be more forthcoming if their own child has left.

Racism

In a multi-cultural society, race can often become an issue, whether your child is one of the majority or from a minority community. All children are entitled to fair treatment in school, and can be damaged directly or indirectly if this is not assured. Parents will want to know how individual schools approach the problem of racism, what policies are in place and how they deal with incidents, should they occur. Solutions cannot be found unless the school recognises that there is a problem: some do not acknowledge the incidence of racism for fear of negative publicity. However, some schools, particularly those with a multi-ethnic population, have ensured that teachers receive the appropriate training, so they can interpret children's behaviour correctly.

The difficulty for schools is that the attitudes of a pupil's family and his or her social background can influence behaviour regardless of any attempts to encourage racial tolerance. Parents who are considering schools should find out about each school's attitudes and policy, and ask what is done to supplement 'citizenship' education (see page 158). Questions to ask include:

- is the existence of racism recognised at the school?
- what steps are taken to monitor and control it?
- have teachers received skills training to improve their teaching methods in multi-ethnic classes?
- are racist incidents, involving other pupils or staff, dealt with promptly and sympathetically?

Academic performance

The most insidious and damaging form of racism is institutionalised and often unwitting. The academic results of ethnic minority groups vary. African pupils and some Asian races, particularly Indian and Chinese children, are achievers. The racial groups most at risk appear to be Afro-Caribbean, gypsy, Pakistani and Bangladeshi children, who are failing to achieve. Afro-Caribbean boys are about six times more likely to be excluded than white children and 50 per cent of gypsy children have special educational needs. Research shows that many children from minority groups are stereotyped as poor performers regardless of their real potential.

There may be problems outside a school's control: for example, overcrowding in the home environment might make study difficult. Cultural differences may impinge on study time where children are expected to be carers, particularly in the case of Pakistani and Bangladeshi children. However, class and gender may be just as important as race. Schools need to work hard to raise their expectations of *all* children if disappointing performance among some groups is to be overcome.

The government's action plan

The government has developed an action plan to tackle these issues, to improve the monitoring of racist incidents and tackle ethnic minority under-achievement. Schools will be required to record all racist incidents and report patterns and frequency to local authorities. As with all bullying incidents, pupils will be encouraged to report the matter to an adult so that appropriate action can be taken. Schools will also be discouraged from down-playing such incidents in an attempt to avoid negative repercussions, and parents will have the right to know when racism occurs and what action the school has adopted to counter it.

Schools will be expected to monitor the performance of all ethnic groups and exclusion policies, and to produce policies to tackle under-achievement and any problems which may arise from institutionalised racism.

Checklist for bullying and racism

(1) Your child may not always feel able to turn to you in case of a problem: children often worry that things could be made worse if their mother or father steps in. Watch out for signs that your child is being bullied.

(2) Try to assess the head's personality and attitude towards bullying. The reactions of staff and children to the head will indicate how he or she is regarded.

(3) Ask how bullying is dealt with, rather than whether it exists. Is there an 'open door' policy to enable victims to seek support? If discovered, how is bullying monitored?

(4) Enquire about the school policy on racism and find out how incidents are dealt with.

(5) Ask whether any staff are specially trained to meet the needs of minority groups.

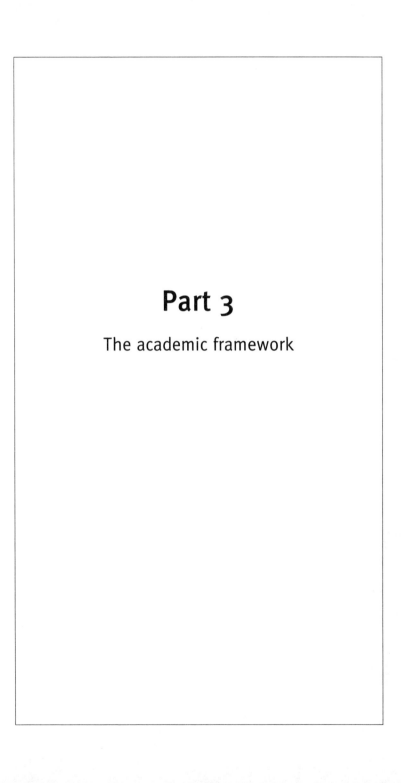

Part 3

The academic framework

Chapter 12

The National Curriculum, assessments and performance tables

Each school is required to design and deliver a school curriculum within national guidelines that meets the needs and abilities of its pupils in the most effective way.

Besides specific statutory requirements (such as the National Curriculum subjects, religious education and those concerning particular Key Stages), the broad curriculum guidelines include general requirements. These are set out in the Education Reform Act 1996, and stipulate that the curriculum for maintained schools should:

- be balanced and broadly based
- promote the spiritual, moral, cultural, mental and physical development of pupils at the school and of society
- prepare pupils at the school for the opportunities, responsibilities and experiences of adult life.

The Act also establishes principles common to all school curricula: namely, that all pupils are entitled to access to learning and to develop skills and knowledge, with continuity and progression provided by a national framework; that all those involved in education can expect standards of attainment to be set and monitored; and that public understanding of the aims and achievements of compulsory education should be promoted.

National Curriculum

The National Curriculum and Key Stage testing, both now firmly entrenched in the English and Welsh educational system, apply to all pupils of compulsory school age who attend state schools. The system is under constant review, with adjustments made where deemed necessary. Following devolution, the Welsh Assembly is to review its position on the National Curriculum and may deliver future amendments.

The new National Curriculum

A large-scale review, coming into force in September 2000, places particular focus on ensuring breadth, balance and flexibility, the development of literacy, numeracy and key skills, and the preparation of pupils for adult life. Increased flexibility will reduce prescription by reducing the amount of obligatory topics and slimming down course content over all Key Stages (see below).

- The relaxation in teaching coverage of the six foundation subjects in Key Stages 1 and 2, which occurred while the literacy and numeracy frameworks were being introduced, is to cease.
- While giving priority to the literacy and numeracy programmes, primary schools must teach all six subjects again (although the overall weight is reduced). Ofsted is due to inspect the content of the entire syllabus in schools from September 2000.
- At Key Stage 3, the slimming down of non-core subjects and the increased flexibility will allow teachers the opportunity for targeted in-depth study of particular topics.
- Flexibility in the post-14 curriculum is to be increased, with exemption to be made easier and vocational options emphasised to allow disaffected pupils the opportunity to pursue employment-related studies and participate in more work experience.
- Information and communication technology (ICT) is to be given greater emphasis across the curriculum generally, from Key Stage 1 upwards.

As subjects and content have been prescribed for pupils up the age of 16 in every maintained school, basic continuity has improved. If you have to move from one part of England or Wales to another and your child has to change schools, the curriculum should still be broadly similar, although GCSE syllabuses can still vary.

Key stages

The National Curriculum details the subjects which must be taught in state schools, and DfEE booklets for teachers, *Programmes of Study*, lay out the skill levels and content for each subject as they apply to pupils in each of the four Key Stages.

The Key Stages are divided up into age groups.

	Age of pupil	**Year group**
Primary school		
Key Stage 1	5–7	1–2
Key Stage 2	7–11	3–6
Secondary school		
Key Stage 3	11–14	7–9
Key Stage 4	14–16	10–11
Post-16	16–19	Sixth form

Foundation stage and early learning goals

Plans are being considered for a foundation stage which will take children from the age of three to the end of the reception year (4- and 5-year olds). It is intended that 'early learning goals', replacing the 'desirable learning outcomes' currently adopted, will link with the baseline tests for pupils entering primary school (see pages 159–60). These goals reflect the key objectives of the national literacy and numeracy programmes (see Chapter 14) and include rudimentary writing skills. They are also intended to focus on social, personal and emotional development in the context of children's relationships with others. The fact that several of these goals are regarded as 'unachievable' by those expected to deliver them suggests that the introduction of this stage will be far from straightforward.

The six key skills children will be expected to have by the end of the reception year include:

- **personal development** The confidence to initiate ideas and to speak and work in a group; concentration; awareness of feelings and the consequences of one's actions; respect for others; understanding of right and wrong; management of personal hygiene
- **language and literacy** The ability to use language imaginatively

and speak clearly; know the alphabet and read simple sentences demonstrating phonic knowledge; hold a pencil correctly and write simple words; write own name

- **mathematics** The ability to count to 100; recognise numbers; understand size and shapes; perform simple addition and subtraction
- **environmental knowledge** Understand where they live, their families and the natural world; be inquisitive about objects around them, how they work and why
- **physical development** Develop co-ordination and movement; importance of health
- **creative development** Use the senses of sight, hearing, smell and touch; explore colour and texture in art; listen to and explore sounds, music, dance and stories.

Although this programme receives support from those who feel that education should be more closely linked to play, fears have been expressed that this is pushing very young children too far, too early and that those who do not attend nurseries as a result of parental choice could be at a disadvantage when starting school.

Primary school

The following National Curriculum subjects are available.

Key Stages 1 and 2
- Core subjects are English, maths and science.
- Design and technology, geography, history, art and design, music and physical education are non-core foundation subjects.
- IT skills are to be developed throughout this stage.
- Welsh in Wales.

Secondary school

The following subjects and options are available at each key stage.

Key Stage 3
- Core subjects are English, maths and science with the addition of one foreign language, usually French.

- 'Citizenship' will be added in 2002 (see overleaf).
- Foundation subjects continue, plus Welsh in Wales.

Key Stage 4

- Core subjects are English, maths, science, design and technology, ICT, one modern foreign language and physical education.
- Maths is divided into 'foundation' and 'higher' programmes to take account of students with learning difficulties and to stretch the more able.
- Science is divided into 'single' and 'double' science; the traditional three separate subjects – physics, chemistry and biology – are still available in some schools.
- 'Citizenship' will be added in 2002.
- Other subjects are optional, and some schools now include vocational GNVQs worth two GCSEs.
- Welsh in Wales.

In addition to the compulsory Key Stage subjects, schools operate optional study programmes which may include design, drama, a second modern foreign language and vocational courses. Timetable restrictions may limit choice, so that some options may be open, allowing virtually any combination of subjects, while others will be closed: for example, at Key Stage 4 pupils can take history or geography but not both.

Religious education must be taught at every Key Stage, although it is not classified as a National Curriculum subject. There is a legal requirement that secondary schools provide sex education as part of PSHE (see below), but at primary level this is at the school's discretion. Parents retain the right to withdraw their child from religious education, communal worship and sex education if they wish.

PHSE

Personal, social and health education (PHSE) aims to give pupils the skills and knowledge to lead confident, healthy and independent lives. At Key Stage 1, it builds upon the early learning goals, and at Key Stage 2 covers pupils' role in the community and their social and moral responsibility. At Key Stages 3 and 4, the programme consolidates previous work and is intended to complement the statutory provision for citizenship. Under this area of instruction, pupils are guided towards becoming informed and responsible members of society by understanding sexual relationships and dealing with personal, social and moral issues. PHSE is not obligatory. However, in many schools it is viewed as part of the pastoral care framework (see page 121).

Citizenship

The government has made instruction in citizenship one of its priorities. The broad aims of the school curriculum – namely to instil values and morals (see page 153) – were previously met through religious education and PSHE. Rather than just incorporate citizenship across the curriculum, the government is now to introduce it as a subject in its own right.

'Citizenship' will be compulsory at secondary schools from 2002, while primary schools will be required to incorporate it into non-statutory PSHE lessons. Schools will be expected to integrate much of the programme from September 2000, although, in practice, they already carry out much of the content. It is proposed that secondary-school content will include awareness of, among other elements, duties and rights, the criminal justice system, central and local government (including the electoral system), and ethnic identities.

The school day

Following the new proposals for curriculum content, the government is considering extending the school day. At present, the average teaching week in England is 25 hours, with primary schools ranging from 20 to over 25 hours, and secondary schools from 22 to over 26 hours. The independent-school day is usually longer, although likely to include more time for sport. Some independent schools operate Saturday-morning school, and a number of state schools are now introducing this feature. Proposed changes to the school year are outlined on pages 214–15.

Independent schools

The National Curriculum is not compulsory in independent schools, but most follow its guidelines in order to avoid unnecessary complications, particularly for children crossing over between the two systems at secondary-school age who are taking GCSE examinations at Key Stage 4 or studying at sixth-form level.

In highly selective schools, you are much more likely to find syllabuses extended over and above the requirements of the National Curriculum and classes working to standards above the levels of requirement in the Key Stages. Parents will also find some schools that incorporate international syllabuses such as the baccalaureate offering complementary exams at GCSE- and A-level stage where they feel that the system is insufficiently challenging.

Assessments

Children are now assessed at various stages throughout their educational career, the first of these occurring within the very first weeks.

Baseline assessment

Within the first seven weeks of starting school, all children except those with special needs statements (see pages 85–6) must undergo baseline testing to assess their level of prior attainment. As children enter school at slightly different ages, allowances are made for 3-, 4- and 5-year-olds.

Children are assessed in reading, speaking, listening, writing, understanding of numbers and personal and social development. Additional avenues of assessment may be covered by some schemes – for example, awareness of the environment or physical and creative development. The results will assist teachers to discover what a child knows, understands and is capable of in order to plan an education programme for him or her and to identify any potential areas of weakness. The assessment will also help to monitor children's progress, to ensure they are achieving as well as they ought.

The assessment takes place like any normal classroom activity, so children are unlikely to be aware they are being assessed and need not become anxious. Parents are advised not to prepare their children, as this could give a false impression of their underlying potential.

You may request the results for your child and will normally discuss the content of the assessment with the teacher at a parent's meeting during the first term of school (see pages 211–12). If you do not feel that the results properly reflect your child's ability, you should bring this to the attention of the teacher.

LEAs may use the overall results to make comparisons in their own area. National comparisons, however, are not possible as the different assessment systems are too diverse. This situation has led to much debate, and it is increasingly likely that a common assessment scheme will be introduced.

Testing at Key Stages 1, 2 and 3

At the end of Key Stages 1, 2 and 3 (ages 7, 11 and 14), all pupils in maintained schools, including those with special educational needs, take National Curriculum tests in English and mathematics. Science is statutorily assessed at the end of Key Stage 1 (age seven) and then nationally tested at Key Stages 2 and 3 (ages 11 and 14). The tests take place in the summer term. Parents receive the teacher's assessment of the standards their child has achieved in classwork together with a report of the results. At secondary school, children at Key Stage 3 (age 14) will receive teacher assessment in the non-core foundation subjects.

The national school test results and the teacher assessments are equally important and carry the same legal status. They can give different indications of the child's aptitude, because the teacher's assessment covers the subject as a whole over a period of time whereas the tests only cover parts of a subject. A teacher may feel that the test has not properly reflected a child's ability.

Attainment targets for each subject define the standards a pupil is expected to reach for his or her age group. In Key Stages 1–3 there are eight attainment levels (referred to as level descriptions) of increasing difficulty, with an additional one above level 8 to recognise exceptional performance. Children are expected to progress through one level every two years, so that they achieve at least level 2 at age seven and at least level 4 at age 11, for example. By achieving the standard expected in the National Curriculum, a child is demonstrating levels of knowledge and skill which are at least equivalent to those of most children of that age.

Other tests include 'age-standardised' test scores, comparing 7- and 11-year-olds with others born in the same month, and new optional tests to monitor the progress of 8-, 9- and 10-year-olds which are based on National Curriculum levels.

As well as the progress report provided to parents, a summary of the school's results for each age group will be published in the school's prospectus and the governors' annual report.

National targets have been set for 11-year-olds in English and maths for the year 2002. These require 80 per cent of pupils to achieve level 4 in English tests and 75 per cent to achieve level 4 in maths.

Prep schools

Independent prep schools are not required to take Key Stage tests, but many now do – not only to show their academic credentials, which can be a significant selling point in a competitive marketplace, but also because in the case of children transferring to state schools at 11, the results of the tests provide additional information.

Key Stage 4 examinations

There are several methods of ascertaining pupils' achievement by means of public examinations. For information on the debate surrounding examination boards and standards, see Chapter 13.

General Certificate of Secondary Education (GCSE)

At Key Stage 4, attainment is judged by GCSE examinations for most pupils. These are normally taken by those secondary-school pupils who are approaching completion of their fifth school year and were 15 at the start of that year. Examinations may be taken earlier if the head teacher considers that a pupil is capable of passing at a younger age. Most pupils take exams based on National Curriculum requirements and options such as RE, PE, drama or a second language tend only to be taken by a minority.

GCSE short courses

These courses, taken over a one- or two-year period, have been developed to ensure greater flexibility and choice. They are of the same standard as the full GCSE and are worth 50 per cent towards a full GCSE. The subjects available are languages, design and technology, history, geography, art, music, PE, religious education, ICT and business studies. Their usage varies from school to school and subject to subject. Less than 10 per cent of schools operate short courses for more than one subject, and RE is the most popular choice. The value of some courses may be limited because coverage is restricted compared to the full GCSE.

Some schools enter their most able pupils for short courses to supplement the number of full courses taken, while others use them to ensure that the less able have some form of qualification before they leave school. In some instances, if a pupil is found to be struggling with a full-course GCSE, he or she may be entered for the examination in the short course.

GCSE tiering

Some GCSE subjects have more than one level of examination paper (or papers). At the time of writing, all pupils sit the same paper in history, art, music and PE, although tiering has been introduced in the majority of subjects in an attempt to allow for different levels of ability. English, science, technology, ICT, modern languages and geography are split into foundation and higher tiers, while maths has an extra intermediate tier.

The maximum and minimum grades obtainable depend upon the tier for which a candidate has been entered.

Tier	Grades obtainable
higher	A*–D
intermediate	B–E
foundation	C–G

When pupils' grades fall below the stipulated range – for example, if a pupil sat the higher tier but failed to achieve at least a D grade – the result is graded as 'unqualified'. Pressure from schools has led to a special dispensation whereby some pupils graded as unqualified have received grade E, but there is no guarantee that this will become a universal policy. Conversely, if a pupil sits the foundation tier, the best grade achievable is a C, regardless of whether that pupil's standard of achievement is higher.

Many pupils likely to fall somewhere in the middle grades are left in a quandary as to which tier to enter for particular subjects. The universities have only the student's GCSE results and projected A- and AS-levels on which to judge his or her academic record. As admissions tutors tend not to give so much credence to lower grades, it may be worth pupils risking the higher tier, if this is realistic. In addition, rather than weighing themselves down with extra baggage of subjects all demanding prime time, it might be better for pupils to reduce the number of subjects attempted, which will increase their opportunity to improve grades.

Tip

Parents should check whether the school provides a full revision plan for students. Many students need help organising their revision timetable, and if support is in place this demonstrates that the school appreciates the stress under which students are placed and is prepared to take a responsible attitude.

General National Vocational Qualifications (GNVQs)

While GCSEs are academic, GNVQs are also part of the national qualifications framework, but more relevant to the world of work. Designed for students between the ages of 14 and 19, they aim to develop the knowledge, skills and understanding required for vocational fields and working life, but do not constitute job training. Pupils have a wide range of disciplines from which to choose, including art and design, business, health and social care, leisure and tourism and the performing arts. GNVQs give students the flexibility to progress to higher education, further training or employment.

Parents should be aware that these qualifications are not commonly found in independent schools, although some sixth forms are offering Advanced GNVQs.

Part One GNVQ

This new qualification is designed for 14- to 16-year-olds but is also available post-16. The course, taken alongside GCSEs over a two-year period, is made up of six units (three of which are compulsory) and is available at two levels:

- **intermediate**, broadly equivalent to two GCSEs at grades A–C
- **foundation**, broadly equivalent to two GCSEs at grades D–G.

While Key Stage 4 requires National Curriculum study in the core subjects, Part One GNVQs may link with these requirements – teachers working in both areas are encouraged to build on common ground. The key skills to be developed within the chosen vocational area are communication and the application of number and information technology. Pupils may work on assignments which take them out into the community and which capitalise on any business links forged by the schools (see pages 215–9).

All units require continuous assessment through projects and assignments and most also have a multiple-choice written examination. The school performance tables (see pages 169–72) include Part One GNVQ results in the same column as the GCSE results.

Children with Part One GNVQs may progress to post-16 studies or to employment. They can take the remaining units required for a full GNVQ at the same level, proceed to the next level of GNVQ or undertake GCE A- or AS-level courses.

GNVQs

GNVQs are for those over 16. Most are available at three levels:

- **advanced**, equivalent to 2 GCE A-levels
- **intermediate**, equivalent to 4 GCSEs at grades A–C
- **foundation**, equivalent to 4 GCSEs at grades D–G.

The full GNVQ qualification may be built up by completing a number of units. Following a review by the Qualifications and Curriculum Authority (QCA),★ various amendments will be introduced in September 2000. These aim to reduce the amount of assessment while strengthening the external element and clarifying the content to be learnt. Final grades will be calculated using a points-based system, with each unit awarded a grade worth a number of points. These will then be totalled to give a grade for the whole qualification. The grades awarded for foundation and intermediate levels are to remain as pass, merit and distinction, but for the advanced level five grades A–E, comparable to A-level, will be used. One-third of the assessments will be externally set and marked by the awarding bodies.

The key skills of communication and the application of number and information technology, common to all GNVQs, will retain their importance, but will no longer count towards qualifications. From September 2000, GNVQs at advanced level will be available as six-unit (3 or 4 compulsory) and twelve-unit (6 or 8 compulsory) awards, allowing students to combine GNVQs with other qualifications, such as A-level. The QCA has also recommended that selected GNVQs should be available as three-unit awards. The aim behind this is to encourage students to combine GNVQs with other qualifications or to follow part-time study and part-time employment.

National Vocational Qualifications (NVQs)

NVQs measure people's ability at work in any job against a national standard. There are five different levels. Although the scheme usually operates within the workplace, some schools are using these to good effect and forging advantageous links with employers. Testing consists of pupils' competency in workplace conditions being recorded and credited towards the final award. There are no written examinations.

GCE Advanced and Advanced Subsidiary levels (A- and AS-levels)

Following advice from the QCA,* ACCAC* and CCEA* (the regulatory authorities for qualifications for England, Wales and Northern Ireland respectively), the government is introducing reformulated GCE AS- and A-levels, advanced GNVQs (including a new six-unit qualification) and intermediate and foundation GNVQs, together with a new Key Skills qualification. These will all be fully implemented from September 2000.

These changes represent a shift towards the continental system of the International Baccalaureate (see page 168), and are intended to increase flexibility, broaden the post-16 curriculum and improve vocational qualifications. The intention is that students taking A-levels will be able to widen their study by adding the new AS qualifications or a vocational subject, while those taking a vocational route will be able to add one or more of the smaller GNVQ qualifications and an AS qualification. The broader framework will entail students taking up to five subjects in the lower sixth (AS-level), before choosing three subjects selected to be taken in upper sixth (A-level). AS examinations are of an equivalent academic standard to A-level, but having half the content they are equal to half an A-level.

Phasing out current qualifications

Existing AS- and A-level qualifications are to be phased out, and a full range of AS examinations will be available in 2001 for those commencing two-year courses from September 1999. The first award of the new A-level will be made in August 2002. Those who have not completed the current modular courses by summer 2001 will be given a date by which to do so. Existing students will not be able to transfer to the new specifications because of the changes to the qualifications.

The new modular A-levels

Following changes to the curriculum, A-levels will become a series of six modules or units spread over two years. Examinations will be held twice a year, with the AS component being taken in the first year of sixth form (see below). The modules can be 'banked' or retaken to improve the original grade – see 'External and internal assessment', below. Concerns have been expressed that modular exams may not provide as broad an overview as traditional courses and that continuity between units could be hindered if pupils have a different teacher for each module.

In future, qualifications accredited to the national framework will be governed by a series of criteria to ensure quality and control by the awarding bodies. A- and AS-level qualifications will normally adopt the following structure:

- each specification, or syllabus, will contain six assessment units – three designated as AS (the first half of an A-level course) and three as A2 (the second half of an A-level course)

- each assessment unit will be separately assessed and certificated
- AS units will be compulsory for candidates taking the full A-level (A2)
- assessment units will carry approximately equal weighting in their contribution to the whole qualification
- each specification will permit assessment units to be taken either during the course (staged assessment) or at the end (end-of-course assessment). In those subjects which attract a small number of candidates and it is uneconomical to offer both staged and end-of-course assessment, only the latter option will be available. However, the option to take the AS-level halfway through the course will generally be available
- each specification for a full A-level will require a synoptic element of assessment (requiring the ability to integrate and apply knowledge, understanding and skills across the subject). This will account for at least 20 per cent of every full A-level and will form part of the external assessment at the end of the course.

Key skills

In all subjects, apart from maths and modern foreign languages, pupils will be assessed in the skill of written communication (currently known as quality of language). Where it is considered essential – for example, in English – it will be assessed as part of the AS- and/or full A-level, and count towards the A-level grade.

A free-standing 'key skills' qualification has been developed and will be available from September 2000. This will recognise pupils' ability to communicate and their application of number and information technology. Those achieving a level in all these skills will receive a separate certificate. Opportunities for learning and assessment in both GNVQ and A-level courses will be clearly pinpointed within the units, to build up evidence towards this qualification.

External and internal assessment

- External assessment will take the form of supervised and timed assignments, tests or examinations.
- Internal assessment may be in any form other than the above (e.g. coursework).
- At the time of writing, the maximum weighting of internal assessment in most subjects is 20 per cent. For some subjects there

is a modest increase in this proportion, provided quality safeguards are in place.

- As A-levels are intended to be predominantly two-year, full-time courses, only one re-sit of each assessment unit will be permitted, although it will be possible to take the whole examination more than once. The 'bankable' duration of an assessment unit will last only as long as the life of each specification.

Examination sessions

These will be held in January and June each year. Specifications must state whether any assessment units are available for examination in January; all modules will be available for examination in June.

Grading

Both AS- and A-levels will be graded A–E for pass grades, with 'U' (unclassified) for fail. The current 'N' (near miss) applied to A-levels will cease to be used.

World-class tests

The government has announced the introduction of these for the most able students. At the time of writing, they are still in the development stage.

International Baccalaureate (IB)

Following changes to the A-level framework, an increasing number of schools are contemplating joining the handful of those already offering the International Baccalaureate. Many consider it a superior academic route, recognised by universities in the United Kingdom and 95 other countries worldwide. More than 90 per cent of students across the globe take their IB in English, and British universities receive more IB students than any other country.

The IB requires that students take six subjects, with three at a higher level (equivalent to A-levels) and three at standard level (equivalent to AS-levels). In addition, students must take a course in the theory of knowledge (philosophy) and write an extended essay. IBs are graded from 7 down to 1, with IB 6 said to be the same as an A-level A/B grade. After the revisions to A-levels come into force, the gap between the two systems will be much less pronounced and switching between the two will be easier.

Both state and independent schools that offer the IB complain that IB achievements are not fully recognised in the performance tables (see below), and claim that their league-table position could be enhanced if a points system equivalent to that for existing qualifications were implemented (see page 171). Parents should therefore check carefully what a school has to offer and assess whether offering the IB may have affected its table position.

Alternative A-levels

Head teachers in several independent schools have become so disenchanted with the current moves in the national A-level framework that they are threatening to set up their own examinations and examination board, to maintain the A-level 'gold standard'. If this is successful, it could mean a dual route for A-levels, particularly if state schools choose to join the alternative.

Assessing special educational needs

Appropriate provision is made for the varying needs of children with this requirement. Flexibility has been built into the National Curriculum so that teachers can make allowances where necessary at each Key Stage. The Certificate of Achievement is aimed at accrediting the abilities of those pupils for whom the GCSE is too difficult. In addition, the Trident Award is designed for those who have spent time in a workplace, carried out community work and experienced education in an outdoor context.

Performance tables

These government tables, which the league tables published in the press are based upon (see Chapter 13), reflect nationally recognised standards. Readers in Scotland, Wales and Northern Ireland are advised to consult the Appendices where appropriate for information on performance tables in these countries.

Primary-school performance tables

Key Stage 2 test and assessment results for state schools are published for England only, in alphabetical order by the DfEE. Although special schools are not listed, their results are included in the local and national averages. Only schools with pupils of 11 years of age are listed, therefore first schools whose pupils transfer to middle school are not included; similarly, junior schools appear, but not infant schools.

Where there are fewer than 10 eligible pupils in a school, the results are not published owing to the possibility that individual pupils could be identified. In this case, it is important to ask such a school how its results compare with the local and national average. You may well find that their results are above the average, as was demonstrated by a government analysis in 1999.

Test and assessment results for level 4 (11-year-old children; see page 161 for an explanation of attainment levels) are shown as percentages of all eligible pupils, with local and national averages published to enable comparisons to be made. Note that children who did not take the tests, for whatever reason, are included and could affect the figures. However, whilst their numbers are shown as a percentage, a comparison with the Teacher Assessment column could prove enlightening. This column gives an overall figure, not just test results. Some teacher assessments differ markedly from the test results; parents should ask why, where this occurs.

Additional information is given in the tables, including school particulars, enrolment numbers and the number of children with special educational needs. The last category is especially significant for parents endeavouring to evaluate a school's strengths, as the greater the number of such children, the greater the affect will be on the results; allowance should be made for this.

The tables are published each year at the end of February, which is too late to help parents make informed decisions for that September's entry. Parents have to rely on tables from the previous year, which may not give an accurate picture of a school's current standing or progress.

Secondary-school performance tables

The results of the Key Stage 4 examinations (GCSE) and vocational qualifications (GNVQs) are published for all schools (including independent schools) in each individual LEA area in England and Wales, in booklet form by the DfEE. For information on Scotland and Northern Ireland, see pages 293–4 and page 303. ISIS publishes its own performance tables for those schools within its membership (see page 178). Both these sets of results form the basis for the league tables published in the national press (see Chapter 13).

Each booklet contains a map of the area covered. The background information on each school includes the type of school; whether it is comprehensive or selective, co-educational or single-sex; the total number of children in the school; the number aged 16–18, if applicable; the number of children with special educational needs (statemented and non-statemented); and the absence record for day pupils of compulsory school age.

The GCSE results recorded for each school show the percentage of children who attained:

- 5 or more grades at A★–C (the standard usually required to proceed to GCE A/AS-level or more advanced vocational qualifications such as GNVQs)
- 5 or more grades at A★–G and
- 1 or more grades at A★–G.

In addition, extra columns provide information on the number of pupils aged 15, the number of pupils in Year 11 (including the number with 5 or more A★–C grades) and the average points score per candidate. Points are now accorded to each grade as follows:

A★ = 8, A = 7, B = 6, C = 5, D = 4, E = 3, F = 2, G = 1 and U = 0.

To help parents make a more informed judgement, additional columns detail improvement measures over the last four years for 5 or more grades A★–C and 1 or more grades A★–G (in other words, the increased percentage of children getting better grades). The progress measure column places a tick against schools whose pupils have made the greatest progress between Key Stage 3 and GCSEs/GNVQs compared to most other schools. The continuance of the progress measure in its present form is in doubt, with changes likely to be made from 2000.

As with the primary performance tables, average percentages and points scores for the schools are provided (excluding independent schools), as well as the average across England (including all schools), to enable parents to gauge performance.

Sixth-form performance tables

Published by the DfEE as 'School and College Performance Tables', these apply to the 16–18 age group. Unlike the secondary-school performance tables which cover the LEA area, a total of 24 booklets are produced for England, each covering a much wider region – for example, one booklet might contain up to 13 LEAs. The booklets are sub-divided into LEA areas and include information about the achievements of the age group at secondary schools and Further Education colleges, together with maps and instructions on how to read the tables. For information on Scotland, Wales and Northern Ireland, see pages 293–4, 299 and 303.

Schools and colleges are listed in alphabetical order and include independent schools. Those special schools that wish to be listed are also included and a section is provided for any sixth-form centres or consortia that pool resources in the area.

Background information includes: the type of school; whether it is comprehensive or selective, co-educational or single sex; the age range of pupils; the number of pupils aged 16, 17 and 18 at the start of the academic year and registered in January of that year.

Results recorded are for those pupils who were entered for GCE A- or AS-level examinations, or who are in their final year of study towards an Advanced GNVQ or other qualifying vocational qualification. The results of modules are also included. Work-related qualifications, such as NVQs, are not included.

A- and AS-level results

The columns record the following information:

- the number of candidates entered for fewer than two A-levels or the AS equivalent (these include those who may be taking an exam earlier than usual)

- the average points score per candidate, for the above category
- the number of candidates entered for two or more A-levels or the AS equivalent
- the average points score per candidate, for the above category
- the average points score per examination entry.

Points for A- and AS-level results are calculated as follows:

Grade	A-level points	AS-level points
A	10	5
B	8	4
C	6	3
D	4	2
E	2	1

Advanced GNVQ results

The following information is given for Advanced GNVQ results:

- the number of candidates in their final year of study to GNVQ
- the average points score per candidate.

Points for GNVQ grades are allocated as follows:

Grade	Points
distinction	18
merit	12
pass	6

Other information

Further columns show the combined results of A- and AS-levels and Advanced GNVQs, stating:

- the number of candidates entered for two or more GCE A- or AS-levels or the Advanced GNVQ equivalent
- the average points score of those candidates
- the average point scores per examination entry of all candidates.

An improvement measure for A- and AS-level enables parents to compare data for the past four years, including the current year. Separate columns record other vocational qualifications. As a few schools offer the International Baccalaureate diploma, these results are also recorded.

Each LEA area section shows the local average statistics, excluding independent schools and, at the foot of each page, the national average statistics are shown for all schools. These enable parents to compare schools with local and national averages.

Information on the Internet

School performance tables for all LEAs are available on the Internet at: *www.open.gov.uk/dfee/perform.htm*

The SchoolsNet web site provides information on over 5,800 schools throughout the United Kingdom, together with teaching materials, exam questions and revision help: *www.schoolsnet.com*

The Qualifications and Curriculum Authority web site contains details of curriculum requirements and the Secretary of State's proposals for the revised National Curriculum: *www.qca.org.uk*

Subject choice

Although it is commonly thought that independent schools offer a wider choice of subjects than state schools, the truth is that many state schools offer a greater variety, because they cater for a wider range of ability.

Subject choice at secondary school

At secondary school, subject choice is inevitable. As different schools group subjects into different timetable categories, you must examine these categories carefully to establish the choice available and avoid a clash.

The restrictions on subject combinations are greater for A-level studies. Although it is difficult to plan far ahead when your child is only 10 or 11 years old, it would be wise to check what is available at sixth-form level. This is also important if you are planning a change of school at sixth-form level. You may find that the choice at one school is too limiting, compared with another. A clash between subjects might prevent one of them being studied. Ask whether the rules are rigidly applied. Some heads will accommodate your wishes where possible.

In addition to curriculum requirements, the more able pupils may be able to study other examined subjects. Additional, non-examined courses may also be offered in the sixth form to broaden the educational base and provide pupils with key skills. Courses cover a range of topics, such as accountancy, current affairs, art appreciation, law, and skills such as communication, money management and careers advice.

Science subjects

State secondary schools teach single and double science at GCSE level, leading to a 'double GCSE'. Some, usually those that apply some degree of selection by ability, will also offer biology, physics and chemistry as separate GCSE subjects. Independent schools generally provide for both combined and separate sciences; girls tend to take the former option. If it is likely that your child might take science at A-level and perhaps university, you should discover how science is taught at the school. Taking individual subjects would probably be preferable for a child who wants to focus on science.

Prep schools

In private prep schools, Latin is commonly offered, but parents should be aware that despite a revival in popularity of the classics, this should not be taken for granted. Some substitute this with a modern-language bias towards German, Spanish and Italian, as well as the usual French, even for young children. Such schools refer to themselves as tri-lingual schools.

Independent secondary schools

At independent secondary school, it is normal to offer Latin, although this is generally an optional subject.

Chapter 13

League tables and academic performance

In order to satisfy the main objective of most parents – a sound academic education – it is necessary to analyse what a school can deliver and compare it with the opposition. This has been made a great deal easier by the introduction of league and performance tables, which have focused public perception on academic status. However, these tables are highly controversial and the information is limited to a narrow range of test and examination results.

League tables

League and performance tables highlight the best- and worst-performing schools, in terms of examination results. Note the distinction between the DfEE performance tables (see Chapter 12) and the league tables published in the national press, which are dealt with in this chapter.

The league tables in the press often cause controversy. As a result of their publication, fierce competition has sprung up between schools at both national and local levels: whether it is state or private, a school's position in the tables will affect its ability to recruit pupils and its financial horizons. Even those schools which deliberately avoid emphasising academic achievement – in favour of outdoor pursuits, for example – have been compelled by parental pressure and league-table purchasing power to prioritise excellent exam results.

Arguments focus on schools at the lower and upper ends of the scale. The top-rated schools benefit most from publication of the league tables, to the cost of those at the bottom end. Naturally, schools at the upper end find little wrong with their published placements (although there is bickering over the odd .01 percentage point, which can make an enormous difference to maintaining position). Those at the bottom claim that the figures do not tell the whole story and that there is much more to them than cold statistics. Of course they are right, but it is a question of how right. Statistics need careful interpretation. They can be manipulated to tell any story, depending upon who compiles them. Parents need to know how to read these tables critically.

Warning

Taken at face value, league tables are extremely dangerous. They provide only bare facts and do not take into account any non-academic care, services or diversity at a school. One crucial factor is whether a school is selective or not. A school that can hand-pick the most able pupils from supportive homes will inevitably achieve better results than a comprehensive that takes all the children in a neighbourhood regardless of ability. All these factors should be considered along with the examination results to gain an overall picture. Do not be panicked by raw figures.

Compilation of the tables

League tables published in the press are based on statistics supplied by the government and ISIS. They resemble the government version but the exact layout will vary according to editorial policy. Emphasis will also depend on whether a table gives priority to GCSE results or A-level results, and which band of grades is highlighted. The tables may give prominence to the number of pupils achieving five or more GCSE passes at grades A*–C. This fine-tuning can make a considerable difference to the portrayal of a school.

This chapter pays specific attention to GCSE/GNVQ (Key Stage 4) and A/AS-level results as covered in the national press. As Key Stages 1, 2 and 3 are compiled and recorded in a different way, these are examined in greater detail in Chapter 12.

The A-level tables are recorded separately, but you may come across these results published in conjunction with GSCE results so you can assess a school's strengths at each exam stage. Tables may also incorporate previous years' grades or points to allow you to compare a school's performance over time.

Note that schools with less than 45 pupils in the sixth form do not qualify for inclusion.

League tables based on government statistics

Government statistics are published for each LEA area in the autumn. These tables rank schools alphabetically and record the percentage of pupils aged 15 at the start of the school year who achieve five or more GCSE passes at grades A*–C. The national press uses these statistics when compiling league tables for publication.

Note that the DfEE tables, and those based on them, include only the GCSE results of children who are 15 at the start of year 11 (the GCSE year) – other children are not counted. The results of the younger pupils will be recorded the following year, but the results of those who are 'over age' are never counted. This factor can quite substantially alter the published results and head teachers are quick to point out if they feel this has resulted in unfair downgrading.

League tables based on ISIS statistics

ISIS tables contain the statistics of private schools that are ISIS members. Arranged in a similar way to the DfEE tables, they will state whether a school is academically selective, but strictly speaking this label may not always be accurate (see page 183).

League-table analysis has shown that the independent sector, which accounts for about seven per cent of pupils, obtains as much as 50 per cent of the A grades awarded at A-level.

In contrast to the government tables, ISIS shows the results of all GCSE pupils, not just those of a certain age (see above). An ISIS survey published in 1999 found that after the application of DfEE measures, some private schools' GCSE points score is up to 10 per cent lower than their true level of achievement – boarding schools, with more overseas pupils, are particularly affected. Parents considering private education are therefore advised to base their judgement on the ISIS tables.

Other methods of comparison

Some national newspapers now compile 'value-for-money' tables based on A-level success rates for the state and independent sectors.

In the state sector, 'value for money' will be based on how much funding the school receives.

There is pressure to make 'value-added' tables available to parents, both nationally and for LEA catchment areas. These would show what each school has achieved with regard to the ability level of its intake each year and outgoing pupils' performance. It has been suggested that these figures would be unfair to schools which are highly selective, as statistically they would not show so much improvement over time, although this should not deter clued-up parents. As support mounts for this information to be officially published, an increasing number of LEAs and independent schools are supplying their own figures to enable parents to compare neighbouring schools.

Added value wins an A grade

At one inner-city girls' school which belonged to a value-added pilot scheme, a fifth were refugees, many did not have English as a first language and over 70 per cent were entitled to free school meals. Although the school appeared low down the league tables in terms of academic results, it took pride in an A grade for value-added performance, a measure which acknowledged the hard work and commitment of the staff.

Factors affecting league-table results

Before you examine an individual school's performance, some of the more common factors affecting league-table results should be considered.

General reasons

You may find numerous valid reasons why a school appears lower down the league tables than the pupils' performance might warrant – these may include curricular matters such as a policy of restricting A-level students to three rather than four subjects, or the encouragement of specialist activities. These factors will not show up on the tables, which cannot relay the unique strengths and weaknesses of a school. On a personal level, one or two external incidents or traumatic events that affect a candidate's performance could swing a close-run placing where results hinge on a fraction of a percentage point.

Examination boards

When competition for pupils is hotting up, the examination-board factor can be more significant than is openly admitted.

Single bodies carry out testing at ages 7, 11 and 14 but after that a number of examination boards offer different examinations in each subject. This lack of uniformity can produce discrepancies in the results obtained.

The boards claim that the system is tightly monitored by the Qualifications and Curriculum Authority (QCA),* which strives to ensure consistency. However, a study of 3,000 pupils by a former chief examiner which was published in 1998 suggested that some boards could be setting simpler GCSE questions than others and boosting pupils' results by up to two grades.

Because examination boards vie with each other for market share they can profit from being seen as less stringent in their grading. A shrewd teacher will play the market by analysing the results from different boards and 'switching horses' in order to boost the league-table position. However, excessive leniency in marking is not to schools' or pupils' advantage. Criticism of unfair leniency one year can result in a backlash the following year when a board will mark strictly in order to counter such claims, and children may suffer as a result if they do not achieve the grades reasonably expected.

In a pilot scheme launched in summer 1999, students were being allowed access to their marked examination papers in order to reduce the number of appeals.

Examinations

Although schools maintain that the quality of intake has remained consistent, the 1990s have seen a dramatic increase in pass rates. Since the introduction of GCSEs in 1986, the proportion of pupils achieving high grades each year has risen steadily.

People whose schooldays are a distant memory remark that exams are getting easier and standards dropping. However, a valid explanation for this phenomenon is that marking procedures have changed. From a position where a fixed percentage of failures was laid down in advance, together with a fixed percentage of grades to be awarded, the goal-posts have been moved so that all candidates achieving a set mark will be awarded the relevant grade. Together with emphasis on positive marking, where points are given for the quality of the answers, rather than being knocked off for mistakes, and moves to grant candidates the benefit of the doubt, this has led to an overall improvement in performance. Moving the boundary between two grades by even one or two marks can make a considerable difference to the number of passes at each grade.

Research undertaken by the QCA into O-level, GCSE and A-level exams dating back to 1976 has failed to provide conclusive proof that exams have got easier. Instead, findings indicate that changes have varied according to individual subjects, some of which have actually become more demanding. The most likely explanation for the perceived shift in examination standards is the differences between GCSEs and the O-level exams they replaced and the trend towards modular A-levels (see page 166); the new exams require students to apply different types of skill.

Schools that emphasise results may short-change pupils

In the present climate where the attainment of top grades is seen as paramount, there is a danger that some schools, eager to achieve excellent statistics, may set greater store by exam technique than the in-depth teaching of a subject. Ask teachers about the approaches they use when you visit a school. If they seem keener to amass good grades than to inspire the children, be wary. Learning for its own sake should not be neglected.

Examination entry

It is claimed that some state and private schools jostling for position in the league-table war actively discourage pupils from registering for subjects if they do not consider the individual capable of achieving at least a 'C' grade. A-level candidates have even been shown the door because their impending failure will affect league-table results, and some state schools have been known to encourage unlikely candidates to stay on for A-levels, only to request their removal after the mock exams once funding has been received for the student. Another problem is that pupils may be encouraged to take unsuitable subjects to boost the amount of subjects passed. Other schools may persuade the parents of less able children to enter their offspring privately for exams rather than including them on the official register, to avoid the school jeopardising its position. This does a serious injustice to the pupil.

Prep-school ploy

A certain prep school openly admits to encouraging children who are very poor academically to drop out of the Common Entrance exam, while simultaneously claiming increased academic success. Observers have suggested a link between the two developments.

GCSE tiering

The different levels of tiering for the majority of subjects at GCSE, and the variation in the grades which can be obtained (see page 162), make further manipulation possible. Pupils are entered in separate tiers for each subject according to ability, so while one student might be able to obtain grade C maximum, grade D will be the lowest achievable mark for another. For example, about 70 per cent of children are entered in the intermediate tier for maths, which means that they cannot obtain an A or A*.

Since press league tables give priority to passes A*–C, schools could be tempted to play safe and enter borderline pupils at the lower foundation level in order to maximise the number of C grades. By doing this they make a 'C' more likely to be achieved and avoid the possibility of a result being 'unplaced' at the higher level.

Foreign nationals

The presence of foreign nationals in independent schools – especially boarding schools, which tend to have more overseas students – can incidentally boost league-table position at A-level. Some schools enter foreign pupils for A-levels in their own language and so obtain a full set of 'A' grades from this group. These could affect the league tables and, more specifically, the school's own performance tables (see overleaf).

Selective and non-selective independent schools

A common misconception is that all independent schools are selective. They are not. Even though they may be listed in the league tables as selective, many are non-selective in practical terms. The main criteria may be whether they are sufficiently well endowed, or whether the parents can afford the fees. Many stipulate a Common Entrance threshold mark below which they will not accept a pupil, but if there are empty desks or beds to be filled, that threshold may be ignored. At the end of the day schools have overheads to cover.

Schools sited in large towns and cities can be choosy about the calibre of pupil accepted, since they have a large catchment population from which to select and competition to fill the given number of places each year will be fierce. These schools are in the position of being able to pick and choose the very best from a group of candidates, and can consequently raise their academic standards. Some have dropped boarding to focus on the classroom and several impose an IQ limit on applicants. The top-rated boarding schools can also exercise the same freedom of choice. Since the advent of the league tables these schools have focused more on enrolling academic highfliers, although the background and wealth of the parents are also very relevant as the majority of parents need substantial means to consider such schools. Some scholarships and bursaries are awarded each year (see Chapter 17).

Conversely, schools in rural areas and those with a limited catchment population in small towns often struggle to make ends meet. In an attempt to fill places they may not impose stiff entry requirements, or any at all, because they need the fees. Similarly, they may not dissuade less able students from attempting A-levels, however unsuited they may seem, as to do so could adversely affect future income from fee-paying pupils.

Some schools use the fact that they are non-selective to excuse poor performance. Bear in mind that where initial entry is not rigorously selective, schools usually stream or set the year groups according to ability so that the slower stream does not hold back the fast track – this can be a more significant factor than selectivity on entry (see page 194).

The tables therefore do not reflect the circumstances of some independent schools or the quality of their intake.

Keeping children's needs in mind

Do all you can to choose a school that will suit your child's academic abilities. A boy or girl of average ability could struggle and feel sidelined at a highly competitive school, while equally a bright child might be unhappy in an environment where the prevailing culture labels studious pupils as 'uncool'. The tables emphasise the attainment of good grades. However, in academic terms, a school should be judged on its abilities to stimulate the students to achieve the maximum qualifications possible for their individual capabilities; for one pupil, getting a grade 'D' may be a far higher achievement than obtaining a grade 'A' is for another. Meanwhile schools that are selective should encourage pupils to take pride in all their accomplishments and ensure that children of below-average ability are not submerged in the race to squeeze good grades out of students.

Schools' performance tables

An individual school's academic tables over the past three or four years will prove of greater value than the generalisations of national league tables. These should supply specific information for each academic subject: namely the number of children taking the exams, the number of pass and fail marks, the grades achieved and percentages overall. You can also ask for the average numbers in each stream (see page 194).

State schools must publish the results for the previous year in the prospectus. You could ask for the results of the year before that for comparison purposes. Independent schools may publish several years' results and possibly also their own comparison tables, which could prove useful if just a few percentage points separate competing schools. If you encounter resistance to a request for details, this is understandable – schools do not want to send results to all and sundry, regardless of the seriousness of your intentions. If the school appears reticent then the most appropriate time to ask is at the interview, which could entail a subsequent meeting to answer your questions.

How to assess a school's performance tables

Study the tables carefully, making the following assessments:

- ascertain, if you can, the strengths and weaknesses of individual departments and whether results are standing still, improving or deteriorating (bear in mind that results will vary to some extent according to the ability of a particular year group). This approach is most usefully applied to core subjects such as maths and English – optional subjects, such as history, will vary according to the ability of the pupils opting for them
- at an independent school, compare the results in the top stream with the numbers of children in that stream taking exams, and then do the same for the year overall. From this you will be able to see how the top stream is performing in comparison with the national level, and whether the lower streams are affecting the school's national position. If there is a significant gap between the top and bottom grades, this could indicate that the school is failing to improve the qualifications of those in lower streams or sets.
- compare GCSE and A/AS-level results. If there is a noticeable falling-off at A-level, this could indicate that the teaching of subjects at a higher level is not the school's forte.

Tip

If you are told that a certain A-level subject is strong because the cleverer children are taking it, this could indicate that pupils have chosen the subject because there is a good teacher – such as Eve (see page 187) – who will help them to get the best results.

Factors affecting academic performance

A number of variables, discussed below, can influence the outcome of the results published in school performance tables.

Choice of subject

At GCSE level there is little choice in the core curriculum subjects, such as English and maths. However, GCSE results for optional subjects – for example, history – will vary according to the ability of the pupils who have chosen them. See Chapter 12 for more on the curriculum.

Science subjects vs arts subjects

Research commissioned by the School Curriculum and Assessment Authority (now the Qualifications and Curriculum Authority) confirms that A-level science subjects are more difficult than the arts. Physics has been identified as the most severely graded, followed by chemistry, mathematics and biology; these are matched in the arts only by foreign languages and General Studies. It is conceivable that some schools might actively discourage pupils to opt for arts rather than sciences in order to improve their league-table position.

Girls' performance vs boys' performance

Information in the league tables suggests that girls are ahead of boys academically and obtaining a larger proportion of top grades at GCSE-level, apart from in physics. Figures for 1999 showed girls obtaining better average results at A-level, although boys still outperform girls in the traditional academic subjects.

Former tendencies to dismiss girls' academic ability and suggestions that exams were biased towards boys have now been replaced by claims that some exams, especially English, favour girls rather than boys. In reality, the discrepancy in results could simply be explained by the fact that girls mature earlier and tend to be more studious.

Neither the national tables nor the school tables differentiate between the sexes, unless a school is single-sex. If you come across improved results when studying school tables, particularly in English, check:

- whether there are girls present
- when they joined the school
- whether their number is increasing
- the ratio of boys to girls.

This alone could be the reason for improved results, rather than an overall improvement in academic standards for which the head may be taking the credit.

Quality of teaching

One of the key influences on academic performance is the quality of the teachers. Popular schools with excellent academic standards attract a high calibre of teacher: many can pick and choose from applicants and some build up staff waiting-lists. By contrast, schools trailing at the bottom of the league tables may find it hard to attract candidates.

However, good teachers are to be found in schools at both the top and bottom ends of the tables and in both the state and the private sector, occupying a position purely through personal choice and producing enviable results through inspired and expert teaching. Their results will be self-evident in the school's tables.

Eve

Eve has for many years taught German at a provincial state school near the bottom of the league tables. Last year, with a class of 33 pupils, she achieved 23 'A' grades at GCSE – the rest were 'B's and 'C's apart from lower grades achieved by two pupils with significant learning difficulties. These results match her success rate in previous years.

University entry

Ask for a list of university entries over the previous few years. This will show the school's general success rate and the number of students destined for Oxford and Cambridge. Although you may not feel that it is relevant to your circumstances, Oxbridge entries bestow a certain amount of kudos on a school. However, Oxbridge students are not necessarily better placed than their peers to obtain work after graduation. Many students choose other universities for their quality of subject teaching and popularity with employers.

The downside of the league tables

Although league-table competition can boost morale in schools positioned towards the top end of the tables, it can have a negative effect on schools lower down the lists which can extend to the pupils. This might manifest itself as disrespect creeping into the pupils' regard for their school – with an ultimate effect on discipline – and/or a reduction in students' self-esteem.

The creation of a competitive culture can have a harmful effect on children already living in a stressful society. Those as young as 10 are being put under so much pressure to excel in exams that failure can lead to despair and even, in rare cases, suicide. Meanwhile, young adults entering the jobs market are finding that some employers have introduced their own rigorous criteria for selection following the expansion of the university base, demanding higher grades and ranking universities and the classification of degrees.

Parental neurosis

One unfortunate development is the panic overtaking parents, particularly in London and other large towns and cities. Some complain that there are insufficient good state primary schools and expose 2- and 3-year-old children to intensive coaching in order to get them into private schools. Nursery and prep schools which are regarded as feeder schools for secondary schools that occupy elevated positions in the league tables exacerbate the hype by encouraging an atmosphere of competition. To whittle down the deluge of applications, many from the parents of newborn children, some of these schools impose 'selection tests' (see page 48).

Selection stress

The stress of selection tests at a young age and the months of waiting involved can create a tense situation for parents, some of whom resort to calling in child psychologists to maximise the chances of a successful application. In addition to the potential harm to family life, this can have a stressful effect on the child.

> **Warning**
>
> It is not a good idea to coach your child intensively or place too much emphasis on selection tests. Too much expectation of a child can be as harmful as too little, and extreme, incessant pushing could seriously damage a child's emotional development.

It is worth noting that these sorts of tests do not take into account individual speeds of development. A high achiever may not show true potential until later. Many parents resent the possibility that their child may be refused a place because he or she has an 'off-day' on the crucial date; others feel that it is more humane not to expose children to selection, and remain optimistic that a non-selective school will nurture talent as well as one with a competitive entry.

The benefits of the league tables

Although this chapter has demonstrated the league tables' inadequacy and their inability to give the whole picture, the tables have none the less performed a valuable service to society and to parents in focusing attention on educational standards. Even schools which outwardly express disdain or criticism feel compelled to advance up the tables. Schools have been galvanised into doing something about providing the level of education they are eager to claim they are capable of and, in the case of independent schools, for which they charge substantial fees.

> **Don't dismiss low-ranking schools**
>
> Many parents, ambitious for their children, have written off a school that has appeared near the bottom of the top 200 league of national schools, or does not appear at all. This is unwise. League tables merely provide an additional means of making an informed choice. They cannot form conclusive evidence or enable a direct comparison to be made between schools with very different intakes.

Checklist for league tables

(1) Obtain published performance tables for schools in the areas which interest you. You should be able to get hold of these from the LEA or the local library.

(2) Acquire the schools' own tables of academic results for the past three to four years, together with a comparison table if available. From these:
   - check which subjects are consistently strong, both at GCSE and A-level, and which are consistently weak in relation to streaming and setting
   - analyse the percentage of pupils taking arts and science subjects at A-level
   - find out the ratio of boys to girls.

(3) The school's tables should show whether there has been a progressive improvement in average grades. Look out for inconsistencies in particular departments. If you spot a downturn, ask whether this is because of a high staff turnover. If this is the case, ask why staff leave regularly.

(4) Check that the teachers who consistently produce the strongest results are not just about to retire or reach the end of their contracts – in other words, are they likely to be teaching for the duration of your child's projected time there?

(5) Ask whether the school caters for any particular range of ability, and how it manages diversity (the school should aim to stretch the brighter pupils while motivating and encouraging the less bright).

(6) Ask what moves are being made to improve weak areas and what measures are already in place.

(7) Ask what initiatives the school is adopting to improve its academic status. In the case of 'cruising' schools which obtain consistently good inspection reports and results, ask how the school intends to maintain this momentum – this is not always easy to accomplish.

(8) Ask what the main priorities will be for the next academic year. Both LEAs and schools must set targets.

(9) Request a list of university entries over the past three years. This will reveal pupils' achievements and whether there are any entrants to Oxford or Cambridge.

(10) Ask if there has been a recent Ofsted or HMC inspection and whether the report is available for you to read.

(11) A school prospectus may refer to a school's league-table position citing the reasons for its placement. Do not forget that this is a sales vehicle.

Chapter 14

Form size and the classroom

This chapter looks at organisation within the classroom, explaining the logistics of form size and streaming and setting, and outlining the major trends in subject teaching that will affect the way your child is educated. Methods for keeping track of pupils' progress are examined, as is the provision of school resources such as books, libraries and computers. Significant differences between the state and independent systems are highlighted where appropriate.

Form size

Many parents see class size as a crucial factor, some opting for the private system to ensure low teacher-to-pupil ratios, and the topic frequently stimulates debate.

Tip

Parents visiting primary, pre-prep and prep schools should do a head count in each class, particularly at the younger end. This will give some idea of the average class size.

State sector

A large number of people are aware of the complaints voiced about over-crowded classes. This has been compounded by a demographic increase in the number of school-age children.

Class size varies across the age ranges. The 7–11 age group has been the most affected, with occasionally 40 or more pupils in a class. Next affected are classes catering for children aged 5–7, which has been attributed to a sharp rise in the birth rate. The situation has been exacerbated by the admission of 4-year-olds to primary-school reception classes in some areas. Teacher shortages and financial restraints have also been responsible for pressure on numbers higher up the age range. Some people have blamed the demise of the Assisted Places scheme, under which children from low-income homes took up subsidised places at private schools (see page 261), for causing the influx of a large number of children. Class sizes in inner-city schools tend to be smaller than those in popular suburban schools.

The response from the government has been to commit extra funding to the task of reducing class numbers for the 5–7 age group, to no more than 15 or 30 infants in a class by September 2001 (see box, page 33). Popular schools subsequently face pressure to maintain larger class numbers from parents who fear their children will be directed towards less successful schools once class-size ratios are achieved.

Education authorities are adopting various solutions to meet this target. Some are building additional classes, or bussing children to alternative schools; others are creating mixed-age classes or 'vertical groups', which entails moving infants into classes with older children. The potential adverse effects for older children, who might be slowed down, are causing some concern. However, the system of vertical or family groups is well established in both the state and independent sectors (see page 121). Some schools believe that the benefits outweigh the difficulties for whole-class teaching: children are said to benefit from the continuity of being with one teacher for more than a year and it is argued that younger children are encouraged to develop more quickly while older children benefit from helping them.

Schools with variable pupil numbers

At schools with large numbers of foreign pupils or refugees, there may be a high mobility rate as pupils arrive and leave at a rapid rate. This factor could also affect league-table results (see Chapter 13).

Teachers

The pressure on class size has been exacerbated throughout all the age groups by a critical shortage of teachers. Many schools have been forced to rely on supply teachers, many from abroad (see page 112), and to assign teachers to teach subjects for which they have not been trained (see page 116). The worst-affected subjects are maths and science. Chapter 8 looks at the role of teaching staff in greater detail.

Class size

The ideal class size is probably 12–15 children, since this allows the teacher to devote adequate attention to each pupil. A group of less than 10 could result in insufficient cross-stimulation between pupils and teacher, although this is offset by greater individual attention. The optimum class numbers differ for language teaching. Language experts agree that the preferred class size is 8–12 pupils, which allows all children to have eye contact with the teacher and actively participate in class.

Independent sector

As a general rule, pupil–teacher ratios are better than in the state sector – which is why many parents choose private education. Usually, you will find no more than 20 children to a class.

Assurances regarding class size may be broken, however. Frequently, numbers rise where a school needs money. Proprietor heads have virtual free rein since they are not responsible to a governing body (see page 103). A technique used in pre-prep schools is to assure parents that if a class rises above 20 it will be split into two of equal numbers, which neatly accommodates the fact that the figures do not add up for an extra three or four children. Sometimes schools are forced to make teachers redundant, resulting in the amalgamation of two classes. If this happens to your child and you are concerned about the potential effect, you could ask the school to satisfy you that the alternative arrangements are not detrimental, on the grounds that you are paying fees for a pre-arranged set of conditions.

If you encounter much smaller classes at the top end of an independent school, you should ask the reason for the disparity.

Sixth-form entry

At sixth-form level, new entrants often substantially increase pupil numbers and make up for any losses following the departure of children who have taken their GCSEs. Many boys' independent secondary schools have extra places for girls in the sixth form (see page 61). Sixth-form group sizes are almost always smaller than those comprising children under 16, and some minority subjects attract only a handful of students.

Foreign student intake

As domestic boarding has shrunk, schools have looked as far afield for students as Hong Kong and America as well as to Europe. In this case the pupils' academic ability may be less important than their ability to pay fees. It is argued that public schools with a large proportion of foreign students are in danger of losing their traditional identity and becoming 'international' schools. For this reason, some have a deliberate policy against taking too many overseas students.

Streaming and setting

These two methods of grouping children by ability are used in state schools and the majority of independent schools, especially at secondary level. Both systems may be used in isolation, or together.

- **Streaming** Pupils are grouped together in classes, either according to ability or in arbitrary divisions, and taught all or most subjects in that group. With a few exceptions, streaming by ability is the norm throughout the independent sector and rare in the state sector.
- **Setting** Pupils are grouped together according to their ability in individual subjects.

These arrangements can relieve stress on teachers, since in a mixed-ability class there may be a tendency to aim for a middle level, to the detriment of the slower and brighter children. However, it is possible that children in the lower streams may not fulfil their potential because expectations are low.

Allowance must be made for fluid movement between the groups if necessary and the process must be efficiently administered. If ability is the main criterion there will be borderline cases, and children will develop at different speeds. Regardless of ability, children can become bored and disaffected if not taught at an appropriate level.

Streaming and setting are applied in various ways for different ages and at different types of school.

State primary schools

Streaming is rare in primary schools. The secondary-school trend for setting has been extended down to primary schools and an increasing number have adopted this practice. Selected subjects only are setted, with maths being the most common, followed by English and science. Early grading has been criticised by some parents.

Prep schools

In independent prep schools, the degree to which setting is applied varies. Some schools are wholly committed to setting in all subjects, while others set only in a few. There may be as many as four different sets for one subject, or only two in another, so, for example, a child might be allocated to set 1 for English but set 2 or 3 for chemistry.

State secondary schools

Many schools commonly use sets for exam classes, particularly for maths and languages. Others still prefer mixed-ability groups, especially for 11- to 13-year-olds. Now that pupils are entered at different levels for GCSE examinations, setting is a logical step in subjects with tiered exams (see page 162).

Independent secondary schools

At secondary school, children are selected according to their results at Common Entrance or scholarship exams and streamed into groups with further setting for individual subjects, some crossflow taking place between the groups. Therefore, although a school may not have a strict selective policy at entry level, selection by ability will normally be carried out internally.

Schools putting on the brakes

Some pre-prep schools operate rigid programmes that must be covered within a given year, with no allowance to extend either laterally or into the next year's programme. The result is that the progress of those who move quickly through the set curriculum will be brought to an abrupt halt. Parents may be told that as a child has covered all the books in the classroom for that year, he or she is too far ahead and will just have to wait until next year to move on. At prep-school level, however, children who are ahead of the year group could be permitted to move into a higher class.

Methods used to monitor academic work

Schools employ a number of techniques to monitor and reward pupils' academic work.

Reports

Schools regularly issue parents with reports on children's academic progress. In the state sector it is usual to provide these at the end of the school year, although some produce termly reports. These reports include Key Stage results, National Curriculum levels reached and vocational qualifications, where applicable. Reports for school-leavers are in the form of a National Record of Achievement (NRA). In the independent sector children receive end-of-term reports.

Progress grades

Progress grades, or form orders (not to be confused with the official assessment tests – see Chapter 12), are used to inform both children and parents whether or not a child is achieving the targets set for each subject. Common in the independent sector, these reports are normally prepared regularly throughout each term, following testing or work assessment.

Reward systems

Some schools operate an effort mark or reward system, but the importance attached to this differs widely. Methods used include marks for individual work which win the earner a book prize or other constructive award; inter-house or team competition; and distinctions or merits which are pinned up in the classroom or on the main school board. In primary, prep and pre-prep schools children may be awarded the distinction of 'worker of the week', for which they are given a badge to wear and perhaps a certificate to take home. In other schools, effort mark grading may appear only on half-term and end-of-term reports and there may be no inducements to encourage better work.

Teaching methods

The teaching methods adopted in primary, pre-prep and prep schools for certain subjects differ a good deal. However, regardless of whether a child is educated in the state or independent system, his or her proficiency at reading, writing and sums will depend to a large extent on the amount of parental encouragement received.

Literacy

Children who have been taught to read at home before school age will have an edge over their peers. Some nursery and pre-prep schools advise parents not to teach reading or the alphabet before starting school as children can be confused by conflicting teaching methods. Most pre-school experts argue that a great deal of preparatory learning needs to be done before formal lessons begin. There is increasing pressure for more formal teaching to take place between the ages of three and five in the state sector, where the literacy hour (see overleaf) has become compulsory for children from Year 1. However, many teachers and parents point to the fact that other countries with higher educational standards than the UK do not start formal teaching until six or even seven. Concentration on pre-reading skills is all the more necessary for children with specific difficulties such as dyslexia.

> **Tip**
>
> When visiting schools, ask to see a reading list and some of the books used in class. Note the quality and quantity of the materials and try to assess whether the programme will stimulate your child.

Literacy hour

A daily literacy hour is now part of the National Curriculum at primary schools. The government intends 80 per cent of 11-year-olds to be able to read and write at the expected level (level 4) by the year 2002. To meet this target, children start a daily programme of work from Year 1, with parents providing support at home. Each child is given reading material appropriate to his or her individual ability, to read at school and also to take home to read with parents.

Evidence suggests that boys are lagging behind girls, who tend to be more enthusiastic readers. The government is making efforts to encourage boys to read more (see page 59).

Teaching methods

The traditional method of teaching reading and spelling using phonics (building up words using the sounds of letters) is now back in fashion, which necessitates retraining for some staff. However, government advisers suggest the use of a variety of methods to ensure that children with different learning backgrounds succeed. The effectiveness of the literacy hour has not yet been evaluated but some early concerns have been expressed about the progress of the slowest learners.

Mathematics

Now that mathematics is becoming one of the more popular subjects at A-level and at university, it is vital for a sound foundation to be in place early in a child's educational career. The government has introduced moves to improve numeracy levels in young children, such as the numeracy session (see below). On a general level, the use of calculators continues to be debated, and the possible loss of number skills has led some maths teachers to be much more cautious of their use. You should ask primary and prep schools, therefore, whether calculators are used and how this may benefit or disadvantage children.

Problems can arise in the teaching of mental arithmetic. Some heads prefer children not to receive tuition at home before starting school, while methods used in class could confuse a child tutored by his or her parents. The learning of multiplication tables is becoming more popular, although opposition to rote learning at one stage led to their demise in state schools. Pre-prep and prep schools by contrast have always tended to promote this method, which is useful for quick day-to-day calculations. Inability to cope with mental arithmetic is a sign of dyslexia in some children (see page 88).

Numeracy session

In a drive to raise standards, a national numeracy strategy has been launched in primary schools under which times tables and mental arithmetic are taught and electronic calculators are discouraged for children under eight. This strategy, requiring schools to teach maths for a minimum of 45 minutes each day, was formulated in response to the government's target of 75 per cent of 11-year-olds reaching the standard expected for their age by 2002.

Funding includes provision for the retraining of primary school teachers in traditional methods and maths revision classes after school in preparation for the National Curriculum tests. Schools which do not adopt the recommended methods will be subject to special scrutiny. Instead of a national target being set for all schools, each LEA has been given its own target according to the existing standard of its pupils. To date, the strategies have been shown to work well, with substantial improvements apparent for boys as well as girls.

Science

In state primary schools science is taught as one subject. It has flourished since it was made compulsory in the National Curriculum in 1988. In prep schools, two different methods have been adopted: either the three separate subjects are taught by individual teachers, or they have been combined and are taught by one science teacher. In senior independent schools both 'combined sciences' and the individual sciences are taught to GCSE level, although emphasis is placed upon the latter. For more information on the curriculum see Chapter 12. Evidence suggests that the emphasis on literacy could be depressing science performance in primary schools.

Tip

At primary, pre-prep and prep level, to get some indication of the standards in subject teaching, ask to see some exercise books in various subjects and examine them. Remember that you will be shown only those of the most able children.

School resources

The quality of the resources provided within a school can make all the difference to how much your child gets out of his or her time at school, in both an academic and a personal sense.

Books

In order to ensure improved standards in reading, access to books is crucial. In 1998, the government provided each school with £2,000 with which to buy textbooks and fiction, but books are still in short supply in some state schools. The shortfall has resulted in some teachers subsidising the lack of government spending out of their own pay packets. It is common for pupils, even in secondary school, to share textbooks in class and to do without them for homework. Some parents buy their children's textbooks to overcome shortages.

The provision of fact sheets is not a solution. Some publishers with an eye to the market are providing books in A4 format for photocopying by schools. However, for the time being some schools are reliant upon the fundraising efforts of parents, teachers and children.

Parents visiting state schools should ask whether there are enough books for pupils, for both classroom and homework use. They should also ask whether they are advised to buy any textbooks themselves – this will indicate whether classes are adequately supplied. It is also advisable to enquire what strategies are being used to overcome book shortages.

In prep schools, one cause for concern is that guidance in reading matter can be haphazard and may differ greatly from one school to another. You should ask to see a reading list; be wary if the school does not have one.

Tip

- Look at the quantity and quality of books in the classroom and school library. Do they look well-thumbed, or are they just display copies?
- Ask how the school promotes interest in and love of books in young children. They should be encouraged to use their imagination within the strictures of the syllabus.

Libraries

Most schools have a library where pupils can read, do homework and borrow books. The facilities and atmosphere vary depending on the resources devoted to its upkeep and the level of supervision.

Public libraries provide a valuable support service to schools, especially primary schools, and have assumed greater importance with the advent of the literacy campaign. Following the introduction of the campaign, children's sections have been redesigned to encourage children to spend time browsing.

Examples of the services provided by public libraries include:

- **awareness instruction** as to how the library works for both primary schools and playgroups, run during closing hours
- **schools library service** Schools buy into this service, which permits teachers to borrow books for the school and receive support. The library will also collate and make up information packs for school projects on request
- **booktrack schemes** whereby badges are awarded to children according to the number of books read. The target number is 100 books, for which a gold badge is awarded. The scheme is open to primary school children from six years and has no time limit
- **information technology links** with schools and playcentres allowing easy access to learning facilities.

During a school visit, you could make a point of asking how the school makes use of the local library.

Keeping up with the news

Check whether the newspapers in the library look well-thumbed. A specific effort on the school's part to encourage pupils to keep abreast of current affairs indicates a responsible, outward-looking attitude. You could also ask what arrangements are in place for pupils to watch news and topical information programmes on television.

Computers

Information and communication technology (ICT) is a compulsory part of the National Curriculum in state schools, but the way it has been provided by schools varies.

Starting in primary school, children will be introduced to the basic ICT skills of word-processing, data-processing and information retrieval, and, increasingly, to use of the Internet. ICT is one of the basic skills to be introduced as part of the new A- and AS-level examinations and vocational qualifications for pupils post-16 (see Chapter 12). Examination boards at all levels now accept, and in many cases expect, computer-generated assignments, and this will also be common on many courses in higher education. In addition, most schools are using subject-based software right across the curriculum, although the quality of this is still variable in some subjects.

Britain is a leader in the provision of ICT in schools. One government initiative is the launch of the National Grid for Learning on the Internet. The aim of this programme, organised by the British Education and Communications Agency (BECTA), is that every school should be connected to the Internet.

However, many schools still have insufficient numbers of computers or are using old machines and software. Some have bought second-hand computers, which are useful for providing young children with an introduction to computer skills, although the age of the machines may cause difficulties if they are incompatible with other systems or not fast enough to access the Internet. To address these problems, the government has allocated £1 billion towards ICT up to 2002, to boost this provision and fund teacher training.

Schools' outlay on computers

It is expected that PCs will constitute 86 per cent of new purchases in primary schools and 91 per cent of those in secondary schools. Following the creation of the National Grid for Learning, it is anticipated that 80 per cent of secondary schools will have access to the Internet. Some schools, such as the city technology colleges (see page 36), provide every pupil with a lap-top computer, and many now have their own web sites on the Internet.

Computer technology is typically seen as the preserve of the young, and a large proportion of teachers admit that their computer knowledge is poor or non-existent. In order to address this deficiency, new teachers are now required to undergo training in computer skills and will be expected to use IT as an integral part of teaching. Teachers who have adopted the new technology report improved concentration and motivation among pupils, who find that online encyclopaedias and Internet sites make homework more interesting.

In order to provide a more professional approach, schools are increasingly using external managed services, through which equipment, curriculum support, management and development are rolled into one ICT service. Perks may include pupils being given access to

---

Tip

Be wary of assurances that a school is plugged in to the new technology, only to find that hardware is regarded with suspicion and left to gather dust in a corner. When touring a school, try to see a lesson in progress where computers are in use. You could also check whether access to the computers is unrestricted and whether they are available throughout the school – as well as the computer room, look in the library, science labs, art room and design and technology block.

---

email and online libraries. Managed services can alleviate teachers' workloads and free them up to do the job of teaching while ICT professionals ensure that the technology works.

Of course, the Internet also has its downside: check that access to undesirable sites is controlled by the school.

Computers have been promoted as a selling point in independent schools for many years, but their actual use has been haphazard. While some schools strive to stay ahead and instigate innovations such as their own intranet systems, others have merely paraded parents through essentially defunct 'computer rooms'. However, there have been some high-profile changes in the sector which have ensured computers' greater availability.

Parents should check whether schools give pupils access to the computers after school hours so that those who do not have access to a computer at home can use them. As boys tend to hog computers, make sure in mixed schools that access for girls is guaranteed.

Checklist for form size and the classroom

(1) At primary schools, ask whether there are any 4-year-olds in the reception class or if there is a separate nursery department. This will tell you whether the school is attempting to stay within class limits for the 5–7 age group and whether it is making appropriate provision for 4-year-olds. It would also be a good idea to ask if the teacher has had extra training for this age group.

(2) Ask whether classes are streamed and whether this is done according to ability. Also, enquire whether subjects are 'setted' and, if so, to what extent.

(3) Find out whether vertical groups are used, and if so, how many children of each age are grouped together.

(4) If your child is at nursery, primary or pre-prep level, ask how reading is taught and enquire about the expected relationship between school and home – for example, does the school discourage any intervention on your part or, alternatively, ask you to assist with your child's reading? State schools should clarify any such requirements in the home–school agreement (see overleaf).

(5) Ask what percentage of children are achieving the required literacy level for their age group.

(6) Ask to what extent calculators are used and what percentage of children are achieving the required level in maths and mental arithmetic.

(7) At secondary level, ask whether science is taught as three separate subjects or as 'combined science', and whether individual subjects are taught by specialist teachers.

(8) Find out whether the school is likely to forbid your child from progressing further once a set amount of work has been covered. At prep school, ask whether a child is permitted to advance into the next class if he or she proves to be ahead of the age group.

(9) Ask whether an effort mark system is operated. This will give you some indication of a school's academic intent and attitude to achievement.

(10) Ask whether pupils are given help with exam techniques.

(11) At a secondary school with a sixth form, ask what percentage of pupils continue into the sixth form and how many enter from other schools.

(12) Check out the computing equipment in the school and ask whether it is fast enough to access the Internet efficiently. Ask the teaching staff how comfortable they are with IT equipment and whether they have received training.

Chapter 15

Classroom support

Education is not confined within the four walls of the classroom, and what goes on outside formal school hours – from homework to extra-curricular activities – may be of equal significance, depending on how well it is organised. Non-academic pursuits present children with opportunities for personal growth and allow them to develop interests that will equip them for adulthood.

A recent trend has been for commercial and other organisations to become involved in the day-to-day life of schools, often by providing facilities or funding.

This chapter explores these issues, together with the role and responsibilities of parents in the education of their children.

Home–school agreements

The School Standards and Framework Act 1998 requires all state schools to draw up a 'home–school agreement' incorporating a parental declaration, which you will be asked to sign. This is a document formulated by each individual school in accordance with its own policies and, theoretically, consultation with parents. The intention is to establish a partnership between school and parents for the benefit of each child's educational development. In essence, the home–school agreement not only defines the school's aims and values and its responsibilities towards your child, but also sets down your responsibilities as a parent and the school's expectations of your child.

Parents' responsibilities

While the school must stipulate its targets for National Curriculum assessments, GCSEs and vocational qualifications, you as a parent must agree to ensure that your child attends school on time, every day of term; inform the school of reasons for non-attendance; and seek permission if you wish to remove your child during term time – for example, for holidays (see page 141). The agreement will place emphasis on the child's behaviour, acceptance of discipline and obedience to school rules, and on the parents' agreement to support homework obligations, where required.

The need for home–school agreements

Research shows that parental intervention and support for learning in the home are vital elements in education. The home–school agreement recognises the invaluable role a parent plays in the educational progress of a child. Being asked to sign may offend both those who feel their own efforts are being implicitly criticised and those with little regard for their responsibility towards their children. However, the agreement should not be thought of as a rebuke or a burden, but as a clarification of the areas where you can help. Without good behaviour and self-discipline, the studies of your own and other children may be disrupted.

Signing the agreement

Not only will you be asked to sign on the dotted line, but your child, if old enough to understand what is expected of him or her, will also be asked to sign the declaration. Signing up is not compulsory, however, and schools must not veto parents or pupils who refuse to sign. Furthermore, the agreement may not be used as a weapon in the admissions game and redress for breaches of the agreement cannot be sought through the courts.

An information leaflet entitled *Home–School Agreements: What Every Parent Should Know* is obtainable from DfEE Publications.*

Homework

Homework is a natural extension of work in the classroom. The ability to work alone outside the classroom engenders self-discipline and constitutes a crucial part of the learning process. As children become older, study without constant adult supervision becomes an increasing feature of their education. The following sections outline the approach to homework in the two educational sectors.

State schools

Non-compulsory homework guidelines have been drawn up for state schools. These recommend that children aged:

- 5–7 must complete 1 hour a week
- 7–9 must complete 1½ hours a week
- 10–11 must complete 30 minutes a day
- 12–14 must complete 45–120 minutes a day
- 15–16 must complete 1½ to 2½ hours a day.

It can be beneficial if the parents provide help and guidance, particularly for younger children.

Home–school agreements highlight the partnership element between school and parents. Under this scheme, schools must consult with parents and explain what homework will be expected of pupils, while parents will be expected to support the school's homework policy.

Homework clubs

The home environment of some pupils is not conducive to study or other school work. To make things easier for these children, home-work clubs, or study support centres, have become a common feature of after-school life. These clubs offer children a studious environment with access to books, computers and, frequently, teaching staff.

Independent schools

Independent schools have traditionally placed strong emphasis on homework. Children may be expected to start home study at pre-prep level (age five to seven), and at secondary-school stage the amount of time spent on homework is unlikely to be less than two hours a night.

Doing homework at an early age can provide a valuable rehearsal for children going to boarding school who will be expected to do prep on their own, and familiarity with the discipline may ease the settling-in period. If your child is due to start boarding school, you could ask the prep-school teacher to set some homework each evening so that your child will be confident and relaxed.

Extra tuition

Growing numbers of parents are paying for extra tuition to improve their child's academic chances. They may be unhappy with the level reached in individual subjects, want to make up lost ground if a child has been ill, or require coaching for an entrance or scholarship exam. It is asserted that children can learn more in an hour with a private tutor than in a week at school. However, coaching cannot necessarily provide a 'quick fix', and long-term tuition may be required in order to give a child a thorough grounding in a subject. Parents are advised to take up personal recommendations or look in libraries and local newspapers for details of tutors. They should always check teaching certificates, take up tutors' references and ask for proof that tutors have public liability insurance. For more information, contact the Association of Tutors.*

Extra-curricular activities

A wide range of these may be offered in both the state and independent systems. The pursuit of non-academic interests allows children to participate in new experiences within a controlled environment, and gives staff the opportunity to share their own enthusiasms with pupils. Sociologists suggest that such activities can help effect an introduction to the adult world and the achievement of independence. Local businesses that forge links with schools can help them to develop a much more extensive programme of activities and clubs than they could achieve alone – for example, a garage might sponsor a motor club, while a firm of solicitors might support a debating society. Some activities continue into the school holidays, and others, such as the Combined Cadet Force (see overleaf), may entail attendance at Easter or summer camps. Many schools also organise skiing trips, educational visits overseas and sporting tours abroad for their top teams. These are usually paid for by parents – see Chapter 17 for more on the costs of schooling.

Type and availability of activities

Parents should check that a good range of activities is on offer, especially at boarding school, where children commonly complain that weekends are boring (see Chapter 4 for more on boarding-school facilities). Some common options are described below.

After-school clubs

These may cater for diverse interests such as sport, chess, debating, dancing, astronomy, modelling or martial arts, depending on the age of the children. Groups may take place at lunchtime or after school. Some establishments refer to these as 'enrichment activities'.

Music

Many schools have choirs, bands and orchestras which rehearse outside lesson time and stage performances, either for parents or the general public. Schools that take music seriously may give pupils the opportunity to go on tour within the UK or abroad. Many schools make provision for individual music lessons on various instruments; this will be an extra cost for parents. The government has promised extra funding for music tuition and groups. For information on specialist music schools, sees pages 70–1.

Community service

Community service gives children the opportunity to help people who are elderly, disabled or disadvantaged. Schools may liaise with external agencies to arrange visits and placements.

Duke of Edinburgh's Award Scheme

Many schools in both sectors take part in this scheme. The programme provides opportunities for personal achievement, challenge and adventure, and allows young people aged 14–25 to aim for three award levels: bronze, silver and gold. The main components are expeditions, skills, physical recreation and service.

Combined Cadet Force

The Combined Cadet Force (CCF) is a corps affiliated to sections of the armed services. CCF training is organised by most independent secondary schools and some state schools operate a modified form of this. Students may attend activity courses and camps. Military skills are taught, although much of the instruction is deskbound. Attendance is usually compulsory in the independent sector for one year, usually the first, and then continues on a voluntary basis.

Young Enterprise

Each year over 2,300 schools participate in this programme, the philosophy of which is 'learning by doing'. It engages pupils in practical business projects, giving them experience of running their own company. Volunteers from the business community provide advice and support, and programmes can contribute towards academic and vocational qualfications. For more on business involvement, see pages 215–19.

Parents' meetings

All schools, from primary or pre-prep level upwards, hold parents' meetings. The way in which these are organised will give you an insight into the efficiency of the school administration and how seriously it takes the event. Parents' meetings should be a constructive exercise for improving pupils' performance, not a public relations exercise.

Organisation of parents' meetings

The two main methods adopted involve parents either queuing up outside the classroom of the teacher concerned, or meeting the staff in a large hall. In the former case, conversations will be confidential; in the latter, teachers sit shoulder-to-shoulder and since there is no privacy conversations can become inconsequential.

Some schools specifically insist that the pupil is present while others ban the pupil. It is arguable that the child's presence is essential, considering that the object of the exercise is to discuss the improvement of his or her education. A three-way discussion between child, parent and teacher could prove valuable and prohibit the child claiming afterwards that the teacher 'does not understand', as well as preventing buck-passing. If the consultation is to take place without the child present, then parents should equip themselves with what information they can glean from their child about each teacher. This will help to put the teachers' comments into perspective.

Tip

At your initial meeting, ask how parents' meetings are organised, whether they are intended as a social gathering or serious discussion, and whether your child is permitted to attend.

Potential problems of parents' meetings

With a large number of parents to process, teachers may be tempted to avoid time-consuming issues, in which case the meeting could become superficial. At the other extreme, teachers may take so long talking to some parents that others find themselves unable to confer with all of the teachers they need to see.

Some prep schools treat parents' evenings as social events and somewhat neglect their real purpose. Teachers may fail to refer to specific results and notes, and the presence of alcohol may also preclude a serious atmosphere.

Parents' meetings are sometimes used as a means of placating parents. At schools where this happens, some parents do not even bother to attend.

Careers guidance

Ideally, careers guidance should start before the sixth form: a pupil's choice of A-level subjects will affect university entrance and, subsequently, choice of exam. For advice on what subjects are needed for different careers, see *The Which? Guide to Choosing a Career*, available from Which? Books.* GCSE results are important in that the initial offer of a university place is dependent on these, but if they are not backed up by the required A-level results, that offer will not be confirmed.

All pupils at Key Stage 4 (see page 155) must receive careers education and guidance. However, some schools adopt a more serious approach than others. A responsible school will organise a parents' consultation for the Year 11 group in order to make parents aware of the options and potential problems regarding subject choices, so they can be better informed when discussing the issues with their son or daughter. It is at this meeting that any problems with subject choice on the school timetable will show up. Subject choice is discussed more fully in Chapter 12.

Secondary schools often cite careers advice as a selling point. Parents should ask whether the school gives students the opportunity to meet representatives from a wide selection of professions and from different universities. There is a risk that some schools, keen to push for a university application, may not promote further education courses where these might suit a pupil better. Careers information must be practical and appropriate to the individual; a degree is not always the best option, nor is an academic subject necessarily preferable to a vocational one.

Consider the following points when visiting the careers department.

- Is it central and accessible?
- Are the students encouraged to use it?
- Does the head of careers seem efficient and well-informed?
- Is guidance provided on how to fill in the UCAS form (for university entrance) and write a *curriculum vitae*?
- When A-level and GNVQ results are published, is the head or a senior member of staff on hand? What action is taken on behalf of pupils who have failed to achieve the results expected or are borderline?
- Look at one of the career sections – preferably one dealing with an area you know about – and check how up to date the information is.
- Overall, is the information wide-ranging?

Work experience

To support a pupil's choice of direction, work experience in a relevant field is recommended. Every pupil in a state school is expected to do a two-week placement at the age of 15 or 16, and most independent schools will arrange this although it is not a requirement. Provided the work is constructive, it can be of great benefit to pupils, and an employer's report from this experience can enhance a university application.

Aptitude tests

Schools sometimes recommend that students sit an externally facilitated aptitude test. Otherwise known as psychometric tests, these highlight interests and suitable career options. The value of such an exercise, for which a charge will be made, is questionable, unless the child and parents are genuinely in the dark about what step to take. Opinions from parents whose children have undergone the tests and been given a career profile has been ambivalent.

Charles

Charles' test results revealed a strong aptitude for engineering and he was accordingly advised to read that subject at university. However, they failed to pick up that he hated maths, making engineering, as a maths-based subject, totally unsuitable. His father subsequently declined the test for his second son.

You might find that an in-depth discussion at home, perhaps with a selection of university prospectuses, could prove equally helpful, given that subject preferences could also be discussed.

The school year

A new debate has entered the world of education: the framework of the school year. The number and length of school terms are under scrutiny. City technology colleges (see page 36) are already experienced in operating a five-term year and other schools are now looking at the viability of this system. The demise of the three-term year is on the cards.

The three-term year, which has its origin in the Victorian agrarian calendar, is increasingly regarded as out of date for city-dwellers. It is argued that one of the advantages to be gained from splitting the year into five eight-week terms will be more focused attention over a shorter timespan. The exhaustion experienced towards the end of the long autumn term would be avoided, and with only a four-week summer holiday pupils should not have time to forget everything they learnt the previous term. The other terms would be split by breaks of two weeks.

If this system were to be adopted, it might not be as straightforward as many suggest. Parents, teachers and children could face considerable disruption and inconvenience if the transition is piecemeal, not least in the case of families with children attending schools using different systems. Meanwhile children's friends may have different school dates. In rural areas, those children who help out at harvest time may face a conflict of interests. The long summer holidays are one of the teaching profession's strongest recruitment incentives. If this were to be swept away, the drive to solve teacher shortages could be affected.

State schools are also discussing the possibility of extending the school week into the weekend. Many independent schools operate Saturday-morning school as a matter of course. However, this is not universal.

Business involvement in schools

For many years, business and industry have been encouraged by the government to support innovation in education. This has manifested itself in a variety of ways, the common theme being a desire to provide education which fits young people for life and work beyond school and simultaneously to forge a greater understanding of business among the educational community.

Education Action Zones

This programme has been set up with the intention of raising educational standards in challenged areas of England, and some participating inner-city schools are among the fastest-improving in the country. An Education Action Zone (EAZ) comprises a small group of local primary, secondary and special schools working in partnership with local and international businesses, LEAs, community organisations and parents. Typically, two to three secondaries and their feeder primaries are involved.

The government will ensure that schools within an EAZ have priority access to its other programmes, such as the specialist schools scheme (see pages 37–9), family literacy schemes and advanced skills teachers. Some schools may also be identified as 'beacon schools', which are recognised for their success and commitment and held up as examples for failing schools to emulate. These schools receive extra funding to enable them to share their expertise with others. The target number of beacon schools to be accredited by 2002–3 is 1,000.

The lifetime of an EAZ is at least three years, but this can be extended to five years in order to give the EAZ sufficient time to demonstrate its effectiveness and, it is hoped, build up enough momentum for the project to continue. At the time of writing, 25 EAZs are in operation and it is expected that more will be created.

Each EAZ is run by an Action Forum, the membership of which reflects the make-up of the partnership. The Forum sets and implements targets, which must be sufficiently demanding to achieve the declared aim of raising standards. Goals must include the improvement of teaching standards by in-service training and the recruitment of skilled staff.

In order to provide for all ranges of academic ability, EAZs may apply to change the National Curriculum requirements and develop their own strategies, provided this is not to the detriment of the literacy and numeracy programmes (see Chapter 14) or the assessment requirements. They may also change the school day, week or year, create links with local education agencies, and make greater use of non-classroom learning facilities.

EAZs are expected to make maximum use of existing local skills and facilities, as well as buying in from outside, in order to achieve their targets. They have considerable flexibility in the provision of education, in accordance with the codes of best practice. The government can provide extra funding to support the initiatives, although it is hoped that business involvement should generate further funds.

Keeping in touch

With the help of financial input from commercial enterprises, schools in one EAZ obtained the technology to set up video-conferencing links. By using this method, children in hospital were able to join in with lessons and avoid falling behind with their work while they recovered.

Business takeovers of failing schools

Through the School Standards and Framework Act, the government has given itself the power to create a pool consisting of private enterprises, non-profit-making trusts and successful LEAs upon which it can draw at short notice. These bodies may then bid to take over certain services from failing LEAs or the day-to-day running of specific schools. Successful applicants will be rewarded with staggered payments as pre-set targets are achieved. At the time of writing, this policy is still in its infancy.

Business sponsorship in schools

The 1990s have seen a shift towards more commercial involvement in schools, leading to accusations that businesses are exploiting a largely captive audience of young consumers and, by extension, their parents.

An increasing number of businesses – both commercial and not-for-profit organisations – produce materials for use in the classroom, and some larger companies also employ education officers. Many businesses see involvement in education as their chance to 'put something back' into the community, and companies that have been involved with schools for a long time echo the concerns of teachers and consumer groups, not wanting their reputations sullied by those that might be less scrupulous in their approach. However, such arguments undoubtedly offer businesses the ideal opportunity to increase consumer awareness of both the company and its brand(s). Research carried out by *Marketing Week* in 1998 indicated that 90 per cent of companies surveyed had engaged in some kind of marketing promotion to schools, and 12 per cent of companies acknowledged that they were targeting parents through school-children. The 'pester power' phenomenon is estimated to generate sales of up to £8.4 billion each year in the UK alone.

Materials produced by businesses and the associated activities tend to fall into two main categories:

- **materials linked to a specific product** These are designed to promote brand/s and company and are often linked to resources or cash for the school. They include: basic information about the company and/or its products designed for consumers in general; factsheets about the company designed for the educational market; industrial placements or visits for teachers and pupils; sponsored gifts and reward schemes aimed at schools (e.g. token collection for equipment); sponsored use of space around the school (e.g. noticeboards); unsolicited publicity material; advertising space in return for payment (e.g. hoardings, free postcards); advertising/resources on the Internet; and sponsored equipment/resources (e.g. science laboratories, computers and exercise books)

- **materials linked to a curriculum area** These are aimed at promoting the company presence and image in general but with the additional objective of improving teaching and learning. They include information packs designed for use by teachers; worksheets and support materials for use in the classroom; videos; CD-ROMs; posters for the classroom; and industrial placements or visits for teachers and pupils.

Although, clearly, well-thought-out materials and activities sponsored by business add value to the taught curriculum, it is necessary to discriminate between these sorts of materials and those which do little to improve the quality of what goes on in classrooms, but provide facilities for schools. In an environment where many schools face financial constraints and some are crying out for resources, the need for guidance is apparent.

The National Consumer Council guidelines

These voluntary guidelines on commercially sponsored materials were last revised in 1996. Their aim is to assist teachers, parents and governors to identify quality resources when assessing materials for use in schools and colleges. The guidelines require testers to apply certain criteria, as follows.

- Is it clear who the sponsor/producer is?
- Does the material's educational value outweigh any marketing message?
- Is its approach to the subject balanced and up-to-date?
- Is it relevant to the curriculum and the children's age group?
- Has it been tested for use in schools?
- Is it free from stereotypes of relationships, religions, age, disability, gender and race?

- Can children and teachers participate without buying the sponsor's products?
- Is it free of messages that encourage children to pester adults to buy a specific firm's product or service?
- Is it free of incentives to children to eat an unhealthy diet or take part in unhealthy/unsafe activities?
- Are the benefits of the sponsored offer worthwhile and achievable for your school?

Research carried out by Consumers' Association, which has looked at ways in which users of educational resources can assess their suitability, has found that parents think external control over such activity in schools is necessary.

The question for parents is perhaps: how far do you want your child's school to go and at what cost? Parents might like to ask schools the following questions.

- Do you accept sponsorship from companies for school resources?
- Do you use a lot of classroom materials which contain company brand names?
- Do you use the NCC guidelines in your decision-making?
- Do you have a policy that allows parents to assess what they find acceptable?
- Do you ever feel there are conflicts of interest? For example, healthy eating messages being circulated while vending machines sell foods high in fat and sugar.

Moves to target inner-city schools for improvement

From September 2000, a programme of measures will take effect in 450 comprehensive schools in inner-city areas of London, Manchester, Liverpool, Birmingham, Leeds and Sheffield. The intention is to raise standards in schools which are seen to be failing consistently, and to reverse the trend of middle-class parents fleeing the state sector in favour of private schools.

The measures are designed to tackle problems across the ability range. Teachers will select the brightest pupils for extra tuition in subjects in which they excel. Extra classes will take place after school and on Saturdays, and, where logistics permit, advantage will be taken of any neighbouring specialist schools. Meanwhile, mentors will be recruited externally to provide individual advice and support to children of below-average ability, particularly those who are falling behind. Learning units for disruptive pupils will be established in one in three of the chosen schools, and all secondary schools in the designated areas will have access to these units.

A network of IT learning centres will be created from existing schools, and it is intended to establish new university summer schools for those of sixth-form age, building upon links already formed between some schools and universities.

Checklist for classroom support

(1) Ask for a copy of the home–school agreement.

(2) Check the school's policy on homework and its attitude towards parental involvement.

(3) Ask whether the school runs extra study periods during lunch break and after school.

(4) Find out how parents' meetings are organised.

(5) Ask what form of careers guidance is offered.

(6) If the school is within an EAZ, ask what targets have been set and how it expects to achieve these.

(7) If the school operates a three-term system, ask whether any changes to the school year are contemplated and consider whether this will be a problem for you personally.

(8) Ask the school whether it has any unusual facilities or features. For example, is it a specialist school (see pages 37–9) or a beacon school (see page 216)?

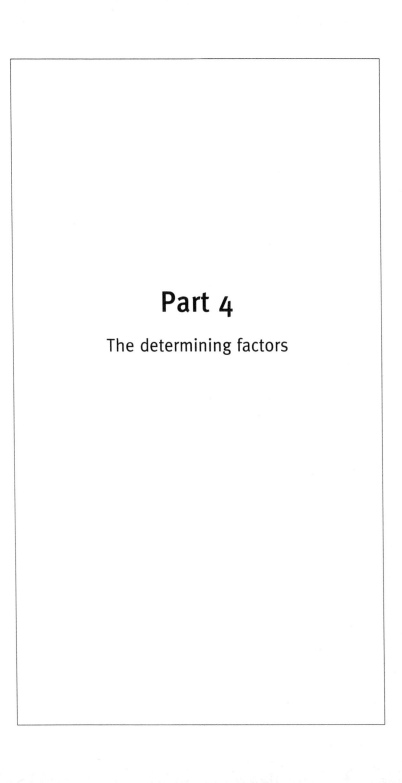

Part 4

The determining factors

Chapter 16

School admission criteria

The admission process for the state and independent sectors is very different. While the former is defined by law, the main criteria for the latter are academic ability and/or the parents' capacity to pay.

Admission procedures at state schools

The introduction of the School Standards and Framework Act 1998 has prompted some alterations in the school admissions system. These will affect arrangements for primary and secondary intakes from September 2000 in England and Wales, and will be administered by LEAs (see page 23) and governing bodies (see pages 104–6).

Likelihood of obtaining a place at your preferred school

The government claims that the majority of parents obtain a state-school place that is acceptable to them. However, not all parents gain their first preference. Schools that offer a high standard of education tend to be heavily over-subscribed – as many as 660 children can chase as few as 90 places at such establishments. In these circumstances, a school will apply certain criteria to determine which children will be admitted (see pages 227–30). Because competition can be intense, it is vital that parents state their first-choice school when making an application (see page 234).

Purpose of the new admission regulations

The government's aim has been to introduce procedures that are clear and understandable, and to ensure that disputes are dealt with fairly. Local admission forums will now decide on admission arrangements through consultation, and disputes will be referred to an independent adjudicator (see page 242). Parents who are dissatisfied with the school place offered may turn to independent admission appeal panels (see page 243), which are to replace appeal committees.

Obligations of the admission authority

The different types of state schools are described on pages 24–6. At:

- **community** (including community special) and **voluntary-controlled** schools, the admission authority is the LEA or the governing body, if this responsibility has been delegated, in which case the governors must implement all LEA arrangements and policies
- **foundation** (including foundation special) and **voluntary-aided** schools, the governing body is responsible for admissions.

All admission authorities within a relevant area are now legally obliged to consult each other before deciding on their admission arrangements, which means that an LEA must consult the governing bodies of schools for which it is the admission authority. The LEA is responsible for defining its geographical area, in consultation with the other admission authorities. In doing this, it must take into consideration parental preferences and schooling patterns and include parts of neighbouring LEAs if common sense dictates.

Admission forums

The DfEE recommends that these should be set up at local level to facilitate consultations between the relevant admission authorities, although this is not a legal requirement. Forums are expected to include:

- the LEA
- school governors
- head teachers
- dioceses representing schools in the area
- Early Years Development Partnerships (see page 44)
- special-interest groups

- City Technology Colleges, if applicable
- local parents.

They should give all those directly involved in the provision of education at local level the opportunity to voice their opinions, and enable all aspects of admission arrangements to be co-ordinated to suit local needs.

Guidelines for admission authorities

The new arrangements aim to ensure that parents understand the admission process fully and are able to make appropriate decisions. Admission authorities are required to make it as easy as possible for parents to exercise their preference. They must also produce clear, fair and objective admission criteria and operate them for the benefit of all parents and children in the community. Authorities will be expected to follow certain guidelines:

- discrimination on the grounds of gender is unlawful (except in the case of single-sex schools)
- the proportion of boys and girls in a co-educational school may not be fixed artificially
- discrimination on the grounds of race, colour, nationality or ethnic origin is unlawful.

The LEA prospectus

Each year LEAs must publish information on the admission arrangements for all schools in their area or the consultative area. This prospectus may be a single publication or in several parts if the area is subdivided. Separate sections may be issued for primary and secondary schools.

Each prospectus will contain the names, addresses and telephone numbers of local schools, as well as details of their classification and religious affiliation and the criteria operated in case of over-subscription. LEAs with a system of feeder primary schools (see page 34) must include details of the relationships between schools. In the case of secondary schools, the information must also include the number of places available – a figure known as the PAN (see page 227) – and the number of applications received in the previous year.

The prospectus will also disclose the arrangements in place to help parents achieve their preference, together with details of the admission appeals procedure (see page 242). The LEA may also include in this document any other information that is considered to be of interest to parents, such as details of measures undertaken to rectify problems found during school inspections. However, LEAs are not obliged to make reports of recent school inspections available. For advice on how to obtain inspection reports, see box, page 98.

Governing bodies that act as admission authorities must publish independently details of their admission arrangements and appeals procedure, although they may delegate this responsibility to the LEA.

The admission regulations for state schools

Parents should be aware of the rules followed by admission authorities when allocating places, since these will affect their application.

School numbers

Regulations prescribe maximum and minimum numbers for the intake at each state school. The new arrangements outline how these figures will be set.

Standard number

Schools must now have a 'standard number' for the age group normally admitted to the school for the first time. It represents the minimum number of pupils the school may admit, provided there are sufficient applications, and will not include children transferring from earlier age groups. The only exception to this rule is in the case of children who attend a nursery class in a primary school and then join others being admitted to the school's reception class: in this case, the standard number will comprise both groups. Where a school has a sixth-form intake from other schools, it is required to have a second standard number appertaining to this group.

Schools can apply to increase their standard number if they have expanded their classroom facilities or accommodation. The government encourages popular and high-achieving schools to increase the amount of classrooms – and correspondingly their standard number – since this makes it proportionately easier for parents to obtain places for their children. In the case of infant classes, expansion may enable the school to comply with class-size limits (see page 192).

Admission number

The admission number is set by the admission authority. It may be fixed at the standard number or increased above this, but not lowered. The admission number is referred to as the PAN (published admission number) in the LEA prospectus. The published admission number includes the number of 'statemented' pupils who must be admitted to a school (see pages 85–6). The effect may be to give precedence to these pupils over non-statemented pupils, if an authority has received a large number of applications from non-statemented pupils. Once the admission number is fixed it must be adhered to, unless the school expands or reduces its capacity.

Over-subscription criteria

Many schools, especially those offering a high standard of education, receive such a large number of applications from parents that they cannot possibly satisfy demand. An authority's published admission arrangements must include the criteria for allocating places in the event of over-subscription, and the order in which those criteria will be applied. Although the definition of these criteria is left largely to the discretion of the admission authority, their operation must be even-handed and the rules must be followed. It is considered good practice for LEAs to provide details of schools in their area which have been over-subscribed in the past, the extent to which this happened and whether it is likely to occur again.

Some commonly cited criteria that can influence admission in a child's favour are:

- residence within a designated transport area
- having a brother or sister at the school
- accessibility by public transport
- compelling medical or social problems
- transfer from a feeder primary school
- parental ranking of preference.

If it proves necessary to make a distinction within a particular category, the methods to be used must be published. The most common method is likely to be the distance between home and school using the shortest available walking route. As there are often instances where a child's home is closer to a school in a neighbouring authority, common sense should prevail.

An LEA must treat applications from parents living outside the LEA area on the same footing as those from parents within that area. Nevertheless, while no initial priority may be given to those from within an LEA area, admission authorities may operate a catchment area as part of their over-subscription criteria.

Catchment areas

A catchment area (sometimes known as a designated area) is a geographical area defined by the LEA within which a number of homes are served by a named school. From time to time circumstances may dictate that the extent of the area undergoes an adjustment – for example, there may be a shift in schooling patterns or the educational structure may be reorganised. Living within a school's catchment area can prove decisive in gaining a school place, and some parents attempt to capitalise on this either by moving house to their target area or employing more devious means (see below).

Audrey

Audrey identified a good school for her daughter, but was unable to satisfy the prime criterion as she lived outside the catchment area. Her mother, however, lived in the locality. Determined to obtain a place, Audrey gave her mother's address and moved her daughter to the grandmother's home during the admission process. As soon as the school offered the girl a place, Audrey moved her daughter back to the family home.

Evidence shows that some movement between the state and independent systems is prompted by the practice of parents 'negotiating' siblings into their state school of choice.

Clare

Clare has two daughters, the elder of whom attended a popular primary school before being moved to an independent school. Her younger sister was due to undergo the admission process to the same primary school, but Clare realised that if the school operated its over-subscription criteria, a successful outcome could well depend on her elder daughter still being there. The older girl was therefore moved back to the primary school on a trumped-up pretext. Her younger sister was duly admitted to the school, at which point Clare moved her older daughter back to the independent school where she would eventually be joined by her younger sister.

Parents tend to justify devious behaviour by reasoning that if they do not 'join the fray', they will be at a disadvantage and left behind. In the scrum for places, it may well be that the most opportunistic parents stand a better chance. However, parents intending to manipulate the regulations should take care (see below).

Warning

Bending the rules is one thing, fraud and cheating are quite another. Head teachers are becoming more aware of dubious practices in the case of catchment areas, and many schools now take steps to catch out those who use false addresses on their application forms.

Where over-subscription criteria are operated at schools with a religious foundation (see page 26), priority is normally given to families of a certain faith or denomination. The adherence to strict rules on religious commitment can vary enormously, ranging from an insistence that the entire family worships regularly to simply the practice of the child in question. If you are contemplating such a school you should ascertain what the requirements are, and whether a reference will be necessary from your family priest, minister or other religious leader.

Some authorities operate waiting lists. Where this occurs, the authority must explain how the children are to be ranked in relation to the published over-subscription criteria. It is important not to place too much reliance on a waiting list and if you find yourself in this position, you should put contingency plans into action.

Points mean prizes

In applying the over-subscription criteria, some admission authorities operate a points system against each factor used to determine eligibility. Applicants with the highest number of overall points will be successful.

Partially selective schools

Some schools allocate a proportion of their intake according to academic ability (this will be indicated in the prospectus). These schools are not allowed to alter their basis for selection or increase the proportion of pupils that are selected by ability, although they may introduce fair 'banding' (see below). The number of these schools will not be added to, with the exception of sixth forms.

Banding

Banding is operated by some admission authorities for partially selective schools. It requires children to take a test to determine the ability band into which they are to be placed. The test is devised by the admission authority and may take various forms – for example, reading or verbal/non-verbal reasoning.

Each school allocates a set number of places per band. Where there are more children than available places in a band, parental preference and then over-subscription criteria will be applied. In the event that places remain unfilled in any band, the school must comply with parental preference and ensure all places are filled, if there is sufficient demand.

Schools that band must ensure that the children admitted are properly representative of the ability range of the children applying in that year. Banding must not be used to select a disproportionate number of high-ability children or to discriminate against children on the grounds of sex or race. Those which already band, but not according to the above conditions, may continue to do so in accordance with the rules laid down for partially selective schools as described above. Complaints about banding at these schools may be referred to the adjudicator (see page 242), and parents may also object if an admission authority wishes to introduce banding.

Selection by aptitude

The School Standards and Framework Act has introduced new methods of selection based on aptitude. The word 'aptitude' side-steps the academic connotations inherent in the expression 'ability'. It is generally accepted that a child with aptitude has the capacity to learn skills and succeed in a subject, and as a result will benefit from what that particular school has to offer. The exact form of the tests is devised by individual admission authorities.

If a school is part of the specialist programme (see pages 37–9), or can show that it has relevant expertise or facilities, the admission authorities may select up to 10 per cent of pupils purely on the basis of aptitude for one of the following subjects:

- physical education or sport
- the performing arts
- the visual arts
- modern foreign languages
- design and technology and information technology.

The same percentage applies if a school has more than one specialism, in which case the admission authority will decide how the proportions will be applied. The admission authority and/or governing body may decide in consultation whether a school can be described as specialist.

If children with special educational needs apply, the tests must be adapted so as not to disadvantage them.

Schools are permitted to combine this selection by aptitude with a banding procedure (see opposite). By combining the two permitted selection procedures, a school may either admit 90 per cent of children on the basis of banding and 10 per cent by aptitude, or band the entire admission and then select 10 per cent from each band on the basis of aptitude.

If the regulations described above are not followed, parents may object to the adjudicator (see page 242).

Pupils with special educational needs

Admission authorities may not discriminate against disabled children or those with special educational needs. The published admission number of each school, explained on page 227, includes the number of 'statemented' pupils who must be admitted. If a school is named in a child's statement, the admission authority is required to admit the child to that school. Where a child has special needs but is not statemented, it must apply the normal published admission criteria, and may not refuse admission because it feels that it cannot cater for the child's special educational needs. If an admission authority gives some degree of priority to such children without statements, this policy must be published in its admission arrangements.

The parents of a child with a statement of special educational needs may appeal against a school named in the statement, or against the LEA's failure to name a school. Complaints should be directed to the special educational needs tribunal (see page 86), not to the appeals panel.

Pupils who behave disruptively

An admission authority may not form an opinion as to a child's suitability for a school, nor may it request that a child be assessed for special educational needs before acceptance. Should a child prove to be disruptive after admission, the appropriate disciplinary action should be taken. This could mean exclusion (see pages 137–8).

A school may be directed by an LEA to admit an excluded child, if it has spare places and the child has been refused admission to other suitable schools located at a reasonable distance from his/her home. In this instance, if a school is generally under-subscribed, it may find that it ends up supporting an unreasonable proportion of pupils with challenging behaviour. Although schools with such pupils receive a Pupil Support grant, this may be of little comfort if a school is attempting to improve its standards. In the case of schools that have a particularly high number of such pupils and are under special measures to raise standards (or have been within the last two years), or those that have been identified by Ofsted or the LEA as seriously weak, an admission authority may refuse a pupil entry because to do so would be prejudicial to the efficient provision of education. For information on Ofsted and school inspections, see Chapter 6.

Pupils from overseas

Admission authorities are obliged to consider the educational needs of these children:

- school places must be kept open for children who are UK nationals temporarily living abroad or accompanying their teacher parents on exchange schemes
- provision must be made for the children of parents participating in a teacher-exchange scheme living temporarily in the UK
- parents who are not UK nationals but have a right of residence may apply for school places for their children
- children who hold a British citizen passport or have right of residence are entitled to an education in the UK
- children who are nationals of the European Economic Area (Austria, Belgium, Denmark, Finland, France, Germany, Greece, Ireland, Italy, Luxembourg, the Netherlands, Portugal, Spain, Sweden and the UK, together with Norway, Liechtenstein and Iceland) may seek a state education in the UK, whether or not they are accompanied by their parents
- children without EEA status may be admitted to a state school on a student exchange-scheme basis, usually for one year only
- families from overseas that are not yet resident in the UK are not precluded from making an application to a school. However, the admission authority will take into account the likelihood of entry being granted, either to the parents or the child alone. Each application will be decided on its merits.

Considerations for parents making an application

When filling in application forms, you should take certain precautions in order to maximise your chances of obtaining a place at your preferred school.

Lack of standardisation

School applications do not all follow the same format, although LEAs and other admission authorities have been advised to simplify the process for parents by standardising their procedures. A standard application form, common deadlines and test dates and one date for the final decision would be preferable, but you should not assume that this will be in place in any one area. This degree of co-ordination is also unlikely between neighbouring LEAs.

Application deadlines

Owing to the discrepancies among different admission authorities, you should double-check all the dates by which you must submit application forms. The date order in which applications are received is not significant, provided they meet the deadline.

Parental preference

Application forms must contain a section where parents can nominate their first-choice school: some forms also make provision for a second choice. Admission authorities are obliged to adopt all possible measures that will enable parents to exercise their preferred choice, in so far as this is compatible with their duty to provide an efficient education within their education budget. This preference must be operated before all other policies when allocating places.

Tip

As the admission authority must give precedence to those parents who have stated a preference over those who have not, it is vital that you mark your first choice on the form and submit it before the deadline. If you do not state a preference, your child will be allocated a school place within a reasonable travelling distance, in line with the policy of the LEA or admission authority.

Some exemptions to the rule of parental preference which will affect admission are listed below.

Overcrowding

This is the most common exemption. Overcrowding may be cited if it would be prejudicial to the provision of efficient education or the use of resources to exercise a parent's first choice. The need for primary schools to comply with infant class-size limits (see page 192) has led to widespread enforcement of the exemption in this age group. Other instances where overcrowding may be cited as a factor occur in the case of schools that are wholly selective, or have a religious ethos.

Second-choice school

Where a parent is allowed to express a second choice, the operation of parental preference is slightly different. If for some reason the first choice cannot be granted, the duty of the admission authority to comply with the parents' wishes shifts to the second. There is, however, no statutory requirement to rank this second choice above all other criteria, and it would not be unreasonable to assume that most, if not all, of the places at that school will have been allocated to other pupils exercising their first preference. If, therefore, you have expressed an unreasonable first choice, you may also risk losing out on your second choice.

Tip

Check early on whether your LEA applies over-subscription criteria above parents' order of ranking. If it does, be very careful when choosing your first preference. Don't throw it away in the belief that your second preference will automatically apply. Unless you are confident that you have a decent chance of success, it may be wiser to play safe and choose a suitable first-choice school where the merits of your case are stronger.

Excluded pupils

Where a pupil has been excluded from two or more schools, parents forfeit the right to exercise parental preference for a period of two years from the start of the last exclusion, unless the child is below compulsory school age or has been reinstated.

Transfer to state secondary school

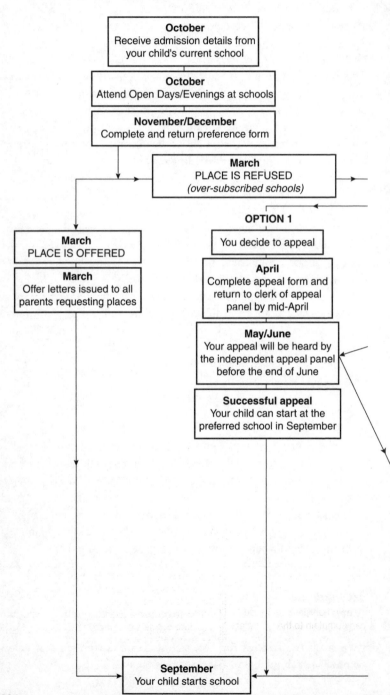

October
Receive admission details from your child's current school

October
Attend Open Days/Evenings at schools

November/December
Complete and return preference form

March
PLACE IS REFUSED
(over-subscribed schools)

OPTION 1

You decide to appeal

March
PLACE IS OFFERED

March
Offer letters issued to all parents requesting places

April
Complete appeal form and return to clerk of appeal panel by mid-April

May/June
Your appeal will be heard by the independent appeal panel before the end of June

Successful appeal
Your child can start at the preferred school in September

September
Your child starts school

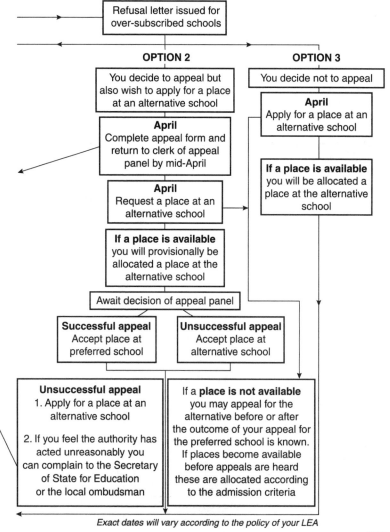

Refusal letter issued for over-subscribed schools

OPTION 2

You decide to appeal but also wish to apply for a place at an alternative school

April
Complete appeal form and return to clerk of appeal panel by mid-April

April
Request a place at an alternative school

If a place is available you will provisionally be allocated a place at the alternative school

Await decision of appeal panel

Successful appeal
Accept place at preferred school

Unsuccessful appeal
Accept place at alternative school

Unsuccessful appeal
1. Apply for a place at an alternative school

2. If you feel the authority has acted unreasonably you can complain to the Secretary of State for Education or the local ombudsman

OPTION 3

You decide not to appeal

April
Apply for a place at an alternative school

If a place is available you will be allocated a place at the alternative school

If a **place is not available** you may appeal for the alternative before or after the outcome of your appeal for the preferred school is known. If places become available before appeals are heard these are allocated according to the admission criteria

Exact dates will vary according to the policy of your LEA

Planning your child's admission to school

Once your child has started school, the school should tell you when and how to prepare your application and what will be required of you at each stage. The LEA will also provide assistance: some operate designated parent information lines. If you want to consider schools within neighbouring LEAs, you must apply for details from those LEAs.

The application process starts in September, at the beginning of the school year, and continues through to November or December depending on area. The flow chart on pages 236–7 outlines the stages of transfer to secondary school. Relevant dates and deadlines will be clearly printed on the application forms and other documentation. In areas where a large proportion of parents do not have English as a first language, forms will be printed in a variety of languages. They may also be available in large-print and braille formats.

Parents are permitted to complete one LEA form per LEA, which may allow them to state one or two preferences (see page 234). Some schools, such as church schools, may require parents to fill in an additional form. If parents fail to achieve admission to their first-choice school (or first and second choices, if this was an option), they will be contacted by the LEA and given a list of available schools.

Lodging an appeal

If you have been allotted a school by your LEA after failing to achieve your preference(s) and you are not happy with the choice, you might want to consider lodging an appeal to try to win a place at your preferred school (see page 243). Failure to act may indicate to the LEA that you are satisfied with the school selected.

Chapter 2 describes the types of state school and ages of admission. The entry specifications for each age group are different and parents need to be aware of the rules on exceptional entry.

Nursery level

Parents who want to arrange nursery care should plan ahead – it is not too early to begin investigations when your child is two. All 4-year-olds are entitled to three terms' free nursery education under a government scheme now extended to include 3-year-olds in some areas. Parents should follow certain steps to ensure their child gets a place under this scheme (for details, see pages 28–30).

Primary school

Parents whose children have not yet started school should either contact the LEA direct or fill in a 'pupil details' form from a local primary or infant school to receive documentation about admission. If your child attends a nursery class, he or she will usually transfer to the reception class of the same school, but this cannot be taken for granted. It will be necessary to make a separate application.

The points of entry to a primary school are in September, January and April. A school may operate a once-, twice- or thrice-yearly admission system.

- Where pupils are admitted into school only **once a year**, the formal intake will be in September for the autumn term.
- In a **twice-yearly system**, the formal intake is in September and January. Children whose fifth birthday falls between 1 September and the end of February will normally be admitted in September, while those whose fifth birthday falls between 1 March and 31 August will be admitted in the January term.
- With a **thrice-yearly system**, in addition to the September and January admissions another intake is added in April, generally comprising children whose fifth birthday occurs between April (or May) and the end of August.

Make sure you are aware of the relevant dates for your area. If you do not take up a school place at the normal time for that particular school or LEA, it may not be kept open for your child. Early admission is generally not permitted unless it can be proved that there are pressing medical or social reasons.

Exceptional admission to primary school

You will find that some admission authorities operate an intake to reception classes before a child is of compulsory school age – sometimes for children as young as three years old. However, if parents do not wish to take up the entitlement to three terms' nursery education but wish to wait until their child has reached school age (by law, the start of the term following the child's fifth birthday), they may accept the offer of a place at the time of the normal intake but ask to defer actual entry until the child has reached school age. This effectively holds the place for the child, provided it is taken up within that academic year. This procedure is at the discretion of individual admission authorities and if offered must be published in the LEA prospectus.

The government has ruled that infant classes should contain no more than 30 children (15 in some LEAs – see page 33). However, exceptions may occur if parents can show that adherence to this rule would prejudice their child's interests – for example, where the authority has made a mistake in implementing the admission arrangements, or an admission appeal panel has upheld the parents' complaint.

If the family has moved into an area after the normal admission date, the parents may request admission for their child if there is no other suitable school within a reasonable distance from home, or the child has a statement of special educational needs naming that school (see pages 85–6 and 232). If a child receives a statement after the normal admission date that names the school, entry must be permitted.

These exceptions may be relied upon only for that school year, after which point the class number must be returned to 30 – for example, by employing another teacher. However, extensions are permitted for children with special educational needs, who will be treated as 'excepted' pupils during their stay in an infant class in a mainstream school.

Secondary school

Parents of children in the top year at primary school will automatically receive a document explaining transfer arrangements to secondary school within the LEA area. Admission authorities must allow at least six weeks for the parents of children transferring to secondary school to collate information on schools and to arrange visits.

Entry to secondary school is in September. For advice on entry outside the normal time, see opposite.

Grammar school

Entrance to these schools, which are wholly selective by ability, is via the 11-plus examination or equivalent. Some schools vary their requirements according to the age of entry: at 16 this may be by GCSE results, for example. Parents will be sent details in September by their child's primary school if teachers believe the child has the potential to attempt entry, so that his or her name can be entered for the appropriate examination.

Not all children who pass the entrance examination will obtain a place, as these are awarded to children with the highest marks first, and then allotted in decreasing order. Children who pass the exam but have low marks may therefore miss out. The demand for places will dictate the degree to which the school selects – if large numbers of bright children are chasing a small number of places, this will be marked.

Applicants who are not successful will be put on a waiting list. As parents frequently enter children for numerous schools, and subsequently decline offers of places once they have made their final decision, it is possible that children towards the top of a list may be offered a place. However, parents should not bank on this happening. In the meantime, parents whose children have been unsuccessful are entitled to appeal (see page 243).

Because grammar schools select only according to academic ability, they are permitted to keep places empty if there are insufficient pupils of the required standard to fill them. If a grammar school is named in the statement of a child with special educational needs, the governing body must admit that child.

From September 2001, local parents may petition to change selection procedures (see pages 35–6).

Admission to state school outside the normal year of entry

Children whose parents have expressed a preference on the application form may join a class outside the normal year of entry, provided the class size is below the published admission number applicable to that age group (see page 227). In this case, an admission authority may not claim that this prejudices the provision of efficient education or use of resources. The same rule applies if the parents can prove that the school's accommodation and/or resources have expanded since publication of the admission number.

As British service families are subject to postings at short notice, LEAs and admission authorities in areas likely to be significantly affected must ensure that suitable measures are in place to provide education for any children of those families when required.

Admission complaints

Grievances concerning general admission policy and specific cases may be respectively directed to either an independent adjudicator or an appeals panel.

The adjudicator

The School Standards and Framework Act set up the Office of the Schools Adjudicator, which has a team of 16 independent adjudicators whose aim is to resolve disputes concerning local admission authorities.

Adjudicators hear complaints on wider aspects of admission policy and practice. Parents' complaints can be heard only if they are submitted by more than 10 families of primary-age children living within three miles of a relevant school who feel that selection is partial or are unhappy about the continued selection process – for example, grounds might exist if children were being denied admission locally and as a result had to travel unreasonable distances to another school.

The adjudicator in effect exercises ultimate control over the admission policy for an area. He or she must take all the local educational interests into account, and determine whether the selective process is detrimental to the provision of efficient education and to parental choice. The adjudicator can direct an admission authority to cease a policy of partial selection, if necessary. The adjudicator's decision is final and binding and can be challenged by judicial review only.

Adjudicators cannot challenge grammar-school selection

Although adjudicators may rule on disputes concerning grammar-school admission arrangements, they may not question the schools' policy of selection according to academic ability.

The appeals panel

An admission authority must by law set up an independent panel of up to five people which will hear appeals that relate to individual admissions only.

You may appeal to this body if your child has been refused a place, unless:

- your son or daughter has been permanently excluded from two or more schools, in which case your right of appeal is suspended for a period of two years from the last exclusion
- your child has a statement of special educational needs and your complaint concerns a school named in that statement or the lack of a named school, in which case you should consult the special educational needs tribunal (see page 86).

The panel is permitted to reverse a refusal of a place on the grounds of class-size prejudice, if it is satisfied that the refusal was unreasonable or that the published admission arrangements were not properly implemented. Places won on appeal are included on top of the published standard or admissions number for the school (see pages 226–7).

Where a decision favours the parents, it is binding on the admission authority and governing body. If it goes against the parents, the parents may request a judicial review or an investigation by the Local Government Ombudsman⋆ if they feel that the panel acted improperly or unreasonably.

Governing bodies may appeal to the panel if the LEA directs that a permanently excluded child be admitted to the school.

Warning

It is very unwise to rely on the appeals process to gain admission to a school. Even if a large proportion of appeals are allowed, the number that actually obtains a place may be very small – for example, at one school in 1998 only 3 out of a total of 113 appeals were successful.

The flow chart on pages 236–7 summarises the stages of the appeals process.

Admission procedures at independent schools

Chapter 3 describes the different types of independent school. Admission policies can vary enormously in the independent sector and the degree to which a school is selective will depend on demand. Some schools are so over-subscribed that they can afford to set rigorous entrance exams or even to impose an IQ level below which they will not consider a child (see page 48). At less popular schools, selection may be more relaxed and the parents' finances will be a key factor. In this case, an interview may be the only admission requirement.

Unlike that of the state sector, a first-come, first-served approach operates to some extent. The demand for some independent schools is so great that you may find it necessary to register your child's name at birth. However, competition is not this intense throughout the sector. Some schools may require only a year's notice while at others parents may be able to place their child at the last minute.

Unlike state schools, independent schools do not limit their intake to a specific geographical area, while boarding schools admit pupils from all over the UK and abroad (see Chapter 4).

Many schools offer scholarships and awards to entrants (these are described in Chapter 17).

Tip

Because independent schools differ greatly in their admission arrangements, when asking for a prospectus you should request details of the admission policy and the age at which children should be registered. You might also want to ask about the pupil numbers for the last three to four years. These will indicate whether the school population is stable, expanding or declining.

Pre-school level

A wide range of childcare and educational facilities is available in the private sector. The types of provision are described on pages 43–52.

Pre-prep school

For these schools, admission is usually by interview, although a few schools receive such a large number of applications that they can afford to be choosy, and therefore set tests.

Prep school

If your child's pre-prep school is a department of a prep school, entry to the upper school should be automatic, although some such prep schools impose entrance tests and/or interviews. If the prep school is not affiliated to a pre-prep school, admission may be via either of these methods. As there is no set formula, you should check with each individual school.

Secondary school

Entry to senior school is normally via the Common Entrance examination. However, some schools set their own papers, so you should establish what is required. If a prep and senior school are under the same management, the transition may be automatic.

Tip

If you have set your sights on the independent sector, keep your options open by registering with more than one school. It may be expensive, but it is advisable. The desperation of parents to get their children into good state schools is widely recognised; it is less well known that popular independent schools can also become over-subscribed, with the result that some children lose out. A number of parents have resorted to fast footwork to gain entry (see overleaf).

Religious schools

The religious affiliation of a school can have a significant influence on its admission policy. Some schools adopt stringent rules in line with their religious foundation, while financially driven schools might admit a majority who belong to that religion but cater for all denominations. If places have to be filled, no child is likely to be turned away because of his or her religious inclinations, or lack of them.

At schools with a religious basis, the organisation, teaching programme and timetable may all reflect the prevailing faith. Check at the outset whether this is likely to conflict with your own beliefs.

Fraudulent entry

Some parents in both the state and independent sectors have been known to go to amazing lengths when devising plans to ensure that their child gets a school place. However, there is a fine line between taking the initiative and cheating, and schools come down hard on those who practise deception. The following example is taken from the private sector, but such behaviour is not confined to private schools (see also pages 228–9).

Gemma

Gemma's determination knew no bounds. After her son was refused a place at an academic school where the competition was stiff, she chose to ignore the verdict. Kitting out her son in the uniform of that school, she took him along on the first day of term, found the classroom for his age group and sat him in it. It was a few days before it was realised that he was not a registered pupil, but by that stage it was felt unfair to oust the boy and so he was allowed to remain.

Parents should note that schools are now keeping a sharper lookout for this type of ruse.

Checklist for school admission

(1) Try to plan the pattern of education for your child as early as possible. You might want to take advantage of the ties between some nursery and primary schools and between 'feeder' primaries and secondary schools. In the independent system, this applies to pre-prep, prep and secondary schools with close links.

(2) Religious schools in both sectors often reserve a proportion of places for pupils who actively practise that religion. You may be able to benefit from this.

(3) If references are required in support of your application to a state school – from the head teacher or church, for example – make sure these are sent in on time. They could work in your favour if over-subscription criteria are to be applied.

(4) If medical or social circumstances dictate that your child be given preference at a particular school in either sector, ensure that you attach any letters from your doctor or social worker to support your application.

(5) Be sure to declare your first-choice state school on the application form – these are allocated first.

Chapter 17

The costs of schooling

Most of this chapter concerns parents considering fee-charging schools in the independent sector; however, parents whose children are in the state system will also incur costs, which they may not have been expecting.

Costs in the state sector

State schools do not charge for tuition. Parents must nevertheless pay for extras – such as uniform, travel and optional activities – which in some cases look remarkably akin to 'backdoor charging', since they effectively have no choice in the matter. The major expenses are listed on pages 262–7.

Donations

The government supplies all state schools with funds for resources such as books and ICT equipment, and may grant lump sums to facilitate the implementation of educational directives such as the literacy strategy (see page 198). This funding is for basic educational tools, and may be insufficient to cover other needs. As a result, an increasing number of schools have been operating a system of voluntary donations from parents. Parents often feel obliged to make whatever donation they can manage, or to contribute towards school appeals (see page 261). Some parents pay as much as £500 per year, while those with low incomes pay nothing. Parents may also have to provide their own children with the textbooks needed for their education (see page 200).

State boarding schools

In the case of state boarding schools (see pages 39–40), parents are required to pay for the boarding element. However, some of these schools offer scholarships and bursaries. Although no one is likely to escape paying any fees at all, there are quite a few ways of keeping these to a minimum (see below in the section on independent schools).

Education maintenance allowance

The government introduced this scheme to benefit youngsters from lower-income families, who are 20 per cent less likely to be in education or training than those from better-off households. The scheme effectively pays teenagers to receive an education. It offers 16- to 18-year-olds a grant of up to £30 or £40 per week (depending on area) to encourage them to stay on at school. To ensure that the recipient pursues an education, pupil and parents must sign a 'learning agreement' with the school or college.

The allowance is means-tested on the parents' income. The maximum grant will be awarded to pupils whose household income is below £13,000, while the allowance will be tapered for those with incomes between £13,000 and £30,000. The scheme was launched in September 1999 in Bolton, Nottingham, Cornwall, Doncaster, Gateshead, Leeds, Middlesbrough, Oldham, Southampton, Stoke-on-Trent and Walsall LEAs and the London boroughs of Lambeth, Lewisham, Southwark and Greenwich. It is expected to run for three years and if successful will be extended nationally. To find out whether you qualify for education maintenance allowance, check with your LEA.

Costs in the independent sector

School fees are the main cost in this sector. These vary widely, depending on whether the school is day or boarding, senior or junior, and may be influenced by the 'going rate' in a particular area. Chapter 3 outlines typical charges at each sort of school. Parents will also have to pay for extras, and may be asked to contribute to appeals (see pages 261–7). Despite the expense, many parents are prepared to make sacrifices in order to buy what they hope will be the best possible start for their children.

Paying for school fees

There is no guarantee that your child will win a scholarship or be granted some other form of financial help (see pages 255–61). It is advisable to prepare for paying full school fees as early as possible – preferably at least three years before your child starts school, and maybe even when your child is newborn.

Warning

Even though schools attempt to keep fee increases to a minimum, you must be ready to see fees rise faster than the rate of inflation. In the late 1990s, fees have risen by about 5–6 per cent per year. Fee increases are often announced by schools at the last moment during the summer term, so make sure you calculate for an increase each year to ensure that you are not taken by surprise.

If you cannot find ways of cutting the cost of fees and you do not think that you will be able to meet the fees out of your monthly income, the options open to you will depend on how soon you will have to start paying the fees.

If you have time to plan ahead, it is worth doing so even if you do not manage to save the full cost of the fees. Although you can use specially designed school-fee plans, there is no particular reason to do so: they are simply a way of investing money in order to make a set of payments some time in the future.

School-fee plans may take the hassle out of planning for school fees – and introduce an element of discipline to your savings – but you could just as easily come up with a do-it-yourself plan using other investments. Which you choose will depend on:

- how long there is to go before you have to start paying the fees
- how much risk you are prepared to take with your money
- how flexible you want to be about how you eventually use the money

- whether you can commit yourself to saving on a regular basis and your tax position
- whether you have a lump sum to invest.

You will find practical guidance on choosing suitable investments and savings plans in *The Which? Guide to Money* and *Which? Way to Save and Invest*, both available from Which? Books.★ You could also consult an independent financial adviser (contact IFA Promotion★ and/or the Money Management National Register of Fee-based Advisers★ for a list of local advisers), or the Association of Investment Trust Companies.★

Tip

One very good reason for avoiding specially packaged school-fee plans is that they are usually insurance-based (they are also called endowment policies). These require a commitment to save a fixed amount of money for a fixed amount of time – typically ten years. If you fail to keep your savings going for the length of time required, you may find that the money you have put aside is worth less than you have paid in. You should definitely avoid these plans if you cannot save on a regular basis, or if there is a chance that you will have to stop or reduce your savings – your income falls when another child is on the way, for example.

If you have a lump sum that you can set aside for school fees, as well as investing it you may have the option of pre-paying fees if you have a particular school in mind. The bursar of the school will be able to tell you if the school runs what are often called 'composition fee schemes'. The advantages are that you may be able to buy fees at today's prices; the disadvantage is that if your child does not pass the entrance exam, you may find that you get back less than you

---

Tip

Many schools permit and even encourage parents to pay school fees by monthly direct debit. Ask if this option is available, as it will enable you to spread payments throughout the year.

---

handed over, unless you can use the money towards fees for another child.

Children's savings

Other ways of coping with fees include creating a trust funded by grandparents or family friends, or making other savings on behalf of the child. As soon as your child is born, he or she is a potential taxpayer and consequently has his or her own tax-free slice of income in the form of a personal allowance. What income can be included in this tax-free slice depends on who donates the money. Gifts of money from friends and family count as the child's income (ask them to send a letter confirming the gift if it is a large amount). If you invest this money, it is likely to be tax-free provided you invest in the child's name. The exception is income from share-based investments, where tax has already been paid by the time the income reaches the child and cannot be reclaimed. If you want to save substantial amounts in your child's name, go for tax-free investments or those that produce capital gains, such as gilts or share investments.

Borrowing to pay for fees

If you do not have the time to plan ahead, and you cannot meet the cost of fees from your income, you will need to borrow to pay the fees (for advice on cutting the cost of borrowing, consult *The Which? Guide to Money* from Which? Books).*

One of the cheapest ways of borrowing can be to re-mortgage your home, which means increasing the size of your mortgage. However, this will be possible only if the lender values your home at a figure which is greater than the total amount you need to borrow. Be wary of extending your mortgage if you will find it difficult to keep up the mortgage repayments, because you risk losing your home.

Affinity cards

Some schools operate an affinity card in conjunction with a bank, which offers parents a credit card with an interest-bearing current account and cheque book. School fees can be paid at the beginning of term with the card and then paid off against parents' monthly statements. The school receives a donation of, say, £5 for each cardholder and a percentage of the amount spent on the card. This is a neat way of raising funds, and is a means of avoiding controversial appeals (see page 261). However, you should compare the annual percentage rate (APR) – the total charge for credit expressed as a percentage – with normal credit-card deals.

Deposits and fees in lieu

Parents should be aware of these two conventions employed by independent schools. In a worse-case scenario, they could leave you out of pocket or even lacking a school.

Deposits

An independent secondary school may ask you to pay a lump-sum deposit by way of confirmation that your child is to join the school. This is usually required a couple of terms before the September entry, but sometimes as much as a year in advance. The amount should be deducted from the first term's fees, but you may find that some schools like to hold on to your money until the very last term, with no interest accruing. This is dangerous: should the school fall foul of its contract with you, you will find it difficult to get your money back and you may have to resort to legal action; and if the school should go into liquidation, you will lose your money for good.

The excuse sometimes made is that this deposit is to cover the cost of possible extras incurred. It is fair to say that some parents do try to default on the payment of the final term's bill, so schools have learned to be wary. However, in most cases the amount vastly exceeds the average extras bill. You should resist this demand firmly and, if the school does not like it and you have a choice, take your money elsewhere. Not all schools require a deposit; some even disapprove of them.

If your child is entered for a scholarship, no financial demand should be made of you beforehand. However, many schools try to get an irreversible commitment from you before they mete out the scholarship awards. This will put you at an obvious disadvantage. If you receive such a demand, do not pay: simply explain politely that if your child does not obtain a suitable award, your finances may force you to reconsider alternatives.

Patricia

Patricia complained bitterly that she had made the wrong strategic move. Having been categorically promised an award for her son after he gained outstanding Common Entrance results, she did not wait for the school's letter offering an award, but paid her deposit. Within 24 hours, she received an apologetic letter to say that there was no money available, by which point it was too late to retrieve her deposit.

Gambling on getting a good deal

If you don't have to make a final commitment to a school until the very last moment, don't – it will weaken your hand. However, you cannot employ this strategy with every school: some – those that are very sought-after – hold all the aces. Nor is a free-for-all system of bartering advocated. If you cannot reduce schooling costs by playing your cards right, you might be eligible for assistance from the school, the LEA or other bodies (see 'Other reductions', pages 260–1).

Fees in lieu

The ramifications of the 'fees in lieu' code operated by independent schools are many and various. If you wish to remove your child to another school, for whatever reason, you are required to give one term's notice, or pay a term's fees in lieu. If you do not pay and you become embroiled in a dispute with the first school, the second school will not be able to accept your child because it is obliged by the regulations of the organisations listed on page 42 to refuse you. You could therefore end up without a school. In view of this financial sanction, choosing the wrong school can hit your wallet badly, as well as being disruptive for your child.

If you are removing your child because of breach of contract on the part of the school, your position becomes untenable. Do you work out a term's notice when the recipient of your money is in breach and your child faces the possibility of unhappiness, or do you take the child away and threaten litigation, which could jeopardise your acceptance at another school? The only way round this is to stick to your guns with the head and be so determined and unyielding (within civilised bounds) that the school will be glad to jettison you. The key sentence to listen out for is 'I suggest you remove your child', or words to that effect: this absolves you from notice since, from a legal point of view, it is at the school's request. However, before you advance down this route, make sure you have selected another school, explained your problems to the new head, and are as sure as you can be that you and the new head are both on the same wavelength. You may hear the standard phrase: 'I cannot accept you if you are in dispute.' Just make it clear that this matter should be left to you and that there will be no dispute with the previous school.

Unjust though it may be, for the time being parents are stuck with this situation. In law, your remedy for breach of contract is in damages: in independent education, 'if they breach, you pay'. A viable solution needs to be worked out by schools to prevent unpleasant encounters – for example, perhaps the first term's fees could be paid into an interest-bearing holding account, to be paid back if a dispute is settled in your favour by independent arbitration.

Until a solution is established, you are advised to bin any school prospectus containing an inflexible stress on the 'fees in lieu' clause.

Some schools use marketing ploys, such as proposing to refund a percentage of fees if a pupil is not accepted by a university after A-levels. This is not a sound reason on which to base your choice of school, and you have no guarantee of holding the school to its promise.

Scholarships and other awards

Many fee-charging schools offer awards to talented pupils. These alleviate or even entirely remove school fees. Scholarships and exhibitions are generally awarded on merit following a competitive test. They may be given for academic or practical subjects, the performing arts, sport or all-round ability: the exact number and type will vary according to the school. Competition among candidates can be intense. Awards are normally held for the duration of a child's time at school, although if his or her performance deteriorates they may be withdrawn.

Scholarships are open to children throughout the UK and are offered mostly by secondary schools for first-year or sixth-form entry, although some prep schools operate a limited number. The monetary value varies considerably from school to school, and in a small number of cases may cover the full fees. Exhibitions (minor scholarships) may be granted as a result of Common Entrance examination (see page 52), and some schools will state that they reserve awards for children who excel in this exam. Awards may also be granted at the governors' discretion, if they feel a pupil deserves recognition.

Most such awards are won on merit in recognition of the recipients' ability. However, some may be bestowed as a result of behind-the-scenes dealings between parents and school heads or governors. The value of these awards may depend on the school's current financial circumstances.

How to increase your child's chances of an award

Your main concern is likely to be finding a school that suits your son or daughter and meets your academic and practical requirements. However, if you are seeking value for money you may want to investigate ways to reduce the fees at schools that satisfy those criteria. This could include targeting schools that appear to offer an increased likelihood of your child getting a scholarship or other award.

If you plan to do this, first decide which schools to focus on. One with a long waiting list and highly competitive entry requirements is unlikely to release an award in your child's direction unless he or she has something special to offer it in return. However, you may find that scope for negotiation exists at schools affected by either or both of the following factors:

- **geographical location** can be significant in determining a school's attitude. A large number of rural schools, particularly boarding schools, have experienced difficulties maintaining pupil numbers and consequently have introduced more flexible entry requirements. At these schools, fee increases may have been kept to a minimum – often below the inflation rate – in an attempt to stall or reverse the decline in the school population
- **financial circumstance** During the boom years of the 1980s, when school fees rose by as much as 10 per cent a year, some

schools became over-ambitious, undertaking costly expansion schemes and other financial commitments. In the wake of the recession of the early 1990s, some have found that the commitments have not disappeared as quickly as some fee-paying parents.

At such schools the methods employed to attract pupils are often quite ingenious, as the schools are compelled to offer incentives that are superior to those of the competition. Since this creates what is essentially a 'buyer's market', parents are at an advantage.

Trying for more than one award

In one of the Codes of Practice laid down by the Headmasters' and Headmistresses' Conference (HMC)★ and the Incorporated Association of Preparatory Schools (IAPS)★ it states that no child may become a candidate for an award at more than one school without permission and that, if given an award at one school, he or she may not become or continue to be a contender at any other school without permission. However, in practice schools do not strictly enforce this ruling.

Kate

Kate failed to achieve a scholarship to the senior school that owned her prep school. She subsequently sat a scholarship exam to another school and won an award. As a result, she was offered the scholarship previously denied to her because the first school considered some fees better than none.

Joshua

Joshua's parents wanted him to attend a certain secondary school. A separate secondary school, which had a surplus of empty places, offered Joshua a 'scholarship' purely on the strength of his performance in a test taken two months before its official scholarship exams, causing understandable dismay among the scholarship competitors. Joshua's parents, disgusted by the school's behaviour, refused to collude. However, their son now had an award which they could declare to their first-choice school.

Trying for more than one award may give the parents a certain amount of bargaining power, depending on their child's success. However, schools will want to know that awards from competing establishments have been turned down before they are prepared to offer a scholarship.

Identifying the best scholarship routes

Some schools provide a more congenial climate in which to gain an award, either because they offer good tuition or have an affiliation with another school.

When visiting a prep school, pay particular attention to the types of awards listed on the scholarship and exhibition boards, and note the names of the secondary schools that have granted awards to graduating prep-school pupils. Focus on the last 10–15 years, not the 'dark ages'. From the quantity and type of awards listed you should be able to judge the effectiveness of the scholarship tuition at the prep school (see below).

Check that the tenor of the awards matches up with any information about subject provision – for example, if the school magazine has devoted a great deal of space to school choirs, bands and concerts but the walls do not boast any music scholarships, you should be cautious.

The number of pupils a prep school 'feeds' into a secondary school can dictate the number and quality of awards granted by that secondary school. Some large prep schools expect a certain number of awards each year from the senior schools they supply. This situation is compounded in the case of schools with financial links or those that are under the same management structure.

One of the major selling points a prep school can claim is close links with a senior school. Not only might the prep school be able to

---

Tip

If your child is at pre-prep stage and your sights are already set on a specific secondary school, consider its main feeder schools carefully. This will enable you to work out which prep school is most likely to procure an award and may therefore provide the best long-term chance for fulfilling your goal.

---

offer automatic entry to the senior school, but parents may be enticed to choose it on the basis that it captures the lion's share of awards.

The operating methods of schools without immediately recognisable connections are less obvious. However, close analysis of the awards may indicate a relationship which you can then confirm with the head.

Preparation for scholarship exams

Methods vary at different schools, so you should ensure that your child is adequately prepared. At prep-school level, staff might refuse to prepare your son or daughter for scholarship exams to an outside school using different methods from those required to gain entry to the linked senior school. Alternatively, a school might fail to prime your child at all – one pre-prep headmistress claims that she does not bother to prepare children for scholarship exams to prep school at all: 'They can either do it, or they can't!'

If you are in any doubt about the school's methods, take the precaution of obtaining previous scholarship papers and go through them with your child. You could also consider home tuition (see page 209).

Common ruses employed in relation to awards

The operation of most scholarship schemes is fair and legitimate. However, leeway for a certain amount of machination does exist, and the giving and withholding of awards can arouse in parents and schools feelings of mutual suspicion and antagonism. Some parents feel that many scholarship or exhibition prizes are merely dangled as a carrot, especially by prep schools. Meanwhile, schools are wise to scheming on the part of parents and are adept at sizing up their financial status early on. The behaviour listed below is not unusual.

- Prep-school heads have been known to persuade senior schools to give awards by threatening their removal from the list of schools recommended to parents.
- Parents have threatened to send children elsewhere unless they receive an award, or demanded one with the threat that they will otherwise remove younger siblings from the linked junior school.
- Some schools console parents whose child has missed a scholarship

with praise about the child's exceptional ability. Suitably flattered, the parents pay for a place at the school.

- Parents avid to secure a scholarship for their offspring dress down for their interview in clothing from a charity shop or jumble sale.

Foundation awards

Foundation awards are scholarships that are available only to children within a certain category, usually those who live locally. The school's founding document will state the criteria and number of awards that can be made in any one year. Foundation awards are usually based on an assessment of the parents' income and applicants' results following an examination or the school's scholarship papers. Parents should contact the school to find out whether they are eligible for a foundation award.

If you are unable to obtain a scholarship, there may be alternative ways to reduce fees.

Bursaries

Most schools operate a bursary scheme as an alternative or addition to the arrangements described above. At the time of writing, the amount of money allocated to bursaries exceeds that donated to scholarships. Bursaries are a reduction in fees, potentially of 15 per cent or more. They can be awarded following Common Entrance exam results or if your child achieves a certain academic standard but are generally based on parents' financial circumstances. Such schemes are an attempt by some schools to target families that need assistance. Sometimes this criterion is very loosely applied and a certain amount of bargaining can take place, particularly with rural boarding schools. Some schools have told parents not to make a final decision in favour of another school without first discussing the matter with them, as a bursary could be accommodated.

Other reductions

Reductions for siblings are common, often ranging from 10 to 20 per cent. Depending on bargaining ability and luck, further reductions might also be negotiated; for example, a huge reduction was achieved by parents who demanded and won education for two of their children for the price of one. Failing that, it may be possible to negotiate payment by instalments, or gain a reduction if you are an old boy or girl of the school. Some schools offer a reduction, often substantial, in fees for pupils living within a certain radius of the school.

Others offer boarding on an *ad hoc* basis, which offers convenience without the committment of full termly fees.

Help may be available from certain employers, the clergy and some professional organisations – further details should be sought from the relevant body. Government grants may be available for the children of members of the Diplomatic Service or the armed forces, or for those with special needs. Note that such financial help may be viewed as a taxable perk, so check with your tax office. However, tax on the benefit will still cost less than paying the fees yourself.

Lists of the charities and trusts that provide educational grants are published in *The Directory of Grant-making Trusts* and *The Education Grants Directory*, which you should find in your local library.

The demise of the assisted places scheme

The assisted places scheme was designed to help pay the school fees of bright children from homes with low incomes. The subsidy was worth £200 million a year before it was abolished by the Labour government. Many private schools have tried to replace the scheme by offering scholarships, bursaries or foundation awards instead. However, the scheme's passing has resulted in the social mix at some independent schools becoming more narrow since many are forced to target parents who can afford the increasingly expensive fees. An ISIS survey in spring 1999 revealed that the number of children entering those private schools which belonged to the scheme from the state sector is dropping: in 1998, 34 per cent of pupils were from state schools; in 1999 this fell to 31.3 per cent with further falls expected.

School appeals

Appeals, common in both sectors, are not in themselves bad news. Many school promotions launched to provide new facilities and update others are organised in an enthusiastic and sensible way. Parents involved in raising funds for IT equipment, books, musical instruments and special needs or sports equipment might be seen undertaking parachute jumps, sitting in a supermarket trolley while being pushed at breakneck speed around car parks, or, more sedately, bidding in special auctions where articles or services have been offered free of charge. School fêtes, and 'bring and buy' events – for example, sales of garden plants – provide an effective way of involving the community outside school and persuading people to part with cash for a good cause.

The downside of appeals

Despite what may be described as initial enthusiasm, appeals often attract censure. Often, the plans are grandiose and the target figure over-ambitious. All the energies of the school may be focused on raising money, rather than concentrating on the job of education, and you might find corners being cut where they should not be. Pressure tends to hit the kitchens first, with the quality and quantity of food deteriorating. This may be followed by other annoyances affecting the incumbent children and parents.

The following examples show what can happen when things get out of control.

- Members of an appeal committee of one school organised a telephone rota to contact parents and demand contributions. Parents paid up to be left alone, yet regardless of their donations the very next term's fees were increased by 14 per cent.

Schools can build castles in the air

Many a school has crumbled in the face of mounting debt under-taken with reckless ambition to fulfil a pet fantasy. When being shown round a school, beware the words 'We shall be building . . .'. Ask: 'How is this to be paid for?' If you receive the answer 'Out of existing school funds', you can relax. If the question is avoided or the answer is that an appeal will be launched, watch out. You may end up being badgered for a donation.

- Another school with an appeal fund did not even bother to play this game, but increased its fees by 10 per cent two terms running, with the second 10 per cent being calculated on the increased figure – a move disguised in the wording – thus totalling an increase of more than 20 per cent in a single year.
- One set of parents who were persuaded to donate towards expensive facilities saw everything disappear as the school went into liquidation, only to be faced by another appeal two years later at their child's next school.

Extras

Often not given the consideration they deserve, such expenses apply to all types of school in both sectors.

In accordance with the Education Reform Act, each LEA and each state school must have a policy on charging. The primary object is to maintain the right to free school education and to ensure that activities in normal school time are available to all, regardless of financial status or willingness to make a voluntary contribution. Schools may charge for optional activities provided wholly or mainly outside school hours, such as after-school clubs (see pages 209–11). Details can be obtained from individual schools.

Although some independent schools claim to make a completely inclusive charge, extras always accrue and can add a substantial amount to the bill. Ask the school for a rough breakdown of probable costs.

School uniform

While many state schools have reverted to a uniform policy in a quest for improved discipline and to encourage bonding and allegiance, independent schools have started relaxing their rules. A few have dispensed with uniforms altogether, although the wearing of a uniform is generally obligatory in this sector.

Nursery schools in both sectors tend not to impose uniform rules, but with children aged five onwards expenditure on uniform is likely to increase.

The compulsory purchase of uniform items from the school shop or designated outfitters can form a significant addition to the bill –

particularly when many schools seem to adopt a cavalier approach to the cost of these garments by specifying large numbers of the same item.

Tip

Ask for a uniform list and enquire whether it is possible to buy second-hand clothes – many schools and some groups of parents run second-hand shops. If you buy from these outlets you can make a substantial saving, particularly if your child regularly wears out certain items – your son gets through a lot of rugby shirts, for example. Alternatively, high-street stores may stock general uniform items such as shirts, skirts, jumpers and trousers for local schools.

Parents of children at state secondary schools who receive income support, income-based jobseekers' allowance, family credit or disability working allowance may claim a small uniform allowance, normally at two-yearly intervals. Grants may also be available for essential clothing and footwear. You can obtain forms from the school or LEA.

There is an increasing tendency in boarding schools for formal uniform to be worn only during classroom hours, with home clothes permitted at other times. This arrangement will, of course, suit your child admirably, but you will be faced not only with a school uniform bill, but also the prospect of equipping your child for the school fashion parade. The freedom to wear what one pleases may be a mixed blessing: when the uniform rule is relaxed, it can be a nuisance having to decide what to wear in the morning.

Examination entry fees

Parents are required to pay examination entry fees at independent schools. At state schools, pupils' first examination attempts are paid for, but subsequent sittings if they fail may not be.

In 1999, the charges for GCSE and A-level subjects were £19.50 and £40 respectively. Modular A-levels (see page 166) are charged on a module basis. A-levels with a practical or performance element, such as music (£50 in 1998), are more expensive than other subjects.

Travelling expenses

These can be significant. It is advisable to calculate your likely fuel costs if you plan to take your child to and from school by car. Choosing a boarding school may mean that you travel greater distances, albeit less often (see page 64). Some schools allow pupils in the sixth form to drive themselves into school. In outlying areas this may be convenient in the case of, for example, parents who are farmers and do not have time to drive their child to school.

A further consideration for those opting for the state sector is that if you have succeeded in getting your child into a school of your choice which is not within the catchment area designated by local admission authorities (see page 228), you are unlikely to find transport laid on by the school – you must provide this yourself or use public transport.

The law stipulates that transport to school should be free where a pupil attends either a school within the catchment area, or the one outside that catchment area nearest to his or her home, provided the home address is beyond a stipulated distance. This distance is two miles for children up to the age of eight, and three miles for those of eight years and over. It is measured using the shortest available walking route between home and school. Some pupils living within the statutory distance may also be provided with free transport for medical reasons.

As the type of transport laid on differs from LEA to LEA, it is advisable to ask your local authority what you can rely upon.

- You may be able to purchase a spare seat in a bus or minibus, if one operates, on a concessionary basis.
- Travel passes for use on public transport may be issued to students aged 11–16 who face a journey of over three miles, provided they attend the nearest suitable school.
- Post-16 students may be required to contribute towards the cost of travel, unless their parents are receiving state benefits.

An item that is not strictly an extra, but one some parents may regard as such, is the cost of buying your way into your first-choice school by moving house to the relevant catchment area. Many parents

Checklist for school costs

(1) At schools in both sectors, ask for a list of 'extras', including a uniform list, if applicable.

(2) In the state system, parents may be entitled to uniform allowance, while some children may qualify for free meals (see page 127) and 16- to 18-year-olds may be eligible for education maintenance allowance.

(3) Ensure that your child has adequate insurance cover, and check the attitude of the school towards your making a claim.

(4) In both sectors, ask about school appeals: are any running at present or likely to be launched in the foreseeable future, and if so, in aid of what?

(5) Ask relevant organisations and employers whether they provide any financial assistance towards independent-school fees.

(6) At a prep school, independent secondary school or state boarding school, find out what scholarships and awards are available from that school, and what awards have been granted to pupils joining senior schools. In the latter case, the schools that grant the prizes will be a more reliable source of information.

(7) Check on the possibility of a bursary or foundation award at the same schools.

(8) Find out what scholarship tuition is provided at the independent school your child currently attends, and ask whether it has experience of coaching children for competitive entrance exams to any of the senior schools you are considering. Keep a close eye on things if the school offers little or no preparation. Take the precaution of obtaining past scholarship papers and go through them with your child, or consider appointing a home tutor.

(9) Check with the school that any scholarship entry forms have been completed and sent off in time.

(10) Check whether any special relationships exist between your child's current independent school and the senior schools you have targeted.

(11) At independent schools, ask whether a deposit is required and when this is payable. If you are being pressurised to pay a deposit, check whether there is any likelihood of a scholarship entry. Prep schools can forget to tell parents when a deadline approaches. A deposit already paid can influence a scholarship result.

who are not prepared to accept what they regard as a less than ideal school place are now pursuing this option.

Additional expenses

Extra subjects such as music lessons, technology project materials, theatre expeditions or other educational trips will add to the end-of-term bill, and you will find an item for 'matron's sundries' if your child boards. At boarding schools, it may be necessary to buy a computer for your child's personal use in his or her study bedroom. Chapter 15 describes some of the extra-curricular activities that may entail extra expense.

Insurance cover

Whatever the type of school, you are advised to take out your own insurance cover for any valuable items your child has at school. A school will have its own cover for valuable items belonging to a third party while on their premises, but you could be hard pressed to pursue this successfully.

In order for a school to claim on its insurance policy in the event of loss or damage, usually a police report must be filed. Most heads will have no qualms about calling in the police if a theft is suspected. However, depending on the circumstances a school may attempt to prevent this since such reports are open to the scrutiny of local newspaper reporters.

If the school refuses to report a stolen or damaged item, it is not a straightforward matter of calling in the police yourself. You could find that the school continues to deny the accusation, and the police

---

Head's two-faced trickery

One head teacher told a parent whose child's property suffered vandalism that it was a pity the school had insurance cover only for theft, not vandalism ... and then told another parent whose child had experienced theft exactly the reverse.

---

may be inclined to believe it unless you can provide concrete proof, or witnesses. You may also have to take into account the possibility of your child being victimised if you stand your ground.

When arranging your own cover, it might be possible to extend your household contents policy. For more information, see *The Which? Guide to Insurance*, available from Which Books.★

Chapter 18

Compiling information on schools

It is a good idea to compile a dossier on the schools you may be considering in order to assess suitable candidates and establish which meet your requirements. This will mean sending off for literature from a variety of sources. If you wish to keep your options open, it is advisable to apply for details from both sectors.

Tip

You can get an impression of what a school's pupils are achieving, and their wider interests, by obtaining the school magazine/ newletter. Many schools now have their own web sites on the Internet which provide general information.

State schools

Your local Social Services department and the Daycare Trust* can provide you with information about childcare and playgroups in your area. Most of the information you require should be available from the LEA.

Information from the LEA

Your local LEA will provide you with a list of nursery schools and primary schools with nursery units. At primary and secondary level, you should contact your LEA before approaching the schools. Make sure you are supplied with all the information it is able to divulge, including the education directory or equivalent for the area. Even if your immediate concern is the nursery or primary age group, it is still worth requesting information on transfer arrangements to secondary school. It can be helpful to find out whether linked or 'feeder' primary schools are operated. With knowledge of all the variations controlling admissions to secondary school, you will be much better placed to take advantage of any over-subscription criteria (see pages 227–30) and to plan a coherent educational path for your child.

The type of information sent out to parents by individual LEAs varies. Apart from the statutory requirements, such as the obligation to publish a prospectus (see pages 225–6 and opposite), it is up to the LEA to decide what constitutes useful information for parents. You may have to do some prompting to ensure that you receive all the relevant material.

Performance tables

Your next step should be to examine the local school performance tables. While some LEAs will send these out to you, others will tell you to find these at your local library. You should make an effort to read the tables. They include independent as well as state schools and will provide you with invaluable basic information on which to plan your strategy. Chapter 12 explains the background to the tables.

Tip

You may find that after identifying a suitable secondary school, the best strategy is to work backwards and identify the primary school that affords the optimum chance of gaining entry to that secondary school.

Ofsted reports

Your public library will contain a selection of Ofsted inspection reports, which are explained in Chapter 6. You may find it useful to read through these before contacting the schools: one of their purposes is to give parents extra information (make sure the reports are not out of date).

Schools are supposed to send copies of the full reports to libraries, but some libraries may not hold all the inspection reports for the local area. If you wish to read more than the summary normally sent out from the school, you can access reports on the Internet (see page 98) or alternatively obtain a copy from the school for a small charge.

The prospectus

Once you have identified the schools that interest you most, contact them direct and ask for their prospectus and any other relevant material.

Some prospectuses have wide-ranging coverage and will provide answers to many of your initial questions. All state-school prospectuses should explain:

- the aims and values of the school
- the content and organisation of the curriculum
- examination and Key Stage test results
- pastoral care and discipline arrangements
- admission procedures.

Summaries of Ofsted reports will be supplied if they are current. You will also be provided with details of Open Days and Evenings arranged by each school. If you want to see the governors' annual report, you may have to request this specifically (for more on the role of governors, see Chapter 7).

Independent schools

At nursery level, the organisations listed on page 44 can supply you with details.

ISIS★ covers independent schools within its membership. This organisation can put you in touch with a regional representative and provide handbooks containing statistical information on member schools. ISIS also holds exhibitions in some areas which parents may attend.

You will find full details of all independent schools that are not ISIS members in the *Independent Schools Yearbook*. This useful additional source of information can be found at your public library.

Inspection reports are to be made available to all parents in the independent sector for the first time in 2000 (see pages 97–8).

Warning

Many of the descriptions in school guidebooks are provided by the schools themselves. As such publications feature the merits of numerous competing schools, many establishments are tempted to make exaggerated claims about their performance and facilities. Much of this is sales spiel and should be treated with caution.

Using the information you have acquired, list the possibilities and arrange them in descending order according to their *apparent* ability to fulfil your requirements – only by visiting a school can you establish whether it lives up to its description (see Chapter 19).

Tip

If you have made your mind up that your son or daughter should go to your old school, scrutinise your preference very carefully before making a commitment and make comparisons with other establishments. This procedure may confirm your choice; alternatively, if your *alma mater* performs poorly it will have given you the opportunity to examine the alternatives.

The prospectus

Once you have made a list of possible candidates, the next step is to obtain the school prospectus and any other data the school is prepared to divulge, such as sports results and academic analyses.

Although this may enable you to narrow your choice still further, it is worth remembering that a prospectus is a sales document which must be treated with the same scepticism as, for example, property descriptions from estate agents. It is likely that certain elements in the prospectus will have been over-exaggerated or included merely to impress. By the same token, aspects that strike you as unfavourable may in practice be insignificant or non-existent. Hints on checking whether a school matches up to its own description appear on pages 280–1.

Prep and secondary schools will usually send you a list of school personnel with the prospectus. It can be helpful to know how to assess teachers' qualifications – for advice on how to do this, see Chapter 8. In the pre-prep field, it can be difficult to obtain details of staff and qualifications without specifically asking for them. Persist in your enquiries, and do not take it for granted that the teachers will have qualifications.

Prospectus descriptions are not binding

Few parents know that they are required to accept a clause in the school's Standard Terms and Conditions which directly affects the prospectus. This is worded along the following lines:

> Nothing contained in the prospectus shall form part of any agreement between the school and the parents or any other person, and the parents confirm that they have not relied on its contents in entering into this agreement.

In other words, having sent you a prospectus upon which it knows you are likely to rely – and perhaps after you have paid a non-returnable registration fee on the strength of this combined with a verbal interview – the school effectively tells you at the last minute that the major written document in your possession is not worth the paper on which it is written.

Schools have been known to fall back on this clause, using the excuse that 'things have changed' to parents misled by false descriptions in the prospectus. It is important to be aware of this loophole. A simple solution is explained on page 281.

A checklist overleaf summarises the main points to bear in mind when gathering details on schools.

Checklist for compiling information on schools

(1) For state schools, telephone your local LEA and ask for all relevant data on the schools within its area, plus the admission information.

(2) For independent schools, obtain the ISIS handbooks and read the *Independent Schools Yearbook*.

(3) Plot the position of the schools that interest you on a map.

(4) Read the local school performance tables and Ofsted inspection reports.

(5) List likely schools in accordance with your priorities. Select at least three or four. Even if a particular school initially jumps out at you, look carefully at one or two others if only to cement your decision.

(6) Phone the schools to request prospectuses and any additional material that is available. Read these documents carefully, while bearing in mind that their content may not be entirely accurate.

(7) Make a list of any queries you want to raise or points that require clarifying and clip these to each individual prospectus.

(8) Check the schools' admission policies and required age of registration.

Chapter 19

Visiting the school

After you have read the school prospectuses and studied staff lists, exam profiles and sports results, you will be in a better position to appreciate what you will see during the Open Day or Evening. Remember that these events are staged to present the school in the best possible light; an interview with the head can be more valuable in helping to crystallise your opinion of the school.

Tip

Be sure to visit a selection of schools before you make any attempt to decide on your first preference. If you are unable to attend an Open Day or interview but wish to tour an establishment, the school will normally be happy to arrange a personal appointment for you.

A significant difference exists between the independent and state sectors with regard to interview policy. An independent school can interview both you and your child, but a state school is precluded from doing so, with the exception of church schools that wish to assess your religious commitment and state boarding schools that need to assess your child's suitability for boarding. If a state school wishes to conduct an interview, the reasons for this must be published and, in the event that an interview does take place, it may be introduced as evidence in an admission appeal (see pages 242–3). To all intents and purposes, therefore, you may interview a state school, but it may not interview you.

Planning a strategy

Make sure that you visit in term time during normal school hours, and that you allow sufficient time to absorb the atmosphere at the school. The reason for your visit is to judge how suitable the school is for your child, and certain crucial factors that will influence your choice can be ascertained only during a conducted tour while the school day is in progress.

Avoid making the classic mistakes:

- an exploratory casual wander around the school grounds observing pupils and their general behaviour before deciding whether to ask for a formal interview: schools do not appreciate the presence of unescorted strangers. At a primary or prep school you would not get far without being challenged, with embarrassing consequences for yourself
- requesting a conducted tour by a pupil in the hope of obtaining secrets from the horse's mouth: although it might be possible to obtain unguarded remarks from pupils untutored in the 'right' answers, such information is likely to be unspecific and of limited value if you are looking for a critical response. Generally, pupils who give tours to parents are carefully chosen, comport themselves like staff members and refrain from saying anything adverse that could get back to the head.

Tours of the school by the head

When making an appointment, ask whether the head will be conducting the guided tour after your meeting (this duty might alternatively fall to the admission officer, a housemaster or a sixth-form pupil). The answer will enable you to plan your visit and questions more efficiently.

If you are allocated only 20–30 minutes with a clock-watching head teacher, you may be faced with the prospect of condensing an extremely important interview into a very short time and the discussion could be perfunctory. However, if the head is to show you around and spend time with you, the atmosphere will be more relaxed. You will be at leisure to develop a rapport and discuss the points that matter to you in unhurried conversation. Chapter 7 outlines how to assess the character of the head.

Taking your child to visit the school

The state and independent sectors have different policies on children's attendance.

- In the state sector, you are likely to be allowed just one tour of the school in which to form an impression, which will entail your child being present if he or she is old enough. However, if you have arranged a separate personal interview it should be possible for you to visit the school alone.

- Independent schools are likely to be more accommodating and to oblige parents with a second interview. When making an appointment, it is a good idea to ask whether your initial interview may be conducted without your child. If this is allowed, it will enable you to make preliminary investigations and shortlist schools without exposing your child to presentations that could prove tiring. You can then arrange tours with your child at schools that warrant a second look (schools are used to this).

- If you are attending an Open Day in either sector your child's presence is advisable, particularly in the case of older children who will want some input into the decision.

The interview

After following the advice in preceding chapters, you should be in a confident position to control the course of the interview and ensure that your specific concerns are addressed.

Take certain precautions to guarantee that the encounter is productive.

- Before the interview, make a list of key points you wish to clarify and produce this if necessary.

- Do not waste valuable time asking obvious questions – you will get obvious answers. For example, rather than asking whether music or drama are encouraged, ask how this is achieved.

- Steer clear of generalisations such as 'Is the school good at sport?' or 'Are your teachers well-qualified?' If you have studied the information supplied by the school and other sources outlined in Chapter 18, you should already know the answers. Instead, ask questions that relate specifically to your requirements. Be critical.

- Do not ask questions to which you can predict the answers (for example, it is pointless to ask about the supervision of excursions since the school is bound to tell you that all outings are well supervised).

- Do not adopt a submissive attitude and just sit there soaking up the sales spiel – you should not feel so cowed that you are unable to challenge the head. There is no need to accept everything he or she says.
- Do not be embarrassed to raise further questions, if any occur once you have covered the major areas. You do not want to leave the interview wishing you had asked more.
- Politely insist on detailed, on-the-spot answers; if you allow any of your questions to be waved aside you are likely to feel dissatisfied afterwards. If the head is confident about the school, answers should be positive and to the point. Be wary of responses that appear to gloss over issues or feed you what you want to hear.

You should temper your approach and your level of questioning to what you feel you can get away with. Not all questions will be relevant to all schools and at others you may feel that the atmosphere precludes pointed enquiries. However, as a consumer you are entitled to pursue all lines of enquiry in the interests of obtaining the best deal for your child, especially if you will be paying fees for the privilege. Being outspoken may pay dividends in the end.

You might be able to get some indication of how to rate your child's chances of a place by observing the demeanour of the head. If the head seems overly charming, this might be because he or she is keen to win over parents as the school lacks pupils. However, if the head appears offhand, this could mean that the school is heavily over-subscribed.

Tip

If you do not like an answer you have received from the head concerning a point that is crucial to your requirements, strike that school off your shortlist.

At schools in both sectors, observe the interaction between the head and your child. This is likely to be limited in the state sector, which does not permit schools to interview prospective parents and pupils. The type of head you are looking for will address him- or herself almost exclusively to your child, while you effectively take a back seat. If, however, little attention is paid to your child and a lengthy monologue is delivered, this could signify a probable pattern of pastoral care within the school and may indicate an unsuitable environment.

Tip

On a practical note, turn up on time for your interview. If you are late this will place you at a disadvantage, particularly if you have a stream of questions to ask. If the head is late for your meeting, this may be a sign of poor organisation and could provide grounds to mark down that school.

Touring the school

After the formal interview in the head's study, you will be given a conducted tour. This should not be rushed. While there will be significant differences across the age ranges of schools and you will be looking for a variety of evidence, you should hope to observe an industrious, lively atmosphere in all strata of schools.

In the younger age groups (primary, pre-prep and prep):

- do the children come up to show you – or the head – their work?
- are you allowed to see pupils' exercise books?
- do teachers point out pupils' work displayed on the walls?
- how do you rate the standard? (you will find this varies greatly from school to school; sometimes only the efforts of the brightest may be on display)
- note the activities of the children in the classrooms and the educational content of the games being played – for example, do any involve counting or number skills?
- is there a large stock of reading material within easy reach and what number of books are being used?
- what other educational aids, such as modelling clay, water and sand, are in evidence?

In senior schools, such disruption of classes will not be permitted but you can still gather useful evidence:

- observe the posture of the children as you pass them in the corridors. Are they walking about purposefully or slouching?
- assess the children's behaviour in the classroom and throughout the school. Do they appear confident and self-assured or do they seem unnaturally quiet?
- if you are being escorted by the head, try to discern what reaction he or she elicits among staff and pupils
- listen to the teacher's tone of voice in class and that of the children as they respond. This can indicate whether there is a relaxed, friendly atmosphere or underlying stress
- observe the number of pupils using the main library and assess the state of the books and newspapers. Do they look well-thumbed?
- read the notices posted on the main noticeboards
- check for any graffiti, particularly in the lavatories and changing rooms. If this is absent, it can signify that the pupils respect the school
- ask to visit the lavatories used by the children (not the visitors' facilities) to check levels of tidiness and hygiene
- if you are being shown around by sixth-formers, ask about their attitudes and aspirations in order to discover how they envisage the world and their role in it. This will give you some insight into the maturity of the teaching and ethos of the school.

Insist on seeing the departments and facilities that matter to you. For example, if the music department is of special interest, ask to meet the head of music instead of just seeing the practice rooms.

Sizing up the prospectus

If you have read the prospectus prior to visiting the school (see Chapter 18), you will be well placed to determine whether or not the school meets the description it gives of itself. There are certain pitfalls to look out for. When comparing a school to its portrayal in the prospectus, beware literary excess. The words 'fully equipped' should be treated with scepticism, as they often denote an exaggeration on the part of the school. For instance, it is questionable whether any school that does not have an astro-turf pitch or indoor swimming-pool can genuinely describe itself as 'well equipped in all aspects of sporting facilities'. Check also that schools advertising extra activities, such as mechanics, in their propspectus really do provide the technical expertise and access to parts (or other specialist facilities) with which to support their claims. This may necessitate asking some probing questions at interview.

Tip

When touring a school, wear comfortable shoes and in winter make sure you are warmly dressed – if you do not feel at ease physically your concentration might be compromised. Some campuses are large and spread out, so be prepared for a lot of walking.

After the interview

If you have several schools to see, you will find that impressions can fade and merge, making it difficult to recall detail when you come to consider the options. Therefore, as soon as you can after each interview make brief notes of any positive and/or negative points the school possesses and jot down the answers given to your specific questions – small but important details can soon be forgotten.

Should you feel strongly about a certain aspect of education or facility offered, it is advisable to take the precaution of including a specific reference to this in a letter thanking the head for the interview. Clearly state that you regard it as a crucial factor in your choice of school. If you have misconstrued the extent of the provision or have been misinformed by the school, perhaps because of misleading emphasis in the prospectus, the head will have no option but to write and reinform you. The letter will then become important documentary evidence should an altercation arise, and of far greater value than verbal assurances. Such a communication in effect overcomes the exclusion clause that refers to the prospectus (see page 273). You will also be in a position to sidestep the 'fees in lieu' provision should any of your written fundamental terms be breached (see page 254).

Beware verbal assurances. They can quickly be forgotten, as the case history below demonstrates.

Julian

Julian moved house and interviewed several new prep schools for his son. One appeared eminently suitable as the head assured him that his son, who was academically advanced for his age, could join the year above his age group in order to continue at the level at which he was already working. Taking the head at his word, Julian failed to confirm this verbal assurance in writing and on joining the school his child was put into the form below. Only after several weeks and an unpleasant exchange was the child moved up to the level commensurate with his ability.

Consolidating your research

At this point, you could try to do some research outside the school. Information and gossip from friends and relations can be useful, but most valuable of all is the 'insider knowledge' of present pupils encountered off-campus, or of recent pupils. Having seen a school for yourself, you should be able to put into context anything external sources may have to say and to judge whether their comments are valid or irrelevant.

Choose the people from whom you gather information carefully, and consider whether your source could have an axe to grind or a vested interest. For example, local shopkeepers or traders may either have a business link with the school, or be excluded from such an arrangement.

Checklist for visiting schools

(1) Make appointments to visit the schools that interest you and prepare a list of questions appropriate to each school. When contacting the school, ask who will be giving you the conducted tour.

(2) If you have not been able to obtain the academic and sports analyses with the prospectus, ask for them now.

(3) Ensure that all your questions are addressed during the interview. Note down the answers afterwards along with any salient points and personal observations.

(4) During conducted tours, look for indications of an industrious and lively atmosphere and observe the body language of the staff and children.

(5) In primary schools, check whether classroom assistants are employed and that there are enough of them to make an effective difference to pupil–teacher ratios and the learning process.

(6) Ask primary-school teachers how they manage to accommodate the remainder of the curriculum once time has been devoted to the literacy and numeracy hours (see Chapter 14).

(7) Ask primary and pre-prep children what they are doing and whether they are enjoying it. Older children can be asked what targets they have been set, how they intend to achieve these, and whether they are interested in the work they are doing.

(8) Ask what communication system is in place between parents and the school so that you can be kept informed of your child's progress.

(9) After the interview, write a letter of thanks making specific reference to any facilities that interest you or assurances made by the school. This could become vital documentary evidence.

(10) Gather as much information as you can from outside sources. Remember that some people's testimony is likely to be unreliable.

Chapter 20

The final decision

Once you have visited the schools on your shortlist and weighed up all the evidence, the person who matters most must be introduced to the decision-making process: your child. The final choice should preferably be a joint effort, where practical.

Involving your child

Although no final decision should be made without your son or daughter's full agreement at secondary level, in the case of nursery or junior school this will be less essential. Young children do, nevertheless, wield surprising powers of observation. What will be uppermost in your child's mind, especially a younger child's, is whether the school seems friendly and non-threatening. In this respect your son or daughter may have reliable instincts about a school that should be heeded. Academic excellence assumes overriding importance to children only as GCSEs and A-levels loom large. At this point the quality of teaching also becomes an issue (see Chapter 8).

Many children will be influenced by the destination of their present schoolfriends and playmates; some may have the reassurance of staying in contact with their classmates, although this will not always be possible. For children who are naturally gregarious, being separated from their friends will not matter too much, but such a loss could adversely affect a child who has difficulty mixing and making new friends. Problems can arise if a large group of children from the same school all transfer to a new school – see box, page 122. However, although it is natural for them to feel a little lost and overwhelmed to begin with, most children eventually settle happily into their new school.

A second tour may clinch the decision

If you are permitted a second tour of a school, it will give you the opportunity to check on points raised by your unofficial informants and to reassess observations from the first visit, described in the previous chapter. On a follow-up tour, do not hesitate to ask questions or raise any queries you have on exam or sporting analyses received following the first visit. The school should be only too happy to accommodate you as you have shown that you are still considering it.

Balancing negative to positive aspects

Acceptance of the negative points of a school is vital when choosing a school. Unless you are exceptionally lucky, the chances are that when investigating a suitable school you will come across certain elements that are not to your liking – whether these concern the head teacher, staff, facilities, pastoral care system or some other aspect is immaterial, the point is that a potential stumbling block may come to light. In the light of this, when picking the best school for your child you will have to decide not only whether the school fits the bill in terms of your specific requirements, but also whether you (and, more crucially, your child) can live with its less-than-perfect aspects. The overall 'fit' is what matters.

Accepting a school's drawbacks

At this juncture, you will have narrowed down your choice by collating information gleaned from as many sources as possible (see Chapter 18). Any one school is likely to invoke equal amounts of praise and criticism. Of course, your own opinion of a school will count most, but it can also be helpful to examine comments from other sources.

- Ignore glowing reports, particularly if these are uncorroborated by factual evidence. Instead, carefully examine a school's drawbacks by weighing up all the criticisms that have accumulated – both your own and those of others.

- Decide whether you are prepared to put up with the minus points. This will be easier if you feel that on balance they will not encroach too much, if at all, upon your expectations of the establishment.
- If you are certain that your ideals will not be compromised through accepting the school's negative factors, you can proceed confidently to make an application (see Chapter 16) or accept an offer of a place, depending on which stage you have reached.
- If you find that the balance of doubt is too great, tread very carefully.

If you feel comfortable about bringing a sticking point to the attention of the school, a discussion may put your mind at rest. It might be worth finding out if the school is prepared to be flexible over issues that bother you. However, if a conversation with the school does not allay your fears it is inadvisable to proceed any further.

Warning

If something about a school comes to your notice that you feel is absolutely unacceptable, no amount of talking-up the positive points will alter that situation. Do not attempt to fight it by donning rose-tinted glasses. It is far preferable to be able to stomach the negatives in isolation than to rely on the positives to outweigh them. Once encountered, negative points tend to become magnified.

Sometimes, a drawback may be so fundamental that it is not within the power of a school to alter it – for example, the location may expose children to fast or excessive traffic. Schools which openly admit to the existence of factors that will turn off parents and go on to explain how they are attempting to ameliorate unattractive aspects deserve respect for their honesty and initiative.

If the path you choose is in the state sector, think long and hard about how realistic your chances are of getting your child into your preferred school (Chapter 16 explains the factors affecting admission).

Commuting distance may preclude entry

Parents should be aware that some heads impose a maximum time limit for commuting purposes, as they consider it unreasonable for children to spend so much time travelling that they are too tired to concentrate properly on their studies. Check the school's position on this before making any decisions.

Unfortunately, no matter how many enquiries you make of a school or how careful you are to cover all contingencies, it is impossible to predict every eventuality. Because of this, it is unreasonable of parents to expect a head teacher to foresee any difficulties that may arise once you have chosen a certain school – for example, staff whose presence influenced your decision might leave or be made redundant. Even if you choose the best possible school, there are no guarantees that your child's educational career will be trouble-free.

Making the right choice

If you have followed the advice in this book, carried out adequate research and been blessed with a certain amount of luck, you should be able to identify a school which fully meets your personal requirements. However, you may find that dropping a school from your shortlist sends you back to the drawing-board. If this is the case, both parents should discuss with each other whether it will be necessary to re-align their imperatives and possibly to forgo certain requirements in order to cast the net wider.

Siblings can have different needs

What suits one of your children may not be ideal for other siblings, even though it might seem convenient to have them all educated at the same school. If your family increases you should carry out the same careful research for each younger child as for your first – it may turn out that the same school is the best place after all, but the decision should not be left to chance.

Few parents experience the luxury of a completely smooth ride through the educational system. Nevertheless, a methodical approach will quickly weed out the least suitable establishments and enable you to reach your eventual decision by eliminating all but one of the remaining candidates. This is a personal choice and one that this book cannot make for you – only you know what you are looking for and can interpret the atmosphere within a school. However, the advice in this guide on finding a good school should provide you with the means to make an informed decision.

Checklist for the final decision

(1) Make a shortlist of suitable schools and discuss your findings with your son or daughter.

(2) If possible, request a second interview and tour with your child. Use this opportunity to confirm or correct your previous observations.

(3) Contemplate very carefully all the negative aspects which come to light. Do not be swayed by the positive ones unless you have decided that the negative factors do not really matter.

Education in Scotland

The organisation of education in Scotland has some significant differences from that in the rest of the UK. Following devolution, the Scottish Executive* is, among various duties in the field of education, able to determine national aims and standards, policy, curriculum guidelines and assessment. The Scottish Parliament has powers to legislate on education.

General organisation

Scottish Local Authorities (SLAs) arrange educational provision in state-funded schools, which are referred to as free public schools. These unitary councils perform a similar role to that of LEAs in England and Wales (see pages 23–4). They have a statutory duty to provide adequate and efficient education, cater for special educational needs and further the teaching of Gaelic in schools in Gaelic-speaking areas. They have responsibility for expenditure on buildings, recreational and sporting activities and for the curriculum. National guidance is issued on a wide range of subjects, including the curriculum, which SLAs will generally follow closely.

Devolved School Management has placed at least 80 per cent of schools' budgets in the hands of head teachers.

School boards

School boards adopt a consultative role and advise the head teacher. They consist mostly of parents but membership also includes staff and co-opted members. Their duties include liaising with and representing parents at the school, approving the head's plans for spending on school books and equipment and involvement in the selection of senior staff. Although schools boards perform similar functions to those of a board of governors in England and Wales (see Chapter 7), they are less able to oppose the head.

School inspections

HM Inspectorate of Schools (Scotland)* operates along similar lines to its equivalent in England, as described in Chapter 6, but carries out all its own inspections rather than subcontracting the task to registered agencies.

The Inspectorate is a distinct unit within the framework of the Scottish Executive, but is to all intents and purposes independent, publishing its own reports on individual schools and on aspects of the national education system. It is headed by a Senior Chief Inspector while Chief Inspectors are responsible for major policy sectors and geographical areas. Senior inspectors hold national responsibility for each subject in the curriculum and for the conduct of inspections in certain districts.

The school year

The school year, which is divided into three terms and lasts for a minimum of 38 weeks, normally stretches from the third week in August to the beginning of July, with breaks of one week in October and two weeks in December/January and March/April. The exact dates are decided by each SLA.

Pre-school education

At the time of writing, over 56,000 Scottish pupils attend pre-school education. In the winter term of 1998, virtually every child of the relevant age had access to a part-time pre-school place. The Scottish Executive has pledged to extend pre-school education to all 3-year-old children by 2002.

Pre-school education is provided in local authority nursery schools and classes, local authority community day nurseries, private nurseries and pre-school playgroups. Some independent schools also have nursery departments. Crèches and childminders may also provide pre-school education if these belong to the free places scheme (see pages 28–30).

Local authority nursery schools and classes are staffed by fully trained primary-school teachers and nursery nurses (who qualify through a two-year college course or through vocational training on the job). In the private and voluntary sectors as well as local authority centres outside the school system, staff may include teachers, nursery nurses and other carers, some of whom may be unqualified. Guidelines issued by the Scottish Executive state that in such local authority centres half the relevant staff must be qualified.

Advice on easing your child's transition to nursery school can be found on page 32.

Types of school

Schools are divided according to age:

Age	Type of school
5–12	Primary
12–16	Secondary
16–18	Post-compulsory secondary (including further education colleges)

Education is compulsory until the age of 16. Leaving dates for pupils who have reached 16 are the end of the Christmas term or the last day in May.

State schools

State schooling is essentially comprehensive and co-educational. Only one state school is single-sex, and Scotland has no grammar schools.

Primary education

There are 2,363 primary schools which educate over 440,000 pupils. Transfer to secondary school is at 12 years (a year later than the rest of the UK).

> **Country schools**
>
> Many areas of Scotland are remote and sparsely populated. While urban schools tend to be large, schools in remote rural areas are small but serve a much bigger area. Some are single-teacher establishments. These schools, which depend for their survival upon sufficient numbers of pupils, are under constant threat of closure.

Classes are organised according to age and range from primary 1 (P1) to primary 7 (P7). There is no streaming by ability (see pages 194–5), but in the larger schools parents may find more than one class for each age group. In smaller schools, several age groups may be combined under one teacher, and in schools with fewer than 20 children one teacher will teach all the children in a single class. The primary class-size limit is 33 pupils (30 for ages 5–7), but if different age-groups are combined this falls to 25 pupils.

The class teacher will cover all or most of the curriculum with support from specialist teachers in subjects such as art, drama, music and physical education.

Secondary education

Secondary education is provided for nearly 315,000 pupils in over 454 comprehensive schools. School size varies from under 100 pupils to about 2,000 and most establishments educate children up to 18 years. Those in remote areas may provide restricted courses or lower secondary education only. In these circumstances, pupils can transfer to a more suitable comprehensive school, which could necessitate residence in accommodation paid for the local authority.

Classes may not exceed 30 pupils in the early years, while 25 is the maximum higher up secondary school. For certain practical subjects, no more than 20 pupils in a class may be permitted. Pupils are subject to continuous assessment according to the internal procedures of each school.

Provision is divided into two stages.

Lower secondary

- **S1 and S2** Years 1 and 2 provide a general education, following national guidelines.

- **S3 and S4** Years 3 and 4 include elements of specialisation and of vocational education.

Upper secondary
- **S5 and S6** Years 5 and 6 provide greater specialisation. Certain courses may require a minimum academic standard.

Not all pupils remain for the full two years: some leave to take up employment or training, while some proceed to higher education or to further education colleges.

Further education colleges

There are 47 further education colleges in Scotland, 43 of which are incorporated colleges responsible for their own management and funded through the Scottish Further Education Funding Council (SFEFC). Of the remaining four, two in Orkney and Shetland are managed by the Islands' Council with a Scottish Executive grant, while two others receive funding direct from the Scottish Executive.

Each college is managed by a board, at least half of whose members will be drawn from industry or commerce. The powers delegated to board members, together with their local business links, enable them to undertake commercial activities.

Most students at further education colleges are over 18 and attend on a part-time basis during the day or on release from employment. Courses are mainly vocational, incorporating both theoretical and practical work.

Performance tables

National performance tables are published for secondary schools in Scotland (including sixth-form results), but as yet are not available for primary schools. The audit unit of HM Inspectorate of Schools (Scotland)★ publishes a series of books designed to provide information for parents. One of these, *The Examination Results in Scottish Schools*, details examination performance for secondary schools over a three-year period. Results in Scottish Grades (GCSEs and A-levels are not included) are grouped by education authority, together with various background information. Graphs compare authorities and national averages. Separate details are also provided on independent schools.

Information on subject performance within individual schools is now available from each secondary school in a booklet entitled *How Good Are Our Results?*.

Independent schools

There are two categories of independent school:

- independent fee-charging schools
- grant-aided special schools providing for special educational needs.

The latter receive state funding or fees from local authorities. Children with special educational needs are catered for in much the same way as those in England and Wales (see Chapter 5).

The majority of independent schools allow pupils to sit both English and Scottish examinations, depending on parental choice. A few independent-school pupils study only for the English examinations (GCSE, GCE A- and AS-levels), while in other schools pupils study only for the Scottish examinations (SCE S-grade, SCE H-grade and CSYS – see page 296).

It is within the power of education authorities to grant bursaries to students who are resident in their area and satisfy prescribed conditions. The exact amount of financial relief awarded is at the discretion of the authority in question. For more information on meeting the cost of school fees, see Chapter 17.

The curriculum

Unlike England, Wales and Northern Ireland, Scotland does not have a compulsory National Curriculum. The education authorities and the schools jointly formulate and deliver a broad curriculum based on guidance from the Scottish Executive, HM Inspectors and the Scottish Consultative Council on the Curriculum (SCCC). The last organisation is charged with responsibility for reviewing and publishing guidance on the curriculum.

Primary education

In primary education a '5–14 development programme' provides guidelines on a variety of issues including:

- the aims of study
- the ground to be covered and progress to be made in each area of the curriculum
- advice on assessments
- a system of national testing in language and mathematics
- information to parents
- a pupil record card.

There are six levels of national testing in mathematics, reading and writing.

Secondary education

Secondary schools adopt Scottish Executive guidelines which have been adapted to local circumstances. In the first two years, the curriculum is made up of eight subject modes:

- language and communication
- mathematics
- science
- social and environmental studies
- technology
- creative and aesthetic activities
- physical education
- religious and moral education.

A modern foreign language is also usually available. Most schools require pupils to take English, mathematics, a modern language and sometimes science too. Beyond the second year, science is usually taught as separate subjects (biology, physics and chemistry).

At the end of the second year, the core subjects remain in place to provide a broad and balanced curriculum. At this point, pupils choose subjects leading to the Standard Grade (S-grade) of the Scottish Certificate of Education (SCE), taken at age 15/16. This examination is suitable for all levels of ability and is equivalent to the GCSE in

England and Wales. It is graded on a scale of 1–7, where 1 is the top mark (grades 1–3 are equivalent to GCSE grades A–C).

Pupils may also take certificated short courses set by the Scottish Qualifications Authority (SQA)★ and/or vocational subjects for the SQA National Certificate.

Pupils who proceed to the fifth and sixth years have a choice of qualification routes. Changes implemented in 1999 are designed to allow pupils to access learning at levels appropriate to their ability and to ensure that they receive proper recognition and attain the highest qualifications of which they are capable.

There are five new levels of post-16 qualifications:

- Access
- Intermediate 1
- Intermediate 2
- Higher
- Advanced Higher.

The first of the new qualifications to be introduced is the new Higher Grade (H-grade). Highers are equivalent to A-levels (three to five Highers roughly equate to two to four A-levels). Highers are normally taken in the fifth and sixth years (S5 and S6), with a minimum of three Highers or three A-levels required for university entry. All levels will have been introduced by 2003. Pupils who are not expected to reach H-grade level will be able to study for Access and Intermediate 1 or 2 qualifications.

Previously it was not always possible for less able pupils to move immediately from Standard to Higher Grades. The reforms offer them the opportunity to approach this level gradually – for example, by studying for S-grade in fourth year, Intermediate 2 in the fifth year and H-grade in the sixth year. The more able pupils who can move directly from Standard to Higher Grade will be able to progress towards Advanced Higher Grade in sixth year.

Pupils who have passed the subject concerned at H-grade can take the Certificate of Sixth Year Studies (CSYS) in the sixth year. It requires in-depth study, including a dissertation, and is recognised by a number of universities in the UK. The last certification year for this will be 2001.

Although schools need not introduce all subjects or levels in a given subject, the ability of small secondary schools to meet such complex requirements remains to be seen.

Vocational qualifications

A variety of vocational alternatives to academic courses are available.

- General Scottish Vocational Qualifications (GSVQs) are equivalent to GNVQs in England, Wales and Northern Ireland (see pages 163–5). They are offered at three levels I–III. These exams are due to be replaced; the last certification date will be 2004.
- Scottish Vocational Qualifications (SVQs) are equivalent to NVQs (see page 165).
- The SQA awards National Certificates at non-advanced level and the Higher National Certificate (HNC) and Higher National Diploma (HND) at advanced level. Courses cover a wide range of technical and business-related subjects and are available in modular form.

Gaelic in schools

The language features at all levels of education in Scotland and as part of teacher training. While not compulsory, education through the medium of Gaelic is well established at pre-school and primary levels – in 1998–9, 56 Gaelic-medium primary units catered for 1,816 children – and provision is growing at secondary level. The Gaelic language and Gaelic-medium education are not confined to the traditional Gaelic-speaking areas of Scotland but are also established in the main urban areas, with 23 local authorities providing some form of coverage with funding from the Scottish Executive.

Admission procedures

School admission is conducted on a similar basis to that used in England and Wales – in other words, state-school entry is governed by the regulations of the local admission authority, while obtaining a place at an independent school depends to a greater or lesser degree upon selection and the parents' financial status (see Chapter 16).

Parents are advised to consult their local authority and the individual schools for relevant details.

In the state system, parents are now empowered to submit 'placing requests' – i.e. to state their preferred school. If a state school is over-subscribed a place may be refused by the admission authority, in which case parents may appeal against the decision. The authority must by law set up an independent appeal committee. Parents should complain to this body, and if this measure fails may make a final appeal to the sheriff.

Teachers' qualifications

All state-school teachers in Scotland must be registered with the General Teaching Council for Scotland (GTC).* To achieve this, a teacher must be in possession of a teaching qualification from a Scottish teacher-training institution or approved equivalent. Misconduct may lead to de-registration.

Teachers in primary schools hold a Teaching Qualification (Primary Education), obtained either via a four-year Bachelor of Education (BEd) degree course at a teacher-training institution or a university degree followed by a one-year postgraduate teacher training course. Primary-school teachers teach across the curriculum.

Secondary-school teachers hold a Teaching Qualification (Secondary Education) obtained either via a university degree followed by a one-year postgraduate teacher training course or a subject-based degree course involving the study of education and practical work experience at school. A Teaching Qualification (Further Education) – highly recommended for FE lecturers – also exists but is not compulsory. FE lecturers may also register with the GTC if they choose.

Education in Wales

Wales operates the same educational system as England. However, parents should be aware of certain differences.

Rural schools

Wales has a large proportion of rural schools. Several rural primary schools teach different year groups in a single class or vertical group (see page 121), and often the head is a full-time class teacher. Some two-teacher primary schools are divided into Key Stage 1 and 2 classes, depending on pupil numbers. At secondary level, fewer staff can mean that pupils are restricted in their choice of subjects.

School inspections

These are carried out along similar lines to Ofsted inspections in England (see chapter 6), under the auspices of Estyn,★ formerly the Office of HM Chief Inspector (Wales).

Performance tables

In Wales, the performance tables for primary schools compare different LEAs; the individual schools' results are not published. It is therefore difficult for parents to draw comparisons in this respect between the schools themselves.

Secondary-school performance tables for Wales, including sixth-form results, are published in the same booklet in Welsh and English.

Additional results are given for pupils who took the CoEA (Certificate of Educational Achievement) instead of the GCSE.

See pages 171–2 for an explanation of the government performance tables.

The curriculum

The National Curriculum is under review by the Welsh Assembly. The Curriculum Cymreig applies across all subjects. This aims to promote in pupils an understanding of the cultural, economic, environmental, historical and linguistic characteristics of Wales.

Welsh in schools

The Welsh language is a statutory requirement from Key Stage 1 up to the end of Key Stage 4 (GCSE level), although children are not obliged to sit the exam. Pupils transferring to a school in the final year of Key Stage 3 or during Key Stage 4 (either within Wales or from outside the country) may request exemption from the requirement to study Welsh, provided they have not studied Welsh for at least one academic year in any of the three preceding years. Exemption will be granted at the discretion of the school. Peripatetic Welsh teachers visit schools where there is no Welsh-speaking teacher. Some primary and secondary schools have Welsh-medium units where all lessons are taught in Welsh, and Welsh is usually the first language in schools in Welsh-speaking areas. In these schools, English is not compulsory for 5- to 7-year-olds and many do not teach English until a child is seven.

Parents who require information about education in Wales should contact the Public Information and Education Service of the National Assembly for Wales.*

Appendix III

Education in Northern Ireland

Although education in the Province is broadly similar to the system in England and Wales, there are certain variations.

General organisation

The Department of Education for Northern Ireland★ is responsible for the provision of education in the province in partnership with the five Education and Library Boards (broadly similar to LEAs in England and Wales – see pages 23–4), the Council for Catholic Maintained Schools★ and the Council for the Curriculum, Examinations and Assessment.★

Nearly 1,250 schools provide education for about 350,000 pupils and 17 colleges of further education offer vocational and non-vocational courses for almost 147,000 full- and part-time students.

Unlike in England and Wales, education is compulsory for children aged 4–16.

School inspections

The Inspectorate is the Department of Education's principle source of advice on all professional educational issues, as well as on standards of educational provision throughout schools, FE colleges and grant-aided institutions. The Inspectorate operates as an integral part of the Department and fulfils a broadly similar role to that of Ofsted in England (see Chapter 6).

Pre-school education

Nursery schools cater for 3- and 4-year-old pupils. A programme to increase the involvement of pre-school children in education from 45 to 85 per cent by 2001–2 is being phased in and the long-term aim is to provide a full year of pre-school education for children of participating parents.

Types of school

Although the school system in the Province has evolved along religious lines, some integrated schools have been established. The government is required by law to encourage and facilitate integrated education.

The four main categories of schools which receive government funding – controlled, voluntary-maintained, voluntary grammar and integrated schools – are known as grant-aided schools. In law, all grant-aided schools in Northern Ireland are open to all pupils, regardless of their religion.

Controlled schools
These are owned by the local Education and Library Board and managed by a board of governors. Most pupils are Protestant.

Voluntary-maintained schools
Trustees own these establishments, most of which are under Roman Catholic management.

Voluntary grammar schools
These schools are similar to grammar schools in England and Wales (see page 35) and come under non-denominational or Roman Catholic management.

Integrated schools
As the name implies, the aim of these schools is to educate Protestant and Roman Catholic pupils under the same roof. They have strong parental support and there are 40 schools educating about 10,000 pupils.

Irish-medium schools
These provide education through the medium of the Irish language (see page 304).

Primary education

Children join primary school in September at the age of four, provided their fourth birthday falls before 1 July in that year. Should the birthday fall on or after this date, the child must wait until the following September, by which time he or she could be five.

Secondary education

At the age of 11, children move to secondary school where they may remain up to the age of 18. Alternatively, those aged 16 years and over may attend a college of further education offering vocational and academic courses full- and part-time.

Performance tables

These are published for state secondary schools only. The academic results of the schools are listed in a booklet divided into two sections on non-grammar and grammar schools. A- and AS-level results are also contained in this document, whereas the DfEE in England publishes these details separately.

The curriculum

Schools in Northern Ireland follow the National Curriculum (see Chapter 12).

In all grant-aided schools, the curriculum covers six areas of study:

- English
- mathematics
- science and technology
- the environment and society
- creative and expressive studies
- language studies (in secondary schools and Irish-medium primary schools).

Religious education has reached a milestone in that the Protestant and Roman Catholic Churches have together formulated a common core syllabus for religious studies which is now being taught in all schools.

Education for mutual understanding and cultural heritage

These cross-curricular themes are unique to Northern Ireland and spring from its complex cultural heritage. They aim to encourage pupils to develop deeper understanding of themselves and others with different views and values. To help promote this, pupils from different sides of the sectarian divide are encouraged to mix socially while the Schools Community Relations Programme, which acts as a supplement to the integrated schools, involves about half of all schools and about 500 youth and community groups.

Irish in schools

Northern Ireland provides for the teaching of the Irish language in seven Irish-medium primary schools, two Irish-medium units within grant-aided primary schools and one Irish-medium secondary school. Other Irish-medium schools which have not satisfied the criteria for government funding operate independently.

Independent schools

Northern Ireland has about 20 independent schools. These operate along similar lines to those in England and Wales (see Chapter 3).

Admission procedures

Although the process is very similar to that in England, as described in Chapter 16, parents should note crucial differences.

Parents of primary-school children are sent two booklets to help them through the steps of the transfer: a pamphlet from the Education and Library Board containing information on local schools and admission criteria, and the Department of Education's school performance information booklet with details of, among other things, examination results and leavers' destinations. If you wish to apply for a school in another Board area, you can ask your own Board for the booklet covering that area. You may also ask schools to send you a prospectus (for advice on how to read these, see Chapter 18).

Transfer procedure tests

When considering which secondary school you would like your child to attend, the first decision to make is whether you wish your child to take these two tests, the results of which are used by selective schools to determine entry. The tests, taken in November, are not compulsory although all pupils applying to grammar schools must sit them. Non-grammar schools are precluded from using these results when determining entry, except for the two secondary schools with approved grammar streams.

You can discuss whether to enter your child for the tests with the primary-school Principal and will be asked to complete Form TRP8 at the beginning of the autumn term stating your decision. The Department of Education issues two leaflets to parents of participating children before and after the tests, explaining what procedures to follow.

If the area in which you live does not have a selective secondary school, it will be presumed that primary-school pupils in the area will not take the tests. If you wish your child to apply for a grammar school elsewhere, this must be made clear in writing to the primary-school Principal, so that arrangements can be made for him or her to take the tests. Children who have been statemented for special educational needs are exempt from this process (see pages 85–6).

Each test lasts one hour and is based on English, maths, and science and technology. They are marked by the Northern Ireland Council for the Curriculum, Examinations and Assessment (CCEA). Allowance is made for younger candidates and children affected by illness or other adverse circumstances may take a supplementary test. In such cases it is vital to inform the school Principal immediately.

Results are published at the beginning of February and are graded according to fixed percentage bands:

Grade	Per cent
A	25
B1	5
B2	5
C1	5
C2	5
D	55

The tests are not pass-or-fail examinations with a set pass mark: rather, they are a competition that ranks pupils based on their performance in the tests.

Grammar schools are required to admit strictly in order of the grade obtained and must not single out any child for preferential treatment. Over-subscription criteria will be operated if schools have to decide between pupils with the same grade; these will be determined by the school concerned (see pages 227–30).

Transfer report form

After the test results have been published all parents will be asked to complete a transfer report form, whether or not their child has sat the tests. It is vital to complete this document. Parents must list all the schools at which they want their child to be considered for admission, in order of preference.

Tip

- You are advised to list at least three schools on the form in case of over-subscription, and to provide any additional information which could have a bearing on the decision, including documentary evidence if necessary.
- Even if you are seeking a grammar-school place, you are strongly advised to name at least one non-grammar school.
- Carefully consider the admissions criteria for each school; they could inform your choice.

Parents are informed of the decisions of the admission authorities in May. They may appeal against a place being refused on grounds of the admission criteria not being applied, or applied incorrectly. The appeal will be heard by an appeals tribunal, set up by the local Education and Library Board.

Addresses

The new telephone area codes and local numbers, which came into existence in June 1999, are given in the contact details below. Note that until 22 April 2000 you will need to use the new area codes *as well as* the new local numbers when dialling locally (e.g. you will need to use the 020 code when dialling within London). After 22 April 2000 it will be possible to use the new local numbers without the area codes.

Advisory Centre for Education (ACE)
1b Aberdeen Studios
22 Highbury Grove
London N5 2DQ
Advice line: (020) 7354 8321
Exclusion line: (020) 7704 9822
Fax: (020) 7354 9069
Email: ace-ed@easynet.co.uk
Web site: www.ace-ed.org.uk

Association of Investment Trust Companies
Third Floor, Durrant House
8–13 Chiswell Street
London EC1Y 4YY
Tel: (020) 7282 5555
Fax: (020) 7282 5556
Email: info@aitc.co.uk
Web site: www.iii.co.uk/aitc

Association for Neuro-linguistic Programming
PO Box 78, Stourbridge DY8 4ZJ
Tel: (01384) 443935
Fax: (01384) 443931

Association of Tutors
Sunnycroft
63 King Edward Road
Northampton NN1 5LY
Tel: (01604) 624171
Fax: (01604) 624718

Awdurod Cymwysterau Cwricwlwm ac Asesu (ACCAC)
Castle Buildings, Womanby Street
Cardiff CF10 9SX
Tel: (029) 2037 5400
Fax: (029) 2034 3612
Email: info@accac.org.uk
Web site: www.accac.org.uk

Boarding Education Alliance
Ann Williamson
c/o Cohn & Wolfe
30 Orange Street
London WC2H 7LZ
Tel/Fax: (020) 8460 4357
Email: annwilliamson@classic.msn.com
Web site: www.boarding.org.uk

British Dyslexia Association
98 London Road
Reading, Berkshire RG1 5AU
Tel: 0118-966 2677
Helpline: 0118-966 8271
Fax: 0118-935 1927
Email: info@dyslexiahelp-bda.
demon.co.uk
Web site: www.bda-dyslexia.org.uk

Childline
Freepost 1111, London N1 1BA
Helpline: (0800) 1111

Children's Legal Centre
University of Essex
Wivenhoe Park, Colchester
Essex CO4 3SQ
Advice line: (01206) 873820
Fax: (01206) 874026
Email: clc@essex.ac.uk
Web site: www2.essex.ac.uk/clc

Citizens' Advice Bureau
Look in the phone book for your
local office

Conference for Independent Further Education (CIFE)
Dr Elizabeth Cottrell
Executive Secretary
2/295 Ladbroke Grove
London W10 6HE
Tel: (020) 8969 0324
Fax: (020) 8686 2540
Email: enquiries@cife.org.uk
Web site: www.cife.org.uk

Council for Catholic Maintained Schools (CCMS)
160 High Street, Holywood
County Down BT18 9HT
Tel: (028) 9042 6972
Fax: (028) 9042 4255
Email: info.ccms@nics.gov.uk

Council for the Curriculum, Examinations and Assessment (CCEA)
29 Clarendon Road
Belfast BT1 3BG
Tel: (028) 9026 1200
Fax: (028) 9026 1234
Email: info@ccea.org.uk
Web site: www.ccea.org.uk

Council of Voluntary Service
Look in the phone book for your area
office

Daycare Trust
Shoreditch Town Hall Annexe
380 Old Street
London EC1V 9LT
Advice: (020) 7739 2866
Fax: (020) 7739 5579
Email: info@daycaretrust.org.uk
Web site: www.daycaretrust.org.uk

Department for Education and Employment (DfEE)
Sanctuary Buildings
Great Smith Street
London SW1P 3BT
Tel: (020) 7925 5000
Fax: (020) 7925 6000
Email info@dfee.gov.uk
Web site: www.dfee.gov.uk

DfEE Publications
PO Box 5050
Sherwood Park, Annesley
Nottinghamshire NG15 0DJ
Tel: (0845) 6022260
Fax: (0845) 6033360

DfEE Public Enquiry Unit
Area 2B, Castleview House
Runcorn, Cheshire WA7 2GJ
Tel: (020) 7925 5555
Fax: (01928) 794248
Email: info@dfee.gov.uk
Web site: www.dfee.gov.uk

DfEE Specialist Schools Division
Technology colleges
Tel: (020) 7925 5837
Language colleges
Tel: (020) 7925 5807
Sports colleges
Tel: (020) 7925 5484
Arts colleges Tel: (020) 7925 5622
Fax: (020) 7925 6374

Department of Education for Northern Ireland
Rathgael House
43 Balloo Road
Bangor, County Down BT19 7PR
Tel: (028) 9127 9279
Fax: (028) 9127 9100
Email: deni@nics.gov.uk
Web site: www.deni.gov.uk

Dyslexia Institute
133 Gresham Road
Staines, Middlesex TW18 2AJ
Tel: (01784) 463851
Fax: (01784) 460747
Email: info@dyslexia-inst.org.uk
Web site: www.dyslexia-inst.org.uk

Education Otherwise
PO Box 7420, London N9 7SG
Tel: (0891) 518303

Estyn (HM Inspectorate for Education and Training in Wales)
Phase 1, Govt Buildings
Llanishen, Cardiff CF14 5FQ
Tel: (029) 2032 5000
Fax: (029) 2075 8182

Further Education Funding Council (FEFC)
Cheylesmore House
Quinton Road
Coventry CV1 2WT
Tel: (024) 7686 3000
Fax: (024) 7686 3100
Web site: www.fefc.ac.uk

General Teaching Council for Scotland (GTC)
Clerwood House
96 Clermiston Road
Edinburgh EH12 6UT
Tel: 0131-314 6000
Fax: 0131-314 6001
Email: gtcs@gtcs.org.uk
Web site: www.gtcs.org.uk

Girls' Day School Trust
100 Rochester Row
London SW1P 1JP
Tel: (020) 7393 6666
Fax: (020) 7393 6789
Web site: www.gdst.net

Girls' Schools Association (GSA)
130 Regent Road
Leicester LE1 7PG
Tel: 0116-254 1619
Fax: 0116-255 3792
Email: gsa@webleicester.co.uk
Web site: www.schools.edu/gsa/

Governing Bodies Association (GBA)
Mr Frank Morgan, Secretary
The Ancient Foresters
Bush End, Takely
Bishop's Stortford
Herts CM22 6NN
Tel/Fax: (01279) 871865
Email: frank.morgan@dial.pipex.com

Governing Bodies of Girls' Schools Association (GBGSA)
See Governing Bodies Association, above

Headmasters' and Headmistresses' Conference (HMC)
130 Regent Road
Leicester LE1 7PG
Tel: 0116-285 4810
Fax: 0116-247 1167
Email: hmc@hmc.org.uk

HM Inspectorate of Schools (Scotland)
Audit Unit
Area 2B, Victoria Quay
Edinburgh EH6 6QQ
Tel: 0131-244 0746
Fax: 0131-244 0653
Email: hmi.auditunit.scotland.gov.uk
Web site: www.scotland.gov.uk

IFA Promotion Ltd
2nd Floor, 113–117 Farringdon Road London EC1R 3BT
Hotline: 0117-971 1177
Fax: (0207) 833 3239
Web site: www.unbiased.co.uk (for email information request form)

Incorporated Association of Preparatory Schools (IAPS)
11 Waterloo Place
Leamington Spa
Warwickshire CV32 5LA
Tel: (01926) 887833
Fax: (01926) 888014
Email: hq@iaps.org.uk
Web site: www.iaps.org.uk

Independent Schools Association (ISA)
Timothy Ham, General Secretary
Boys' British School
East Street, Saffron Walden
Essex CB10 1LS
Tel: (01799) 523619
Fax: (01799) 524892
Email: isa@dial.pipex.com

Independent Schools' Bursars Association (ISBA)
Mr M J Sant, General Secretary
5 Chapel Close, Old Basing
Basingstoke, Hampshire RG24 7BZ
Tel: (01256) 330369
Fax: (01256) 330376

Independent Schools Council (ISC)
General Secretary
Grosvenor Gardens House
35–37 Grosvenor Gardens
London SW1W 0BS
Tel: (020) 7798 1590
Fax: (020) 7798 1591
Email: abc@isis.org.uk

Independent Schools Information Service (ISIS)
National ISIS
Grosvenor Gardens House
35–37 Grosvenor Gardens
London SW1W 0BS
Tel: (020) 7798 1500
Fax: (020) 7798 1501
Email: national@isis.org.uk
Web site: www.isis.org.uk

Local Government Ombudsman (England)
21 Queen Anne's Gate
London SW1H 9BU
Tel: (020) 7915 3210
Fax: (020) 7233 0396

Local Government Ombudsman (Wales)
Derwem House
Court Road
Bridgend CS31 1BN
Tel: (01656) 661325
Fax: (01656) 658317
Email: rgombudsmanWales@btinternet.com
Web site: www.ombudsman-Wales.org

Local Government Ombudsman (Scotland)
23 Walker Street
Edinburgh EH3 7HX
Tel: 0131–225 5300
Tel: 0131–225 9495
Email: commissioner@ombudslgscot.org.uk

**Mensa Foundation for Gifted
Children**
Mensa House
St John's Square
Wolverhampton WV2 4AH
Tel: (01902) 772771
Fax: (01902) 422327
Email: mensa@dial.pipex.com
Web site: www.mfgc.org.uk/mfgc/

**Money Management National
Register of Fee-based Advisers**
Maple House
149 Tottenham Court Road
London W1P 9LL
Tel: (0870) 0131925

Montessori Society
26 Lyndhurst Gardens
London NW3 5NW
Tel: (020) 7435 7874
Fax: (020) 7431 8096
Email: mariamontessoriamiuk@
compuserve.com
Web site: www.montessori-ami.org

National Assembly for Wales
Public Information and Education
Service
Cathays Park, Cardiff CF10 3NQ
Tel: (029) 2082 5111
Fax: (029) 2082 5350
Web site: www.wales.gov.uk

**National Association for the
Education of Sick Children
(PRESENT)**
8 Victoria Park Square
London E2 9PF
Tel: (020) 8980 8523
Fax: (020) 8980 3447
Email: naesc@ednsick.demon.co.uk
Web site: www.sickchildren.org.uk

**National Association for Gifted
Children (NAGC)**
Elder House, Elder Gate
Milton Keynes MK9 1LR
Tel: (01908) 673677
Fax: (01908) 673679
Email: nagc@rmplc.co.uk

**National Association of Head
Teachers**
1 Heath Square
Boltro Road, Haywards Heath
West Sussex RH16 1BL
Tel: (01444) 472472
Fax: (01444) 472473
Email: info@naht.org.uk
Web site: www.naht.org.uk

**National Association of Special
Educational Needs (NASEN)**
NASEN House
4–5 Amber Business Village
Amber Close, Amington
Tamworth B77 4RP
Tel: (01827) 311500
Fax: (01827) 313005
Email: welcome@nasen.org.uk
Web site: www.nasen.org.uk

National Childminding Association
8 Masons Hill, Bromley
Kent BR2 9EY
Tel: (020) 8464 6164
Information line: (020) 8466 0200
Fax: (020) 8290 6834
Email: natcma@netcomuk.co.uk
Web site: www.ncma.org.uk

National Early Years Network
77 Holloway Road
London N7 8JZ
Tel: (020) 7607 9573
Fax (020) 7700 1105
Email: nationalearlyyearsnetwork@
compuserve.com

Ofsted
Alexandra House
33 Kingsway
London WC2B 6SE
Tel: (020) 7421 6744
Fax: (020) 17421 6707
Web site: www.ofsted.gov.uk

Parents for Inclusion
Unit 2, 70 South Lambeth Road
London SW8 1RL
Tel: (020) 7735 7735
Helpline: (020) 7582 5008 (*10am–2pm, Tuesday and Thursday*)

Pre-school Learning Alliance
69 Kings Cross Road
London WC1X 9LL
Tel: (020) 7833 0991
Helpline: (020) 7837 5513
Fax: (020) 7837 4942
Email: pla@preschool.org.uk

Qualifications and Curriculum Authority (QCA)
QCA Publications
PO Box 99, Sudbury
Suffolk CO10 6SN
Tel: (01787) 884444
Fax: (01787) 375920
Email: qca@prologistics.co.uk
Web site: www.qca.org.uk

Reach National Advice Centre for Children with Reading Difficulties
California Country Park
Nine Mile Ride, Finchampstead
Berkshire RG40 4HT
Tel: 0118-973 7575
Fax: 0118-973 7105
Helpline: (0845) 6040414
Email: reach@reach-reading.demon.co.uk
Web site: www.reach-reading.demon.co.uk

Scottish Council of Independent Schools (SCIS)
21 Melville Street
Edinburgh EH3 7PE
Tel: 0131-220 2106
Fax: 0131-225 8594
E-mail: scis@btinternet.com
Web site: www.scis.org.uk

Scottish Executive
Education Department
Victoria Quay
Edinburgh EH6 6QQ
Tel: 0131-244 0650
Fax: 0131-244 7124
Email: education@scotland.gov.uk
Web site: www.scotland.gov.uk

Scottish Qualifications Authority (SQA)
Hanover House, 24 Douglas Street
Glasgow G2 7NQ
Tel: 0141-248 7900
Fax: 0141-242 2244
Email: email@sqa.org.uk
Web site: www.sqa.org.uk

Service Children's Education (UK)
Trenchard Lines
Upavon, Pusey
Wiltshire SN9 6BE
Tel: (01980) 618244
Fax: (01980) 618245
Web site: www.army.mod.uk

Society of Headmasters and Headmistresses of Independent Schools (SHMIS)
Mr. I D Cleland, General Secretary
Celedston, Rhosesmor Road
Halkyn, Holywell
Flintshire CH8 8DL
Tel/Fax: (01352) 781102
Email: gensec@shmis.demon.co.uk
Web site: www.shmis.demon.co.uk

Standing Conference on Drug Abuse (SCODA)
32–36 Loman Street
London SE1 0EE
Tel: (020) 7928 9500
Fax: (020) 7928 3343
Email: info@scoda.demon.co.uk
Web site: www.ncvo-vol.org.uk/
scoda.html

State Boarding Information Service (STABIS)
DfEE Publications Centre
PO Box 6927, London E3 3NZ
Tel: (0845) 602260
Fax: (0845) 603360
Web site: www.stabis.org.uk

Steiner Waldorf Schools Fellowship
Kidbrooke Park, Forest Row
East Sussex RH18 5JA
Tel: (01342) 822115
Fax: (01342) 826004
Email: mail@waldorf.compulink.co.uk
Web site: www.cix.co.uk/
~waldorf

Which? Books
PO Box 44
Hertford X, SG14 1LH
Tel: (0800) 252100
Fax: (0800) 533053
Web site: www.which.net

Bibliography

Chapter 2 Schools in the state sector

Chubb, J., Moe, T. 1992. *The classroom revolution.* Brookings Institution/*Sunday Times*

Department for Education and Employment. 1998. *Education and training statistics for the UK 1998.* DfEE Publications

Department for Education and Employment. 1998. *Specialist schools – education partnerships for the 21st century.* DfEE Publications

Department for Education and Employment: Fair Funding. 1998. *Improving delegation to schools.* DfEE Publications

Department for Education and Employment: Fair Funding. 1998. *Plans to extend local management of schools.* DfEE Publications

Education Yearbook. Pitman

National Association of Head Teachers. *Survey of LEA education budgets 1999–2000.*

National Early Years Network. 1998. *Choosing what's best for your child.* DfEE Publications

State Boarding Information Service/Boarding Schools Association. 1998. *Parents' guide to maintained boarding schools.* DfEE Publications

School Standards and Framework Act 1998. HMSO

Chapter 3 Schools in the independent sector

Independent Schools Yearbook. A&C Black

National Early Years Network. 1998. *Choosing what's best for your child.* DfEE Publications

North American Montessori Teachers' Association and Association Montessori Internationale. *A parent's introduction to Montessori pre-school.* AMI

Chapter 4 Key concerns for parents

Armstrong, N., Welsman, J. 1997. *Young People and Physical Activity*. Oxford University Press

Department for Education and Employment: Specialist Schools Division. *Sports colleges 1998*. DfEE Publications

Hendry, L.B., Welsh, J. 1981. Aspects of the hidden curriculum: teachers' and pupils' perceptions in physical education. *International Review of Sport Sociology*, 4, 27–42

Hendry, L.B. 1978. Conflicts in the curriculum: an example from physical education. *Educational Research*, 20, 174–180

Hendry, L.B., Thorpe, E. 1977. Pupils' choice, extracurricular activities: a critique of hierarchical authority? *International Review of Sport Sociology*, 4, 39–50

Hendry, L.B., Douglass, L. 1975. University students: attainment and sport. *British Journal of Educational Psychology*, 45, 299–306

Mireylees, J. 1998. *Under achievement by boys: is this a problem in the primary language learning classroom?* La Jolie Ronde

National Foundation for Educational Research. 1999. *Boys' achievement, progress, motivation and participation*. NFER Publications

Qualifications and Curriculum Authority. 1999. *Review of the National Curriculum in England 1999*. QCA Publications

Rae, J. 1998. *Letters to Parents*. HarperCollins

Riddoch, C. 1998. *Young and Active? A Policy Framework for Young People*. Health Education Authority

Chapter 5 Children with special requirements

Department for Education and Employment. 1994. *Special educational needs – a guide for parents*. HMSO

Gaffney, T. 1995. *The Dyslexia Institute: an introduction for parents*. Dyslexia Institute

Gould, S. J. 1997. *The Mismeasure of Man*. Penguin

Murray, C., Herrnstein, R. 1994. *The Bell Curve*. Free Press

Warnock., M. 1985. *The question of life: the Warnock report*. Blackwell

Association of Teachers and Lecturers. 1998. *Achievement for all.*

Chapter 7 Head teachers and governors

Bingham, D. 1994. *Your School's Image*. John Catt Educational

School Standards and Framework Act 1998. HMSO

Rae, J. 1998. *Letters to Parents*. HarperCollins

Chapter 8 Teaching staff

Hendry, L.B., Welsh, J. 1981. Aspects of the hidden curriculum: teachers' and pupils' perceptions in physical education. *International Review of Sport Sociology*, 4, 27–42

National Union of Teachers. 1999. *Associate staff support for teachers.*

Chapter 9 Pastoral and domestic care

Armstrong, N., Welsman, J. 1997. *Young People and Physical Activity.* Oxford University Press

Blythman, J. 1998. *The Food Our Children Eat.* Penguin

Department of Health. 1998. *The health of young people 1995–97.* HMSO

Donovan, N., Street, K. 1999. *Fit for School.* New Policy Institute

Chapter 10 Discipline

Barton, J. 1998. *Young teenagers and smoking in 1997: a report on the key findings from the teenage smoking attitudes survey.* Office of National Statistics

Children's Society. 1991. *Problematic adolescent behaviour*

Department of Health. 1994. *Drugs – a parent's guide.* HMSO

Health Education Authority. 1999. *Drugs and solvency – a young person's guide.* HMSO

Hendry, L.B. 1993. Learning the new three Rs? Educating young people for modern society. *Aberdeen University Review*, 189, 33–51

Hendry, L.B., Glendinning, A., Shucksmith, J. 1996. Adolescent focal theories: age-trends in developmental transitions. *Journal of Adolescence*, 19, 307–320

Ofsted. 1998. *Drug education in schools.* TSO

Ofsted. 1993. *Achieving good behaviour in schools.* HMSO

Standing Conference on Drug Abuse (SCODA). 1999. *The right approach: quality standards in drug education.*

Chapter 11 Bullying and racism

Macpherson, W. 1999. *The Stephen Lawrence inquiry.* TSO

Ofsted. 1999. *Raising attainment of minority ethnic pupils: schools and LEA responses.* Ofsted Publications

Chapter 12 The National Curriculum, assessments and performance tables

AQA. 1998. *Broadening your horizons: an introduction to GNVQs.* City and Guilds

Department for Education and Employment. 1999. *The review of the national curriculum in England.* QCA Publications

Ofsted. 1999. *The quality of nursery education.* Ofsted Publications

Sharp, C., Hutchison, D. 1997. *How do season of birth and length of schooling affect children's attainment at Key Stage 1?* National Foundation for Educational Research

QCA. 1999. *Qualifications 16–19: A guide to the changes resulting from the Qualifying for Success consultation.* QCA Publications

QCA. 1998. *Is your child about to start school?* QCA Publications

QCA. 1998. *Part one GNVQ – a brief guide.* QCA Publications

Scottish Executive. *Examination results in Scottish schools: information for parents.* HMI Audit Unit

Welsh Office. 1999. *How is your child doing at primary school? A parent's guide.*

Welsh Office. 1999. *How is your child doing at secondary school? A parent's guide.*

Welsh Office. 1998. *Welsh in the National Curriculum.* HMSO

Chapter 13 League tables and academic performance

QCA. 1996. *Standards in public examinations 1975 to 1995.* QCA Publications

Chapter 14 Form size and the classroom

Aston, M., Hinder, A. (eds) 1999. *The OrbIT report – information technology provision in primary and secondary schools in the group of eight (G8) nations and other representative nations.* The Advisory Unit: Computers in Education

Bierhoff, H., Prais, S.J. 1995. *Schooling as preparation for life and work in Switzerland and Britain.* National Institute of Economic and Social Research, discussion paper 75

British Educational Suppliers Association. 1998. *Information and communication technology in UK schools.*

Coleman, J.A. 1996. *Studying Languages: A Survey of British and European Students.* CILT Publications

Jamison, J., Johnson, F., Dickson, P. 1998. *Every pupil counts: the impact of class size at Key Stage 1.* National Foundation for Educational Research

Local Government Association. 1998. *Class size reduction study: report*

Ofsted. 1996. *The gender divide: performance between boys and girls at school.* HMSO

Ofsted. 1993. *Boys and English.* DfEE Publications

Roberston, J. 1998. *The use of refurbished computers in schools: evaluation of the Dumfries pilot project.* Scottish Office.

Sainsbury, M., Schagen, I., Whetton, C., Hagues, N., Minnis, M. 1998. *Evaluation of the national literacy project.* National Foundation for Educational Research

Sukhnandan, L., Lee, B. 1998. *Streaming, setting and grouping by ability: a review of the literature.* National Foundation for Educational Research

Chapter 15 Classroom support

Atherton, M., Middleton, B. 1999. Commercial materials in schools: parents' views. *Consumer Policy Review*, 9, 42–5

Atherton, M., Wells, J. 1998. Business involvement in schools. *Consumer Policy Review*, 8, 180–4

Department for Education and Employment. 1999. *Meet the challenge: education action zones.* DfEE Publications

Department for Education and Employment. 1998. *Home–school agreements: guidance for schools.* DfEE Publications

Department for Education and Employment. 1998. *Home–school agreements: what every parent should know.* DfEE Publications

Funding Agency for Schools. 1999. *Making a Break.*

Hendry, L.B., Shucksmith, J., Glendinning, A. 1996. Anticipating adolescence? Some social implications of the organised sports and leisure involvement of pre-adolescents. *Corpus, Psyche et Societas*, 3

National Consumer Council. 1996. *Sponsorship in schools: good practice guidelines.*

Ofsted. 1999. *Homework: learning from practice.* Ofsted Publications

Ofsted. 1993. *Access and achievement in urban education.* HMSO

Weston, P. *Homework: learning from practice.* TSO

Sainsbury, M., Caspall, L., McDonald, A., Ravencroft, L., Schagen, I. 1999. *Evaluation of the 1998 summer schools programme.* National Foundation for Educational Research

Chapter 16 School admission criteria

Department for Education and Employment. 1999. *School admissions code of practice.* DfEE Publications

Welsh Office. 1999. *School admissions: Welsh Office code of practice.*

Chapter 17 The costs of schooling

Association of Investment Trust Companies. 1999. *Investing for children.* AITC

Boarding Education Alliance. 1999. *Value-for-money in modern boarding Independent Schools Yearbook.* A&C Black

Appendix I

Scottish Council of Independent Schools. *Which school? A directory of independent schools in Scotland 1997–8.* ISIS

Scottish Office. 1999. *Education and training in Scotland: a summary*

Appendix III

Department of Education Northern Ireland. 1998. *The procedure for transfer from primary to secondary education 1998–99.* DENI

Department of Education Northern Ireland. 1998. *Transfer procedure, considering schools and applying for a place: advice to parents.* DENI

Department of Education Northern Ireland. 1998. *Transfer to secondary school, arrangement for 1999: a guide for parents.* DENI

Index

WHICH? BOOKS

General reference (legal, financial, practical, etc.)

Be Your Own Financial Adviser
401 Legal Problems Solved
150 Letters that Get Results
The Which? Guide to an Active Retirement
The Which? Guide to Changing Careers
The Which? Guide to Choosing a Career
The Which? Guide to Computers
The Which? Guide to Computers for Small Businesses
The Which? Guide to Divorce
The Which? Guide to Domestic Help
The Which? Guide to Employment
The Which? Guide to Gambling
The Which? Guide to Getting Married
The Which? Guide to Giving and Inheriting
The Which? Guide to Home Safety and Security
The Which? Guide to Insurance
The Which? Guide to the Internet
The Which? Guide to Money
The Which? Guide to Pensions
The Which? Guide to Renting and Letting
The Which? Guide to Shares
The Which? Guide to Starting Your Own Business
The Which? Guide to Working from Home
Which? Way to Beat the System
Which? Way to Clean It
Which? Way to Buy, Sell and Move House
Which? Way to Buy, Own and Sell a Flat
Which? Way to Save and Invest
Which? Way to Save Tax
What to Do When Someone Dies
Wills and Probate

Action Pack (A5 wallet with forms and 28-page book inside)

Make Your Own Will

For credit-card orders phone FREE on (0800) 252100

The Which? Guide to Money

How can you cut the cost of your current account? How do you stop a cheque? Is it worth changing banks – and how do you go about it? What is the cheapest way to pay for things when you're abroad? What is the most cost-effective way to finance your child's education? *The Which? Guide to Money* answers these and many other questions to do with day-to-day spending.

It looks at the basic financial tools you will need through-out your life, such as current accounts, savings accounts and credit cards, and examines the options for: paying bills; renting or buying a home; financing holidays; buying a car; company cars; financial survival as a student; pensions; debt; what to do with a windfall.

Using handy calculators, case histories and tips, this no-nonsense guide will help you keep in control of your money at every stage of your financial life, from first bank account to retirement and beyond.

Paperback   216 x 135mm   448 pages   £9.99

Available from bookshops, and by post from
Which?, Dept TAZM, Castlemead,
Gascoyne Way, Hertford X, SG14 1LH

You can also order using your credit card
by phoning FREE on (0800) 252100
(quoting Dept TAZM)

The Which? Guide to Children's Health

Good health in childhood sets us up for life. This guide shows how parents can help to ensure that their child has the best start possible, looking at general development, eating habits, exercise, immunisations and health checks.

An A–Z of common illnesses gives details of each condition, including what to do in an emergency, together with action you can take and treatment options. Complementary therapies and self-help measures are included wherever appropriate.

The book, compiled by a team of health professionals including GPs, a dentist, a health visitor and others whose daily work focuses on children, also covers: pre-natal care and the first 12 months; care of your child's teeth; behavioural and emotional problems; and accident prevention and first aid.

Another section describes how to get the best for your child from your GP and other health professionals, both in and outside the NHS, and your child's rights under the Patient's Charter.

Paperback   216 x 135mm   288 pages   £9.99

Available from bookshops, and by post from
Which?, Dept TAZM, Castlemead,
Gascoyne Way, Hertford X, SG14 1LH

You can also order using your credit card
by phoning FREE on (0800) 252100
(quoting Dept TAZM)

The Which? Guide to Domestic Help

The demand for au pairs, childminders, carers, cleaners and other domestic help is higher than it has ever been. But employing someone, usually a stranger, to look after your children, care for your elderly dependant or even just to clean your house when you are at work can be fraught with difficulties. Where do you find someone reliable and trustworthy? How can you check that references are genuine? What can you do if you suspect your cleaner of stealing, the nanny batters the children or your dog bites the carer?

The Which? Guide to Domestic Help offers advice on how to tackle the practical, emotional and financial aspects of finding and employing help in the home.

Using checklists and case histories to highlight the pitfalls, the guide covers: how to decide what sort of help you really need; where to find suitable help – from personal recommendations to advertisements and agencies; how to interview an applicant; how to match your expectations with those of your potential employee; employing foreign nationals; drawing up a contract; and how to get redress if something goes wrong.

All in all, *The Which? Guide to Domestic Help* should save both potential employers *and* their employees a good deal of heartache and misery.

Paperback   216 x 135mm   208 pages   £9.99

Available from bookshops, and by post from
Which?, Dept TAZM, Castlemead,
Gascoyne Way, Hertford X, SG14 1LH

You can also order using your credit card
by phoning FREE on (0800) 252100
(quoting Dept TAZM)